Acknowl

First publication of essays in this book, in different versions, was as follows: 'Seeing Place', *In Black and Gold: Contiguous Traditions in Post-War British and Irish Poetry*, ed. C. C. Barfoot (Amsterdam: Rodopi, 1994); 'One is trying to make a shape', *The David Jones Journal* Summer 1998; 'Ceridwen's Daughters: Welsh Women Poets and the Uses of Tradition', *Welsh Writing in English* Vol. 1, 1995; 'The Tree of Life: Explorations of an Image', *The Green Book*, Vol. 111, 6 & 7; 'To Fit a Late Time: A Reading of Five American Poets', *P. N. Review* 109; 'Roy Fisher: Magician of the Common Place', *P. N. Review* 107; 'Christopher Middleton: The Poem as Act of Wonder', *P. N. Review* 114; 'Poets, Language and Land: Reflections on English-Language Welsh Poetry Since the Second-World War', *Welsh Writing in English* Vol. 8, 2003; 'Adventurers in Living Fact: The Poetry of Dick Davis, Robert Wells, and Clive Wilmer', *The London Magazine* December/January 2007; 'A Story of a Poem and a Sculpture', *Planet* 99; 'The Experience of Landscape, painting and poetry', South Bank Centre, 1987; 'Natural Magic', *Modern Painters* Spring 1996; 'Gathering All In', *Modern Painters* Winter 1995; 'Flooded with Light: on the art of Elizabeth Haines', *Planet* 194; 'Ground', Zobole Gallery, University of Glamorgan, 2007. 'Truth of Experience: the Paintings of David Tress' appeared on the *Resurgence* website. I am grateful to the editors and publishers of all of these. 'Putting the Poem in Place' is the text of my Inaugural Professorial Lecture, given at the University of Glamorgan, 11 December 2007.

I wish specially to thank the following friends and editors for their reading and critical support: C. C. Barfoot, the late Sebastian Barker, John Barnie, Tony Brown, the late Anne Cluysenaar, the late Roland Mathias, Michael Schmidt, Ned Thomas, and the late Peter Thomas. Professor M. Wynn Thomas kindly read an earlier version of the text and commented on it helpfully. Mieke, my late wife, was always my closest reader. I am grateful to Deborah Price for her skill in transcribing the text, to Tony Frazer, for his patience and consideration as a publisher, and to Liz Mathews for her cover image.

Art of Seeing

Also by Jeremy Hooker:

from Shearsman Books

Upstate: A North American Journal
Openings: A European Journal
Diary of a Stroke

Ancestral Lines
Word and Stone
Selected Poems 1965–2018

from other publishers

Poetry
Landscape of the Daylight Moon
Soliloquies of a Chalk Giant
Solent Shore
Englishman's Road
A View from the Source
Master of the Leaping Figures
Their Silence a Language (with Lee Grandjean)
Our Lady of Europe
Adamah
Arnolds Wood
The Cut of the Light: Poems 1965–2005
Scattered Light
Under the Quarry Woods

Prose
Welsh Journal

Criticism
Poetry of Place
The Presence of the Past: Essays on Modern British and American Poetry
Writers in a Landscape
Imagining Wales: A View of Modern Welsh Writing in English
Ditch Vision

As editor:
Frances Bellerby: *Selected Stories*
Alun Lewis: *Selected Poems* (with Gweno Lewis)
At Home on Earth: A New Selection of the Later Writings of Richard Jefferies
Alun Lewis: *Inwards Where All the Battle Is: Writings from India*
Mapping Golgotha: A Selection of Wilfred Owen's Letters and Poems
Edward Thomas: *The Ship of Swallows*

Art of Seeing

Essays on Poetry, Landscape Painting, and Photography

Jeremy Hooker

Shearsman Books

First published in the United Kingdom in 2020 by
Shearsman Books Ltd
PO Box 4239
Swindon
SN3 9FN

Shearsman Books Ltd Registered Office
30–31 St. James Place, Mangotsfield, Bristol BS16 9JB
(this address not for correspondence)

ISBN 978-1-84861-708-7

Copyright © Jeremy Hooker, 2020

The right of Jeremy Hooker to be identified as the author of this work has been asserted by him in accordance with the Copyrights, Designs and Patents Act of 1988.
All rights reserved.

CONTENTS

Acknowledgements / 7

Introduction: Learning to see / 9

'Awakening the mind's attention':
Lyrical Ballads and the Art of Seeing / 20

Seeing Place / 34

'One is trying to make a shape' / 52

Ceridwen's Daughters:
Welsh Women Poets and the Uses of Tradition / 66

Heartlands: On the Poetry of
Ruth Bidgood and Christopher Meredith / 85

The Tree of Life: Explorations of an Image / 95

American Visions of England:
Ronald Johnson and John Matthias / 110

To Fit a Late Time:
A Reading of Five American poets / 118

Building with images:
'Jerusalem the Golden' and 'Of Being Numerous' / 130

Roy Fisher: Magician of the Commonplace / 143

Christopher Middleton:
The Poem as Act of Wonder / 151

Taking Words for a Walk:
The Recent Poetry of Philip Gross / 161

Poets, Language, and Land: Reflections on English-Language
Welsh poetry since the Second World War / 168

'Adventures in Living Fact': The Poetry of
Dick Davis, Robert Wells, and Clive Wilmer / 174

A Story of a Poem and a Sculpture / 193

Mametz Wood: The Photographs of Aled Rhys Hughes / 200

The Experience of Landscape: Painting and Poetry / 213

Natural Magic / 221

Gathering All In / 226

Truth of Experience:
The Paintings of David Tress / 233

Flooded with Light:
On the Art of Elizabeth Haines / 236

Ground / 242

Putting the Poem in Place / 246

Index / 262

Introduction: Learning to see

My love of poetry began in childhood, before I could read. It began with nursery rhymes, but also with poems my mother read or recited to me, which she had loved from her childhood. These were English lyrical or narrative poems, from a book similar to Palgrave's *Golden Treasury*, which she had studied at school before and during the First World War. This is where I must begin in introducing the essays in this book, which is a work of criticism that also comprises a chapter of aesthetic and spiritual autobiography. The main subjects I address are modern British and American poetry, Welsh poetry in English and British landscape painting, together with aspects of my own work as a poet. Since the emphasis is upon a personal view of things, I will begin by outlining and exploring the influences that have helped to shape my thinking and my practice as poet and critic.

I developed an early awareness of seeing – especially seeing nature – from my father. Looking at his landscape paintings, initially without really taking them in, I responded to his sense of colour. He was an 'amateur' painter, in the sense that he made a living by other means. He left school while still a boy to work with his father as a gardener; following the Second World War he became horticultural advisory officer to the New Forest area. But from boyhood he had had a passion for paint and colour, for *seeing as an artist*, which for him meant love of nature, and he painted landscapes all his life, until he went blind in his eighties. His conversation, as well as his art, brought me to love John Constable and the tradition of British landscape painting. Both my parents came from generations of labourers who worked on the land. They themselves kept throughout their lives a love of growing things and of country life.

I have retained my feeling for Constable while falling under the spell of Samuel Palmer and the Neo-Romantics, a tradition of British painting that artists such as David Tress continue into the present. My father inadvertently introduced me to the work of Paul Nash, but he had no sympathy with Modernism in any form. I had to learn to see modern art for myself. Later, my friendship and collaborations with the sculptor and painter Lee Grandjean introduced me to a whole new world of making and seeing. This was a new world and an old one, with lines of communication between them, since Lee apprehends sculptural and painterly image making as a continuum, not a series of discontinuous movements. No one is more aware than Lee of the artist's need to make it new. But it was he who taught me about Cubism by showing me a thirteenth-century stained glass window.

In school, I was introduced to Shakespeare and Milton and a range of Romantic and modern poets. As a student in the early 1960s, at the same time as I was reading metaphysical poetry under the tuition of the poet F. T. Prince, I was responding enthusiastically to Beat literature, to Ginsberg's *Howl* and Ferlinghetti and Kenneth Patchen. At the same time, I was beginning to read British contemporaries, such as Charles Tomlinson, R. S. Thomas, and Ted Hughes. I wrote a thesis on W. H. Auden's early poetry, and read my way into his influences, Freud and Jung, Marx, Groddeck and Homer Lane, D. H. Lawrence and William Blake.

My move to Wales in 1965, to teach modern English literature at the University College of Wales, Aberystwyth, was decisive for the way in which I subsequently developed. The figure of the major Welsh-language poet Gwenallt, who had, ironically, a room in the English department, excited my curiosity. It began to dawn on me that there was a living Welsh poetry. Through *The Welsh Extremist*, by my colleague and friend Ned Thomas, and through contact with Welsh writers and intellectuals, I began to understand the critical situation of the country I had come to, so near and yet so far from England. Gradually, through translation, I learnt something of the great tradition of Welsh literature. In reading poems by Gwenallt and Waldo Williams and Saunders Lewis I encountered a live current of cultural and national concern, and passionate political and religious conviction. Through my neighbour Gwyn Williams and his selection and translations from 'the first Thousand Years of Welsh Verse', in *The Burning Tree*, I learned about the poetic tradition that began with Aneirin and Taliesin more than a thousand years ago and continues today. Due in part to the prison of monolingualism – I have failed to learn Welsh on several occasions, and have only a rudimentary grasp of any language other than English – Welsh-language poetry has remained for me a challenging 'other'. I could not hope to make the kind of contribution to Welsh culture that other incomers, such as my friends Tony Conran and Peter Lord have made. Nor could I bridge the two literatures of Wales, or move between Welsh and American literature, as M. Wynn Thomas does with such authority. My opportunity to give something back came with Welsh writing in English, or 'Anglo-Welsh' literature as I learnt to call it.[1]

---

[1] This contested term has usually been replaced nowadays by 'anglophone Welsh literature', or 'Welsh writing in English', either of which I will sometimes use.

In my early years at Aberystwyth, some time in the later 60s, I met Roland Mathias, who befriended me. Roland gave me books to review for *The Anglo-Welsh Review* and published my first essays. One book that I reviewed, *The Lilting House,* an anthology of Anglo-Welsh poetry, introduced me to the work of David Jones. At roughly the same time, I discovered the novels of John Cowper Powys. Within the next five years I published monographs on Jones and Powys, and a comparative study of their work. Both were great writers who, at that time, had received relatively little attention. From that time, one of my primary motives as a critic has been to illuminate neglected work in the hope of helping it to become better known.

Fiona Sampson introduces her book, *Beyond the Lyric*, by saying of contemporary British poetry: 'At times it seems like a kind of club: only if you're already a member can you locate the entrance'.[2] In my view the best poetry of our time is rarely clubbable. More often, in the absence of a widely shared, authoritative sense of *what poetry is*, it involves a struggle with language and form to articulate an individual vision. In the wake of Modernism, and in response to the complex and dangerous world in which we live, poets who are my contemporaries, such as the American John Matthias, explore ways of 'fitting a late time'. The problem is compounded for the writer in Wales. As Diana Wallace says of Christopher Meredith, a Welsh writer with 'a growing international reputation', the fact that he is 'barely known in the rest of the UK… tells us something about the geographies of literary reception and the domination of a London-focused literary scene'.[3] As a result of this focus, writers in Wales have been especially subject to neglect or condescension. One of the worst recent examples occurs in Sampson's book, where, in the space of two pages, she manages to insult the major poet, Ruth Bidgood, by speaking of her 'unstoppable name-calling', and proceeds (misspelling two names in the process) to dismiss the generation of 'Anglo-Welsh poets… who emerged in the Seventies'.[4] I should admit that my name

---

However, I remain most comfortable with the earlier formulation, of which Dafydd Johnston writes: "The term 'Anglo-Welsh' should not be taken to imply any dilution of Welshness; indeed, it is most fittingly used of those writers who assert their Welsh viewpoint most vigorously". Dafydd Johnston, *The Literature of Wales* (Cardiff: University of Wales Press, 2017), 121.
[2] Fiona Sampson, *Beyond the Lyric* (London: Chatto & Windus, 2012), 1.
[3] Diana Wallace, *Christopher Meredith* (Cardiff: University of Wales Press, 2018), p. vii.
[4] Sampson, op. cit., pp. 80-81.

appears in Sampson's ample list. What angers me more, however, is my knowledge of the work of the poets whose names she lumps together so carelessly, work marked by considerable individual differences. I find it incomprehensible that an accomplished poet such as Sampson should want to pass this kind of thing off as literary criticism.

Starting to write criticism, I was naturally drawn to writers who were, in a sense, 'borderers' between England and Wales, such as Edward Thomas, David Jones, and John Cowper Powys. An interest in Powys was the occasion of my meeting Gerard Casey. Gerard, from an Irish Catholic family in Maesteg, had married into the Powys family. He was a man with a profound Christian vision, and author of *South Wales Echo,* one of the few outstanding Anglo-Welsh modernist long poems. His wife, Mary Casey, was a major lyric poet. More than anyone, Gerard helped me to take an independent stance towards contemporary intellectual fashions.

It was through Roland Mathias's encouragement that I began to write literary criticism regularly. At the same time that I met Roland, at Gregynog, I met Glyn Jones, John Tripp and Leslie Norris. In this early period, I also met Gillian Clarke and Emyr Humphreys, John Ormond and Raymond Garlick. On several occasions I shared a platform with R. S. Thomas. As an Englishman living in a Welsh-speaking area, I felt keenly the reasons for anti-English sentiments. During the 1970s my first wife and I lived at Llangwyryfon, in Ceredigion, where an ancient pattern of Welsh life continued, but was under threat from influences brought in from outside. Awareness of being intruders was a factor in our decision to leave Wales. When I returned some fifteen years later it was to the anglicised south.

At Aberystwyth, while I was learning something of the two literatures of Wales, I was also encountering twentieth-century American poetry. It was the American poet, Bill Sherman, then a lecturer in American literature in the English department, who taught me to 'hear' Charles Olson and understand Black Mountain poetics. I had loved Walt Whitman since student days, but now I became excited by Ezra Pound and William Carlos Williams. Gary Snyder delighted me, at the same time that his sense of American wilderness stimulated me to think of its contrast with the different experience of nature within the British Isles. T. S. Eliot, on whom I lectured regularly, had been part of my inner world since 1959, when my girlfriend had given me a copy of his *Collected Poems.*

Naturally, I found marked differences between American and Anglo-Welsh poets. There were, however, two important common factors. The first was a passionate concern for place, for 'heartlands'. In Anglo-Welsh writers, this often focuses upon a sense of belonging, or desire to belong, and includes an element of *hiraeth*, with Welsh-speaking Wales perceived as the culture from which, without the primary language, they live in internal exile. Roland Mathias's metaphor of Wales as a house which he stands outside, looking in but unable to enter,[5] is a particularly moving representation of this condition. The prevalence of place names in Ruth Bidgood's poetry shows the poet's love and respect for a deep, historical landscape, in which she wishes to ground herself, but without assuming an automatic right.

I understood the feeling well, because my own sense of belonging, to my original home in the south of England, was strong, and now I was seeing the loved ground from the outside, with longing to return, in spite of all that my life in Wales meant to me. Home territory in the south of England – country of Richard Jefferies and Thomas Hardy and Edward Thomas, powerful emotional influences on me from my youth – became the subject of my first books of poems. It remains a world to which I shall always return imaginatively, as one does to places that are part of one.

Returning briefly to live in southern England in the early 1980s, I formulated an idea of 'a poem like a place':

> Entering a place that is new to us, or seeing a familiar place anew, we move from part to part, simultaneously perceiving individual persons and things and discovering their relationships, so that, with time, place reveals itself as particular identities belonging to a network, which continually extends with our perception, and beyond it. And by this process we find ourselves, not as observers only, but as inhabitants, citizens, neighbours, and locate ourselves in a space dense with meanings.[6]

From living in Wales, I had absorbed a traditional idea of the poet as a functioning member of the community. But I had yet to take full measure of how much things had changed, in Wales as well as England, and consequently how difficult it is now for a poet to write *from* the life of place, as distinct from as a marginal figure, a stranger.

---

[5] Roland Mathias, in Meic Stephens, ed. *Artists in Wales* (Llandysul: Gwasg Gomer, 1971), p. 163.
[6] Jeremy Hooker, *Master of the Leaping Figures* (Petersfield: Enitharmon Press, 1987), p. 76.

The second common factor I became aware of between the situations of American and Anglo-Welsh poets was a sense of poetic possibility. In American poetry, the 'open field' offers an escape from tight formal structures, and from a limiting irony. It continues the cosmic outreach of Whitman's poetry. Anglo-Welsh poetry, largely from its contact with the Welsh literary tradition, and from its position on the 'border' between that tradition and Anglo-American modernism, is potentially a source of large imaginative possibilities. Only consider the work of Tony Conran, a great translator of Welsh poetry into English, who has drawn upon his knowledge to produce a body of major innovative poetry in English. Poets such as David Jones have lamented their inability to speak Welsh. But it is the feeling for the language and native culture just beyond their reach that enables them to bring something excitingly 'other' into poems in English. My friend Anne Cluysenaar, another incomer like myself, was drawn to Gwyn Williams's description of the designs of 'old Welsh poetry'. Williams extended the sense of design to Dylan Thomas and David Jones, claiming that the Welsh poets 'were not trying to write poems that would read like Greek temples or even Gothic cathedrals but, rather, like stone circles or the contour-following rings of the forts from which they fought, with hidden ways slipping from one ring to another'.[7] This highly suggestive image indicates one way in which the very form of poetry influenced by living in Wales may relate to the physical, historical landscape. The situation of the poet in Wales is enhanced by access to realms of myth and 'British' history closed to most English poets. I do not claim that all Anglo-Welsh poets realise the imaginative possibilities of their position as 'borderers' between cultures – far from it. I do claim that such possibilities exist, in tension with conventional ideas of poetic craft.

I must emphasise that it is not my intention to suggest that Anglo-Welsh poetry shares no common ground with English poetry. It would be absurd to do so. Clearly, poets in Wales, in both languages, have drawn profitably upon both English and European poetic influences. What I do wish to stress is that English-language Welsh poets, with their access, however partial, to Welsh-language culture, as well as to other non-English sources, have had alternatives to the narrowing mentality of post-war English verse. For poets in both languages in Wales, the democratic spirit of *Lyrical Ballads*, which I discuss in this book, is integral to a specifically Welsh heritage with a strong communitarian spirit. My aim

---

[7] From Preface, Gwyn Williams, *The Burning Tree: Poems from the First Thousand Years of Welsh Verse* (London: Faber and Faber, 1956).

here is to emphasise the potential openness of Anglo-Welsh poetry to diverse powerful streams of native and foreign influence, and to counter the idea – unfortunately, still not uncommon both inside and outside Wales – that it is necessarily a product of provincialism.

I share with some other poets of my generation the need to construct a poetic tradition, in the absence of one that is given, and in opposition to prevailing conventions. Coleridge's idea of Wordsworth's object in *The Lyrical Ballads*, to awaken 'the mind's attention from the lethargy of custom', is fundamental to what I call 'art of seeing'. Wordsworth's attention to the wonders of the real world was strongly supported by his sister, Dorothy's eye for details of natural life. Behind these and other Romantic poets, with their close, loving perception of their native localities, stands the great, humble figure of Gilbert White of Selborne. White fathered the ecological vision that connects British and American poets with whom I feel close affinities.

As discussed in my book *Ditch Vision*, my personal introduction to this way of seeing, based on close attention to the natural and human life of home territory, was through the essays of the Victorian poet-naturalist Richard Jefferies, which I read when I was a boy. Jefferies has been a potent influence on certain writers, especially Edward Thomas and Henry Williamson, but he has never been accorded the importance in England his work deserves, which should be seen as equivalent to that of Thoreau in America. He has affinities with the Romantics but is also in certain respects a peculiarly modern writer, in whose 'art of seeing' I have come to recognise a close connection with the localism, clarity and care for particulars in William Carlos Williams and the Objectivists. A similar spirit animates poetry of place and love of the creaturely in David Jones and other Welsh poets.

Spirit is the key word connecting, across times and cultures, poets that are formally and in use of language very different from one another. It is noteworthy, for example, that different critics have detected a 'Franciscan' spirit in Thomas Hardy and William Carlos Williams. Both are poets in whom a strongly developed sense of self coexists with responsiveness to, and a tender regard for, the life around them.

It was probably from my early reading of Jefferies's essays that I first developed the conviction that everywhere is a 'centre'. By this I mean centre of life, both human and natural, the 'world' of each locality, as valuable as any metropolis. I grew up to be stubbornly parochial, in the sense that the Irish poet Patrick Kavanagh defined. While 'the provincial has no mind of his own, ... the parochial mentality ... is never in any doubt about the social and artistic validity of his parish'.[8] By this definition Homer is a parochial poet, as are Hardy and Williams. In Wales one thinks of the poet's *bro*, the known and loved locality in which universal meaning is to be found.

Learning to see, in ways that I am outlining here, I focused my attention as a critic on writers for whom their places were a centre, Anglo-Welsh writers, but also English and American poets, neglected or undervalued by critics with a metropolitan – that is to say, provincial – point of view. In the 1970s Anglo-Welsh writers were often neglected, and at times derided, even in their home country. A symptom of this was the difficulty Ned Thomas had in establishing a module in Welsh writing in English in the English department at Aberystwyth. How things have changed! Aberystwyth now hosts the David Jones Centre. I think of this ironically when I remember the relative isolation of my own early work on David Jones, when, studying in a caravan on the edge of a field in Welsh hill country, and feeling intense excitement while reading *The Anathemata*, I was astonished to receive one of David Jones's marvellous long letters, inspired by gratitude for something I had written about his work. This was humbling for a young writer to receive. It also made me realise the critical isolation that he, a great artist in old age, was experiencing. While such writers remained relatively neglected, I realised there was important work for a critic to do.

John Ormond once predicted for me a crisis from trying to pursue the twin roles of poet and critic. Thinking of myself as an academic, in Aberystwyth, certainly brought on a considerable strain in this respect. Later, while working in universities, I preferred to think of myself as a teacher – a role that I loved, indeed an art that can nurture the practice of other arts. Like most writers, I have experienced 'blocks'. Sometimes I have blamed them on the demands of my university work. At best, however, I see my roles as complementary. There are, no doubt, two 'voices' to be heard in my essays. Some are quite informal; others, with an academic context, use the first person singular sparingly, if at all. But in every instance when writing about others, I aim above all to be an attentive, careful *reader*. Naturally, I am drawn most to writers who speak to me as a poet, but I write to *see* their work, and to help others to understand and value it. Like Matthew Arnold in his study of Celtic

---

[8] Patrick Kavanagh, *A Poet's Country*, ed. Antoinette Quinn (Dublin: Lilliput, 2003), p. 237.

literature, I disclaim a 'passion for finding nothing but myself anywhere'. Learning to see through encountering what is other than oneself is one form of autobiography. In Martin Buber's words, which encapsulate his *I and Thou* philosophy, 'All real living is meeting'.

According to Oscar Wilde's preface to *The Picture of Dorian Gray*, 'The highest as the lowest form of criticism is a mode of autobiography'. To that I would like to add one of my favourite quotations from John Cowper Powys: 'It is hard to be impersonal in a cosmos that runs to personality'.[9] Autobiography is by definition a personal matter. In our time the idea of the person is under siege from theories that replace the 'I' with constructs formed by various power structures. Persons as centres of experience, let alone traditional concepts of 'soul', are seen as illusory. It therefore behoves someone who aspires to write personally to give an idea of what he means by it.

At my first meeting with Glyn Jones he reacted, as I later realised, quite out of character. At the time I was in a highly nervous state, and was recovering from a breakdown. This was the subject of a poem that I read to the group at Gregynog. I talked about the experience behind the poem. Characteristically, John Tripp liked my emotionalism, but it made Glyn angry. He told me, with feeling, that a poet should *use* disturbing inner experience as a source of imaginative energy, *not* talk about it. We were both shaken by the outburst. Whenever we met afterwards, Glyn would refer to it apologetically, and I would tell him he had done me a great service.

An idea of poetry I'd drifted into, partly in response to the 'confessionalism' of the 1960s, was what I would later regard as poetry of the brittle ego, concerned primarily with states of mind. Afflicted by what Edward Thomas in his book on Richard Jefferies called 'the terror' of self-consciousness, I found release through Martin Buber's philosophy, which foregrounds the relationship between self and other. Inspired in part by Glyn Jones's words to me, and influenced by Buber and by traditions within Welsh and American poetry, my settled aim has been to explore ways of objectifying the personal. This does not mean denying the 'I' of lyric poetry. It means, rather, an emphasis upon relationship, in the meeting between self and other.

In the 1970s I first encountered the work of the American poet George Oppen, who wrote:

---

[9] John Cowper Powys, *A Glastonbury Romance* (London: John Lane The Bodley Head, 1933), p. 909.

> 'Thought leaps on us' because we are here. That is the fact
>   of the matter.
> Soul-searchings, these prescriptions
>
> Are a medical faddism, an attempt to escape,
> To lose oneself in the self.
>
> The self is no mystery, the mystery is
> That there is something for us to stand on.[10]

Oppen's Marxist ethic places the self in society, in the humanly created world. His vision is not social only, but shares with Whitman a sense of the elemental cosmos. His idea of the self in relation to 'something for us to stand on' is not an idea imprisoned in a political dogma, and in my view, it can be placed alongside ideas arrived at from quite different starting points. Thus, Keats's idea of the world as 'The vale of Soul-making' also emphasises self as process formed in relationship with what is outside it. I would also invoke David Jones's words about his writing of *The Anathemata*, which for me are a talisman: 'one is trying to make a shape out of the very things of which one is oneself made'.[11]

My thinking is not bound by any of these definitions, though all matter to me a great deal. All have to do with self in relationship, and bring modern complications to Wordsworth's idea of the poet as one who carries 'every where with him relationship and love'. The question posed by Hölderlin, and interpreted by Heidegger, What is poetry for in a desolate time? haunts serious modern poets. Whether explicitly or implicitly, it troubles a number of the poets that I write about in this book. The Welsh poet has been traditionally a *man* with a strong sense of responsibility to his people. Both the rise of women poets, which has been one of the most exciting developments since the 1970s, and the breakdown of communities in Wales have complicated the relationship between poet and people for their Anglo-Welsh brothers and sisters. George Oppen agonised over his distance as a passionately committed, independent Marxist poet from the people whose social and political causes he espoused. This is one reason why his poetry matters so much. In the very texture of their work, in their sense of language, major modern

---

[10] George Oppen, 'World, World', *New Collected Poems,* ed. Michael Davidson (New York, NY: New Directions, 2002), p. 159.
[11] David Jones, *The Anathemata* (London: Faber and Faber, 1952), p. 10.

poets confront radical questions about communication between self and other, and poet and people.

This has a bearing on why I think of poetry as a learning to see. For me, it is an essentially exploratory act, or art. In my work I seek what I have come to think of as 'ground'. As I use the word, 'ground' is a metaphor – but not only a metaphor – which has evolved from my thinking about place. The idea began for me with the actual ground under foot, and extended to the total local environment, place comprising geology, ecology, history, culture, ancestry and family – forces that together with intimate experiences make the world that 'shaped' me. I had lived for some ten years in Wales before I felt that my sense of Welsh 'ground' – the place with which I had formed a relationship – was deep enough for me to be able to draw upon it as a poetic subject. Instead of beginning and ending with the brittle ego, I think of 'art of seeing' as an opening both outwards and inwards. As it explores the outer world – what Oppen refers to as the 'something' we stand on, and I think of as ground – so it is simultaneously a self-discovery and a self-enlargement. Through the personal the poet who sees in this way seeks to reveal common human depths. His or her art is necessarily questioning. It is also always unfinished, and any statement of it, such as this, provisional.

In introducing the essays in this book, I am attempting to speak objectively of personal matters. This isn't easy when talking about my mother's gift of the love of poetry, or the sense of colour I received from my father, or any of the writers, artists or thinkers from whom I continue learning to see. It is always perilous to talk about one's own poetry, which is a continuing process, subject to new discoveries, not a completed product. Nor are the essays about other writers in this book intended as complete summaries of their work. My critical writing represented here covers a period of some thirty years. In many instances it is about writers who have gone on to produce a considerable body of work. What I offer here, therefore, is a view of parts of an ongoing process: a partial view of aspects of certain poets' work, not an attempt at a definitive vision of any one writer. As a critic, I aim for objectivity. I should say, though, that there's nothing objective in my feelings for Wales and the literatures of Wales. Friendships across the generations have enriched my life in Wales. Having said which, I must add that no poet I know would be other than horrified to be told that he or she belongs to any kind of poets' club.

'Awakening the mind's attention':
Lyrical Ballads and the Art of Seeing

The title of this essay comes from chapter X1V of *Biographia Literaria*, in which Samuel Taylor Coleridge recalled 'the plan of the "Lyrical Ballads"'. The importance of his description of William Wordsworth's part in this demands quotation at length.

> Mr. Wordsworth ... was to propose to himself as his object, to give the charm of novelty to things of every day, and to excite a feeling analogous to the supernatural, by awakening the mind's attention from the lethargy of custom, and directing it to the loveliness and the wonders of the world before us; an inexhaustible treasure, but for which in consequence of the film of familiarity and selfish solicitude we have eyes, yet see not, ears that hear not, and hearts that neither feel nor understand.

Coleridge is alluding to the reason Jesus gave for speaking in parables: 'because they seeing see not; and hearing they hear not, neither do they understand' (Matthew 13: 13). The religious allusion is not inappropriate to *Lyrical Ballads*. It does, however, bespeak Coleridge's Christian orthodoxy, rather than 'a new style and a new spirit in poetry', which William Hazlitt recalled in 'My first acquaintance with poets' sensing as a young man in reading poems from *Lyrical Ballads*. For Hazlitt, it had 'something of the effect that arises from the turning up of the fresh soil, or of the first welcome breath of Spring'.

Awakening the mind from the lethargy of custom is a marvellous description of the art of seeing which contributed to the newness of *Lyrical Ballads*. I should say that a leaflet advertising the conference paper, which was an earlier version of this essay, contained a misprint, calling it 'Act of Seeing'. Happy error, indeed, since perceptual and imaginative acts determine the dynamic art of *Lyrical Ballads*. To emphasise the mind's activities is not to contradict Wordsworth's recommendation in 'Expostulation and Reply' of 'a wise passiveness'. The new thinking behind *Lyrical Ballads* centres upon interrelationships between the mind and nature, both perceived as active powers. Key terms, which distinguish the mental awakening of *Lyrical Ballads* from the defamiliarization of a later age, are *human* and *nature*. The philosophy and moral vision invested in these concepts make it a revolutionary book, which transforms both the pastoral tradition and conventional ideas of humankind and its relations with nature.

Lyrical Ballads is in most respects a profoundly optimistic book. As Stephen Gill says of the period 1797-98, Wordsworth and Coleridge 'were increasingly in love with one another, and daily contact, endless talk, madcap walking expeditions, and, most important of all, writing and planning poems made them, simply, very happy'.[1] William's sister, Dorothy, was of course an intimate part of this love relationship. There is a sense in which *Lyrical Ballads* should be seen as a collaboration between the three young people. Hearing William say, 'How beautifully the sun sets on that yellow bank!', Hazlitt thought, 'With what eyes these poets see nature!' It was Dorothy, however, who, as her brother and their friend acknowledged, had the finest and quickest eye for nature. Both poets benefited from what Coleridge called her 'eye watchful in minutest observation of nature'.

But it wasn't only in her seeing that Dorothy Wordsworth contributed to *Lyrical Ballads*. It was also in what she was. In Thomas De Quincey's words, 'she was the very wildest (in the sense of the most natural) person I have ever known; and also the truest, most inevitable, and at the same time the quickest and readiest in her sympathy with either joy or sorrow, with laughter or with tears, with the realities of life, or the larger realities of the poets'.

'It is the hour of feeling.' Wordsworth 'addressed' the line to her. It applies not only to the hour but also to the 'moment' of *Lyrical Ballads*, especially in the volume belonging to the Alfoxden period. Dorothy Wordsworth was a source and a catalyst of feeling. She is a presence in a number of the poems. A presence acknowledged as an influence, she is associated with wildness. In 'Lines written a few miles above Tintern Abbey', for example, Wordsworth speaks of 'the shooting lights/Of thy wild eyes'. These are eyes that see, but they also disclose her inner being. The poets of Lyrical Ballads value wildness. Not the wildness of lawless or immoral behaviour; rather a wildness synonymous with the natural, and appertaining to human kind's 'home' on Earth. In this respect, Dorothy, at once wild and homely, is used to support the faith of *Lyrical Ballads* that the universe is home to human beings.

---

[1] Stephen Gill, *William Wordsworth A Life* (Oxford: Clarendon Press. 1989), p. 122.

'Nutting' provides an example of Dorothy Wordsworth's presence in *Lyrical Ballads*. Here, Wordsworth disturbs himself with his memory of what he did to the 'virgin scene' of the hazel copse:

> Then up I rose,
> And dragg'd to earth both branch and bough, with crash
> And merciless ravage; and the shady nook
> Of hazels, and the green and mossy bower
> Deform'd and sullied, patiently gave up
> Their quiet being:

From his 'sense of pain' at what he had done he turns to his sister:

> Then, dearest Maiden! move along these shades
> In gentleness of heart with gentle hand
> Touch, – for there is a Spirit in the woods.

On the face of it, giving this advice to his sister is rich, for it wasn't Dorothy who needed to be told to be gentle. Her invocation here only makes sense as calling up a presence that stabilises the poet, shaken by a memory of his own lawless, violent passion. Dorothy doesn't need to be told 'there is a Spirit in the woods'. She herself is in league with that Spirit, which here brings her brother comfort and forgiveness.

Coleridge, in the passage with which I began, depoliticises *Lyrical Ballads* by speaking only of 'the loveliness and the wonders of the world before us'. The world before the friends in 1797 was that of their country at war, a country in which the democratic spirit inspired by the French Revolution was in retreat, and in which the poets, who remained democrats, harboured feelings and ideas that the authorities would have regarded as dangerous. There is a double irony in the fact that these observers, with their compassionate social vision, were themselves being observed, but for the wrong reason. Servants gossiped about them and in consequence an officious doctor was responsible for a Home Office informer descending on the Quantocks. The agent, James Walsh, reported that 'the inhabitants of Alfoxton House' (as he called it) 'are a Sett of violent Democrats'.

As Hazlitt saw, Wordsworth at this time did undoubtedly have a levelling Muse. In some respects, life in the Quantocks must have been uncomfortable for the poets. The Wordsworths were faced with the prospect of homelessness, since their lease on Alfoxden was not renewed;

they and Coleridge were objects of suspicion. Wordsworth evidently saw himself very differently from the ways in which both his neighbours and the authorities saw him. He had, he said, 'at all times endeavoured to look steadily at my subject'. He chose his 'subjects from common life'. His idea of the Poet is of course his idea of himself: 'a man speaking to men'; 'the rock of defence of human nature, an upholder and preserver, carrying every where with him relationship and love'.

The democratic poet sees things that hadn't been seen in quite that way before, even by George Crabbe, writing about 'the poor laborious natives of the place': things pertaining to real people in real landscapes, as distinct from the objects of traditional pastoral. Things we still need to see. I remember with shame being amused as a student by Wordsworth's simplicity, as in his words about Simon Lee's ankles: 'For still, the more he works, the more/His poor old ancles swell'. And by his description of old Ruth, who 'works out of doors with him, /And does what Simon cannot do;/ For she, not over stout of limb, /Is stouter of the two'. I was not amused by the disabling conditions, but by the poet's plain recording of them. In consequence I failed at that time to realise the revolutionary nature of the verse, which has helped to shape our seeing and feeling of common life.

Consider the following, for example:

> – This woman dwelt in Dorsetshire,
> Her hut was on a cold hill-side,
> And in that country coals are dear,
> For they come far by wind and tide.

Plenty of picturesque tourists admired rustic huts on hill-sides, but how many, before Wordsworth, *saw* what it must be like to live in them, or thought with any concern about the price of coal, or considered what the distance of Dorset from the coalfields might mean to a poor old woman? Who took such mundane considerations seriously? By the same token, we may know about the harshness of laws relating to the theft of wood from hedges, but would we feel how 'alluring' 'an old hedge' could be if we hadn't seen it through Goody Blake's needy eyes?

The democratic Wordsworth isn't a middle-class ideologue. He is a poet who loves the life of human beings, and knows that individuals with souls manifest it, men and women who are essentially like him. *Lyrical Ballads* are thus poems of encounter, of meetings which generate a sense of relationship. As Wordsworth says in *The Prelude* (1805):

> When I began to inquire,
> To watch and question those I met, and held
> Familiar talk with them, the lonely roads
> Were schools to me in which I daily read
> With most delight the passions of mankind,
> There saw into the depth of human souls,
> Souls that appear to have no depth at all
> To vulgar eyes.

Lyrical Ballads record meetings not with idealised types, as in traditional pastoral, but with real people with souls, in whose depths Wordsworth reveals passions that bind them to one another and to their native places. This is the main source of a stream of influence that flows through the nineteenth century, through Charles Dickens and George Eliot and John Ruskin, for example, and feeds a radical politics that counters materialism, as well as reactionary ideas.

The poetry of relationship and love in *Lyrical Ballads* stands in a dialectical opposition to isolation and solipsism. Happy as the poets were in one another's company they formed a small beleaguered group. As E. P. Thompson says: 'the democrats, in 1797, were being driven into small and personal survival groups'. Thompson relates the forms of writing to this, 'the personal dialogue with one intimate friend', or the interior monologue.[2] The poets were also in process of grounding themselves again, and Wordsworth, in particular, was in recoil from a rationalism which, earlier, had all but robbed him of his imaginative powers. The poetry of encounter, therefore, is juxtaposed with poetry of isolation. More often, poems work through isolation towards relationship, or dramatize failures to do so. Objects in the landscape are often revealed to have been the sites of such conflict.

Thus, 'Lines left upon a Seat in a Yew-Tree' begins, like 'Michael', with a man-made object. The pile of stones recalls to the poet its maker, 'one who own'd/No common soul'. Evidently, he was an idealist, one who, disillusioned, turned from the world, 'And with the food of pride sustained his soul/In solitude'. He appears to have been an intellectual, 'big with lofty views', but though in his solitude he *sees* the loveliness of the scene, and 'the world, and man himself', 'he must never feel'. The injunction seems to be a consequence of his morbid self-isolation, and the poem warns the reader,

---

[2] E. P. Thompson, *The Romantics* (Woodbridge: The Merlin Press, 1997), p. 50.

>   that pride,
> Howe'er disguised in its own majesty,
> Is littleness; that he, who feels contempt
> For any living thing, hath faculties
> Which he has never used.

'Littleness' denotes a double action: sympathy is diminished, and its weakening atrophies the faculties of the one who does not feel, or who feels contempt.

It seems to me reasonable to suppose that here, as in other poems with a similar theme, Wordsworth is analysing what could have been his own fate, if he had retreated into himself following his disillusionment with the French Revolution. The poet sees a poet's temptation, a permanent temptation in troubled times (Seamus Heaney acknowledges it in 'Exposure') and in a fragmented society. In effect, it is to turn poetry into a private indulgence. The man in 'Lines', 'On visionary views would fancy feed, /Till his eye streamed with tears'. He is an example of how 'the visionary' (traditionally an ennobling designation of the poet), instead of seeing and feeling 'the primary laws of our nature' in 'the incidents of common life', can become an escapist, isolating himself from the world and blinding himself with self-indulgent tears.

Coleridge treats a similar theme in 'The Nightingale', where he proposes that, 'In nature there is nothing melancholy'. It is the melancholy man who apprehends the nightingale's song as melancholy, thereby revealing nothing of the truth about nightingales or nature, but displaying the human propensity for egotism:

>   some night-wandering Man, whose heart was pierc'd
> With the remembrance of a grievous wrong,
> Or slow distemper or neglected love,
> (And so, poor Wretch! fill'd all things with himself
> And made all gentle sounds tell back the tale
> Of his own sorrows) he and such as he
> First nam'd these notes a melancholy strain;

Coleridge goes on to say: 'And many a poet echoes the conceit'. The effect of this statement is to distinguish the new poetry of *Lyrical Ballads* from imitative verse. The former arises from self-surrender, in which the poet shares in the spirit of nature. This is the 'different lore' Coleridge has learnt together with 'My Friend, and my Friend's Sister', who do not 'profane/Nature's sweet voices always full of love/And joyance!' The fundamental pre-Darwinian faith of *Lyrical Ballads* rests on this perception of the universality of joy. In Wordsworth's words in 'Lines written in early spring':

> 'tis my faith that every flower
> Enjoys the air it breathes.

This optimistic philosophy does not deny the existence of suffering, but makes it, rather, the responsibility of humankind. In the words of the same poem, Wordsworth grieves 'to think/What man has made of man'.

A sympathetic perception of human suffering is of course one of the principal features of *Lyrical Ballads*. Usually it is suffering with a human cause, which reflects upon social injustice. But whether social or natural, the suffering treated in the poems involves awakening: both actual seeing and moral vision. Nor is it always the reader's eyes that are being opened. Those who most need to be woken and enlightened are intellectuals, and these, in the first instance, are the poets themselves.

The fourth poem of 'Poems on the Naming of Places' shows Wordsworth and 'his two beloved Friends' in a critical light. They are described walking in the mountains above Grasmere in playful and 'vacant mood', in which they hear 'the busy mirth/Of Reapers' from the fields below. The poem so far has elements of conventional pastoral, and the poet and his friends are 'Feeding unthinking fancies'. Then they see, from behind, a man fishing, a Peasant, who doesn't fit into their idea of what he should be doing:

> with one and the same voice
> We all cried out, that he must be indeed
> An idle man, who thus could lose a day
> Of the mild harvest, when the labourer's hire
> Is ample.

This seems rich in view of *their* idleness. Then the man turns his head, and, with a shock, the whole conventional scene is shaken up and rearranged:

> we saw a man worn down
> By sickness, gaunt and lean, with sunken cheeks
> And wasted limbs.
> …

> Too weak to labour in the harvest field,
> The man was using his best skill to gain
> A pittance from the dead unfeeling lake
> That knew not of his wants.

The experience is an awakening for the friends, and a reproach to their 'unthinking fancies', which match a conventional pastoral vision to a lack of feeling, natural in the lake but not in human beings. The sobering lesson is one appropriate to poets:

> Nor did we fail to see within ourselves
> What need there is to be reserv'd in speech,
> And temper all our thoughts with charity.

So, they called the place 'Point Rash-Judgment'.

I take this poem as a paradigm of the art of seeing in *Lyrical Ballads*, which is concerned with the frivolity of intellectuals who substitute a vision of the world – here, distinctively a pastoral vision – for the reality of the natural and human landscape. Here those intellectuals are the poet and his companions, who receive a shock from encountering an actual human being, who does not correspond to their literary image or ideal. The experience is humanizing, and has important implications for their seeing, which refocuses on thought tempered with charity, requiring a change in their use of language. This moral vision connects a steady look at the subject with 'the real language of men'. Respect and self-respect are equally involved in this; by his language the poet participates in the reality of human life, or removes himself from it.

In the words of 'Tintern Abbey' *Lyrical Ballads* is about learning to look on nature in its connected natural and human forms. By contrast, 'A Moralist', as 'A Poet's Epitaph' says, 'has neither eyes nor ears;/Himself his world, and his own God'. He is

> One to whose smooth-rubbed soul can cling
> Nor form, nor feeling, great or small;
> A reasoning, self-sufficing thing,
> An intellectual All-in-all!

To him the poet says: 'Sleep in thy intellectual crust'. As Wordsworth himself might have slept, in the reason divorced from feeling which he had imbibed from Godwin's philosophy, if he had not learnt to hear 'the still, sad music of humanity', and behold

> the mighty world
> Of eye and ear, both what they half-create,
> And what perceive; well pleased to recognize
> In nature and the language of the sense,
> The anchor of my purest thoughts, the nurse,
> The guide, the guardian of my heart, and soul
> Of all my moral being.

Wordsworth acknowledged that his 'both what they half-create, / And what perceive' closely resembled a line from Edward Young's *Night Thoughts*: 'And half-create the wondrous world they see'. In Wordsworth, however, the idea that eye and ear partly create and partly perceive the world is an originating thought of Romantic philosophy. The idea is central to the poetry of relationship and love, of connectedness, of joy common to nature and human life. In my view, the finest expression of this reciprocal relationship between nature and mind in *Lyrical Ballads* is 'There was a Boy', in which the opening line deceptively states the truth that the poem as a whole subtly images:

> There was a Boy, ye knew him well, ye Cliffs
> And Islands of Winander!

In what sense can material places, cliffs and islands, be said to have 'known' a person? Is this merely a sentimental association of boy and place, because he was native to it? Or a loose description of his familiarity to the people of the place? It is neither of these, I think, but rather an expression of belonging based on subtle reciprocity.

Standing 'alone', the boy 'Blew mimic hootings to the silent owls/ That they might answer him'. And they did, shouting 'responsive to his call'. A charming scene, but one that hardly prepares us for its development:

> And, when it chanced,
> That pauses of deep silence mock'd his skill,
> Then, sometimes, in that silence, while he hung
> Listening, a gentle shock of mild surprize
> Has carried far into his heart the voice
> Of mountain torrents, or the visible scene

> Would enter unawares into his mind
> With all its solemn imagery, its rocks,
> Its woods, and that uncertain heaven, receiv'd
> Into the bosom of the steady lake.

The boy calls forth echoes from nature. Then silence ensues, and in that silence he listens ('hung/Listening' is what Wordsworth says, imaging an acute suspense). It is an actively passive state, in which the boy receives 'the voice/Of mountain torrents, or the visible scene/Would enter unawares into his mind'. By the attention he has given he has prepared himself to receive nature's response. One might say there is a philosophy here of how the mind is in the world, and the world in the mind. But that would be a clumsy abstract of the experience that Wordsworth images. And what of 'that uncertain heaven, receiv'd/Into the bosom of the steady lake'? Does this perhaps relocate the Christian heaven in a state of being attainable only in this world, 'the very world which is the world/Of all of us, the place in which, in the end,/We find our happiness, or not at all'? Again, it seems to me the abstract idea does not meet the case.

De Quincey says, marvellously, of the lines about the boy listening: 'This very expression "far", by which space and its infinities are attributed to the human heart, and to its capacities of re-echoing the sublimities of nature, has always struck me as with a flash of sublime revelation'. The profound 're-echoing' reveals a universe that is receptive and responsive to its human inhabitants, but only if they attend to it, as the boy did, forming a reciprocal relationship, calling, listening, opening himself to nature's 'voice'. In this special sense, the 'Cliffs/And Islands of Winander' 'knew' the boy 'well'. In the boy's experience Wordsworth apprehends a sense of profound belonging, of being at home in place and in the universe.

This reciprocity between mind and nature is central to *Lyrical Ballads* and determines the hostility towards the intellect in the poetry. The hostility arises from Wordsworth's experience of Godwinian reason, which had cut him off from nature and turned him into a complete sceptic, leading to a period of deep despondency in the mid-1790s, from which Dorothy and Coleridge had rescued him. Coleridge's subsequent terrible remorse in his 'Dejection' Ode (first drafted in April 1802) reflects his knowledge that he had destroyed the faith of *Lyrical Ballads*, the 'lore' he shared with William and Dorothy. Coleridge restates the faith: 'we receive but what we give', at the same time recognising that he has divorced seeing from feeling, a divorce which poems in *Lyrical Ballads* showed leading to hellish states of solipsism and isolation.

The two finest poems in the book, 'The Rime of the Ancyent Marinere' and 'Michael', may seem to have little in common. However, there is in each a terrible experience of loneliness, against which each poet defines the community of human feeling, that is to say, men and women feeling for and with each other, and for objects among which they live. To my mind this is the primary subject of the book, and it involves the art – and act – of seeing.

True to Coleridge's orthodox Christianity, the Mariner's slaying of the albatross severs his bond with the divinely ordained Creation, completely isolating him:

> Alone, alone, all all alone
>   Alone on the wide wide Sea;
> And Christ would take no pity on
>   My soul in agony.

All horror follows from this severance, until the Mariner is able to feel again. Seeing the beauty of the water-snakes he is able to bless them. It is an instinctive act: 'I bless'd them unaware' – unlike the solipsist of 'Lines left upon a Seat in a Yew-tree', who sees beauty, but thinks 'that others felt/What he must never feel'. The isolated intellectual is outside the community of the living, not only human society but the whole natural order, but the Mariner is restored to it by his capacity to bless.

At this point I should acknowledge that in *Lyrical Ballads* the seeing that awakens the mind's attention is grounded upon a kind of blindness – not physical or moral impercipience, but the blindness of life itself. We can feel the being that we share with all living things, but we cannot see it. At least, we cannot see life directly, although we may perceive it through images or symbols, and apprehend it through objects.

This, I think, is implied in Wordsworth's words about Michael's landscape:

>   these fields, these hills
> Which were his living Being, even more
> Than his own blood – what could they less? had laid
> Strong hold on his affections, were to him
> A pleasurable feeling of blind love,
> The pleasure which there is in life itself.

It has often been observed that there isn't much original description in Wordsworth's poems. It was Dorothy who had the 'eye watchful in minutest observation of nature'. Her brother has been criticised for lacking this, and Dorothy credited with influencing him, when he does observe. In this context, though, I would like to ask why Michael's 'love' should be 'blind'. He isn't presented as being a dull, thoughtless man, incapable of knowing what he sees or feels, or less capable than other people. What Wordsworth is showing in this case, I think, is that love is integral to being, and therefore cannot be represented by visual descriptions or abstract reasoning.

Love is blind because it is in the blood. It is 'that instinctive tenderness, the same/Blind Spirit, which is in the blood of all'. It forms relationships and is manifested by them; it lies between Michael and the fields and hills. How then can it be shown? Not by adjectives, or descriptions, whether Michael's or Wordsworth's. Not in terms of conventional literary pastoral which depicts types in ideal landscapes, not real men and women in actual country.

Wordsworth claimed the language he has adopted is that of men who 'hourly communicate with the best objects from which the best part of language is originally derived', that 'such a language arising out of repeated experience and regular feelings is a more permanent and a far more philosophical language than that which is frequently substituted for it by Poets'. In Wordsworth's view, 'Poets' use poetic diction, and real men use the language of objects. This doesn't mean that he has a naïve philosophy of the relation between words and things. It means that he values substantives: 'these fields, these hills'. This is the language love speaks, and learning it is what made Wordsworth a poet:

> And hence this Tale, while I was yet a boy
> Careless of books, yet having felt the power
> Of Nature, by the gentle agency
> Of natural objects led me on to feel
> For passions that were not my own, and think
> At random and imperfectly indeed
> On man; the heart of man and human life.

There are links between Wordsworth and eighteenth-century poets such as Crabbe and Goldsmith. Wordsworth didn't invent compassion or social conscience. The main difference between him and them, despite the humanitarian sympathy they share, is the depth and peculiar tenderness of his sense of the home instinct. His landscapes are full of humanized objects, objects which reveal the community of feeling between people, living and dead, and between people and things.

In more simple terms, Wordsworth's landscapes are landscapes of objects that tell tales. 'Michael' begins with 'one object you might pass by, /Might see and notice not': 'a straggling heap of unhewn stones'. By the end of the poem we know the tale of Michael and Isabel and their son, Luke; of Michael's great love for the boy, who left home in order to save it, but 'in the dissolute city gave himself/To evil courses' 'so that he was driven at last/To seek a hiding-place beyond the seas'. We know, now, that the heap of stones is the remains of the sheep-fold, which Michael tells Luke is 'An emblem of the life thy Fathers liv'd', and which is 'a covenant' between Michael and Luke. The heap of stones, the sheep-fold, which Michael, because of his son's fate, was unable to complete, is an object of indescribable significance. It signifies ruined hope, the suffering of the man who loved his son, broken continuity of ancestral and familial life in place.

How does Wordsworth show this?

> and 'tis believ'd by all
> That many and many a day he thither went,
> And never lifted up a single stone.

Here the last line has a sublime simplicity, giving us an action, or rather inaction: the inability of the old man to lift 'a single stone' – an inability that bespeaks his feeling – and an object, the partly built sheep-fold. The heap of stone has the meaning that the whole tale has invested in it. It is a meaning grasped by the community – those who believed that he never lifted up a stone because they knew what he felt. Wordsworth doesn't need to show us what Michael saw in looking at the sheep-fold; but in any case, he couldn't. Instead, he has activated 'that instinctive tenderness, the same/Blind Spirit, which is in the blood of all'. We are unable to see the spirit because it is integral to what we are; we can however recognise it in objects that link us to one another and to nature.

At the beginning of Chapter X1V of *Biographia Literaria*, preceding the passage I began by quoting, and which gave me my title, Coleridge speaks of his conversations with Wordsworth during the year when they were neighbours in the Quantocks. These conversations turned frequently on the two cardinal points of poetry, the power of exciting the sympathy of the reader by a faithful adherence to the truth of nature, and the power of giving the interest of novelty by the modifying colours of imagination. The sudden charm, which accidents of light and shade, which moon-light or sun-set diffused over a known and familiar landscape, appeared to represent the practicability of combining both. These are the poetry of nature.

It is characteristic that Coleridge (or both poets) should have seen the new poetry they were contemplating and actively composing as a 'landscape' and in terms, no doubt, of the 'known and familiar landscape' they were seeing in their walks by day and night and in all weathers. The poems in *Lyrical Ballads* are as various as the actual landscapes in which they walked together and with Dorothy. But they have too a common bedrock, which Coleridge calls 'the poetry of nature'. It would be more just, I think, to call it the poetry of human nature. *Lyrical Ballads* compose a landscape in which our minds are awakened by an art that teaches us to see the human significance of natural objects.

Seeing Place

Landscape paintings were associated with landscapes in my mind from an early age, through my father's paintings of our surroundings in the south of England. He loved the work of Constable most of all; he admired the Impressionists, especially Pissarro and Monet; he was either indifferent or hostile to Modernism in its various forms. He emphasized the need for first-hand knowledge of the subject: seeing in depth, based on love. More often than not, his subject was a river: flowing colours of light and water, of clouds and shadows and vegetation. A world of colour, at once stilled and moving. I paid tribute to his art in 'Paintings':

> Avon weir pouring
>
> suspended, the race
> brushed still, river
> and sky, shadow,
> sunlight and trees rushing
>
> enclosed, opening
> the house on water.
>
> Slow Boldre,
> slower Stour:
> gold shallows;
> dark, Forest pools
>
> or where they run
> dammed – white whorl
> of an eddy, or flow
> barred – green, brown
>
> pass from seclusion
> of leaf and earth,
> blue oils spreading
> contained:

>   Christchurch fluid
>   on the wall,
>   the shore at Keyhaven
>   where an easel stood.[1]

The movement described is at once dynamic and stilled: art at once encloses nature in the frame and opens the house in which the pictures hang to the natural world. The expanding movement of paint contains the fluidity of landscape, river and shore.

The world of the poem – which is also the world of the paintings – is one in which opposites are resolved: movement and stillness, dynamic energy and peace, the fluid and the static, enclosure and openness, form and flow. Colour is integral to this world, not ornamental. It is part of the dynamic rhythms of both the paintings and nature. This is a world in which that which contains – the paintings – opens the human space – the house – in which they are contained; a world in which nature and art exist in a close relationship; in which art has qualities – movement, rhythm, colour – of nature, and nature is seen in terms of an artistic vision.

A close relationship between art and nature should not confuse them with one another. Landscape is man-made, but the nature of which it is made is not. Nature is both created and a continuous process of creation. The poem or painting is an object made of paint or words, not, in any literal sense, a mirror or a window on the world. I do, however, think of both poetry and painting as arts of seeing which, by obeying or creatively breaking their respective rules of object-making, quicken, deepen, and enlarge our imaginative vision of the world.

When, in 1982, I published a selection of my essays and reviews written during the preceding decade, I called it *Poetry of Place*. The title was deliberately ambiguous. On the one hand it referred to writers – not all of them poets – who were, in one way or another, concerned with place: Edward Thomas, David Jones, John Cowper Powys, Ivor Gurney, Frances Bellerby, Charles Olson, and others. On the other, it could be taken to mean the poetry inherent in place. In this sense, it could allude to the particular local identities produced in time by the interaction of human and nonhuman forces, by nature and history.

---

[1] Quotations from my poetry in this book will be taken from the substantial selection of my work, *The Cut of the Light: Poems 1965–2005* (London: Enitharmon Press, 2006), and designated *CL* in the text. 'Paintings', a poem of the 1970s, appears on page 74.

The ideas explored in the book both arose from close reading of the writers discussed and expressed my personal experience and need. From early on, I had been strongly attached to places, and had looked at things closely. This was partly a result of learning to see in terms of a particular literary and artistic tradition, through the attention to detail of Thomas Hardy and Richard Jefferies, and of English landscape painters. And it was partly a result of the vulnerability of all things and all places which was felt by all who grew up in the shadow of the Bomb. When I first saw place, in the early 40s, it was a theatre of war. Place was a channel of creativity, but it was also exposed to potential destruction. Nor was the threat only external. Darkness wells up within.

Later, distance helped to clarify and sharpen my sense of home ground. Living in Wales, where I moved to teach in the university at Aberystwyth in 1965, I looked back to the part of the south of England in which I had grown up, and saw it as though for the first time. This was partly because I was among people who see their own places feelingly. Now, too, I learned about the vulnerability people feel not only because they share in a general threat of annihilation, but also because they feel the ground slipping from under their feet, as their language and culture are eroded. It was not a feeling with which I could simply identify, as one who could look back to places he was no longer part of. Rather, learning British history anew, in the light of the Welsh experience of internal colonialism, my seeing of both England and Wales was complicated. I was familiar, however, with the influence of metropolitan centralism in England, which determines ideas of the 'provincial', and marginalizes all local experience. And in Wales I met a resistance to this that I found profoundly congenial, and a living idea of the poet as a voice of resistance, who celebrates and commemorates the things of place.

As Emyr Humphreys in *The Taliesin Tradition* has demonstrated, the tradition of Welsh praise poetry descends from the sixth century AD. It is a tradition that has adapted to the needs of a changing society, but which, through all its adaptations, has been instrumental in 'defending a realm under siege',[2] and sustaining the Welsh people's sense of identity. It is a tradition rooted in the Welsh language, but which a number of Welsh poets and novelists writing in English in the twentieth century, including Emyr Humphreys himself, have brought to bear on Wales through the English language. Thus, for the 'Anglo-Welsh' writer, a stance

---

[2] Emyr Humphreys, *The Taliesin Tradition* (London: Black Raven Press, 1983), p. 6.

of alienated or confessional self-expression is not automatic, and the idea of the poet as a man speaking to men, within a community, offers what is still to some degree a practicable alternative. I should also say that this is no longer an exclusively *male* idea, and the strength of Welsh women's poetry, in Welsh and in English, in recent years, owes something to their access to 'the Taliesin tradition'.

In Wales, I wrote first about the south of England, in *Soliloquies of a Chalk Giant* (1974), and *Landscape of the Daylight Moon* and *Solent Shore*, both published in 1978. The materials of the poetry were things of place, which I was now able to see and grasp because I was standing at a distance from them; and the distance was necessarily part of the 'matter'. After ten years of living in the Welsh hill country, I wrote about Wales, out of the experience of living there, in *Englishman's Road*. Seeing place, I had found, is also a matter of knowing its deep rhythms, which are embodied in the land itself, through the long interaction between human life and language and the physical groundwork of place; and to know its rhythms, it may be necessary to live in a place for years, or, as Richard Jefferies said, like the oaks. Yet I was aware, too, of a contrary truth, and wrote, in 'Hill Country Rhythms':

> Sometimes I glimpse a rhythm
> I am not part of, and those who are
> could never see. (*CL*, p. 120)

As I learnt about what seeing may owe to the distance between the observer and the things seen, and how much seeing place may depend upon one's no longer being part of it, so I came to feel the obstacles, in the society and in the language itself, to a praise poetry in English.

I had started with poetry of place as an expression of primary feeling for the things one loves and knows – a source from which it must always be able to draw – but had come to see it, not in terms of 'roots', but as profoundly affected by displacement, and by loss. In *Poetry of Place*, I wrote about this as follows:

> Poetry of place after Wordsworth cannot be understood, I believe, outside a context of loss. The loss is comprehensive, of shared belief in an ideal of order, mainly Christian in derivation, but shaped by local cultural conditions, which include a sense of nationhood, the Church, the English language.[3]

---

[3] Jeremy Hooker, *Poetry of Place*. (Manchester: Carcanet Press, 1982), p. 181.

The loss of a common world, based upon shared beliefs, affects the poet intimately, through his or her sense of language. The crisis of meaning is fundamental; ultimately, it reflects the failure of *any* centre to hold in the twentieth century. Poetry of place both shares in the crisis and explores possibilities of renewal; its hope is, as I have written in *The Presence of the Past,* to start 'again humbled and caring from the actual ground we occupy'.[4]

'Only the neurotic/look to their beginnings.'[5] The remark of the Tribune, in David Jones's 'The Tribune's Visitation', is of a piece with the Tribune's political dogma, which subdues the love and memory of place and local culture, even in Italy, to the world-plan of the Roman Empire. He is visiting 'troops of the Roman garrison in Palestine in the early decades of the First Century A.D.', but the poem, first printed in *The Listener* in 1958, speaks also of the modern world, and especially of imperial Britain, as few English poems have done. The Tribune is a man who serves 'contemporary fact', as those who boast of being realists invariably claim to do; but he has to subdue his own 'remembered things of origin and streamhead, the things of the beginnings', to 'the fact of empire'. Thus, his discourse to the troops is fraught with emotional tension, even as he speaks for the imperial idea.

The conflict in the poem, which works on several levels, is central to all David Jones's writings. It may be described as a conflict between local culture and imperial or megalopolitan civilization, between utilitarianism and the sacramental apprehension of reality, and, more problematically, between male and female modes of perception. If we are to treat it as a theme, however, we must first understand that it was a conflict which David Jones knew in the very texture of his experience – as a soldier on the Western Front from 1915 to 1918, as a Catholic and an artist living in a secular society, as a Londoner with a fierce attachment to Wales. This is one reason why David Jones's sense of place is profoundly significant; because he lived the history of his time, and apprehended place in terms of the tensions affecting it. There is a sense in which 'Only the neurotic look to their beginnings' is true. For example, it is manifest in the escapist pastoral nostalgia that is a weakening influence on English art and writing in the nineteenth and twentieth centuries, and which sometimes touches authentic work, such as Edward Thomas's and Paul Nash's. In so far as David Jones romanticizes Wales, as a pre-industrial culture, which

---

[4] Jeremy Hooker, *The Presence of the Past* (Bridgend: Poetry Wales Press, 1987), p. 213.
[5] David Jones, *The Sleeping Lord and Other Fragments* (London: Faber and Faber, 1974), p. 51.

he opposes to the English oppressor's mechanical world-view, he, too, is guilty of sentimentality. But this effect is more apparent than real, since his symbolic and mythological treatment of the relationship between England and Wales, in 'The Sleeping Lord' and 'The Tutelar of the Place' for example, also addresses the political and historical situation.

There are several reasons why, in my view, David Jones is the most significant post-war British poet, and one of the greatest poets writing in English in the twentieth century. This is not the place to make a case for this view, and I wish, here, to say only two things. First, that David Jones, on formal and linguistic and rhythmic grounds, is at best an intensely exciting poet, and the one who, with Ezra Pound, has done most to extend the possibilities of poetry in English in the twentieth century. Secondly, that his response to secular and imperial (then post-imperial) Britain has significantly illuminated our situation.

David Jones problematizes the relation between centre and periphery in modern Britain, and therefore the sense of place. This has to be understood, however, in the context of what he loves and knows, and of what he attempts to bring together. According to Coleridge, writing in *The Friend,* 'To carry on the feelings of Childhood into the powers of Manhood, to combine the Child's sense of wonder and novelty with the Appearances which every day for perhaps forty years had rendered familiar ... this is the character and privilege of Genius'. This is an apt description of David Jones. For example, it describes the continuity between his earliest known drawings, such as *Dancing Bear* (1903) and the tenderness of his mature literary and artistic renderings of nature and human beings and other creatures. In a more complex fashion, it describes the connection in his work between his ancestral and personal beginnings and the geological and cultural origins of the British Isles. Although this is not an explicit theme of *The Anathemata,* it is a feeling that animates a significant part of that work.

The Anathemata is 'about one's own thing', David Jones writes in the Preface; 'which *res* is unavoidably part and parcel of the Western Christian *res*, as inherited by a person whose perceptions are totally conditioned and limited by and dependent upon his being indigenous to this island'.[6] The word "thing", used both in this sense and to refer to concrete objects, made by human or divine means, is important in David Jones's work. His most succinct description of his working process also occurs on the same

---

[6] David Jones, *The Anathemata* (London: Faber and Faber, 1952), p. 11. Hereafter referenced *A* in text.

page of the Preface: 'One is trying to make a shape out of the very things of which one is oneself made'.

In *The Anathemata* it is making itself, geological, artistic, and cultural, that returns us to the beginnings. In the following short passage referring to the making of the South Wales coal measures and the glacial shaping of Dalriada and North Wales for example:

> Before the slow estuarine alchemies had coal-blacked the green dryad-ways over the fire-clayed seat-earth along all the utile seams from Taff to Tâf.
>
> Before the microgranites and the clay-bonded erratics wrenched from the diorites of Aldasa, or off the Goat Height in the firthway, or from the Clota-sides or torn from either Dalriada, with what was harrowed-out *in via*, up, from the long drowned outcrops, under, coalesced and southed by the North Channel.
> (*A*, pp. 72-73)

Here is place present, so to speak, in its making: through the names, in the processes ('slow estuarine alchemies') and in the materials and things which disclose their making ('the microgranites and the clay-bonded erratics'). This is an intensely physical writing, in which scientific terms are poetic images. It is language both sounded and wrought, and poetry of fact. It is earth poetry, too, as we may sense in 'harrowed-out', with its echo of 'the rat of no-man's-land' in *In Parenthesis,* which we hear 'harrow-out earthly, trowel his cunning paw':[7] the poetry of a man with a tactile imagination, and bodily sympathy with the things and processes he re-presents. Love of place is a physical experience; seeing with the eye can be overvalued if it does not work together with a sensing and feeling of rhythms which underlie appearances.

When I first read *The Anathemata*, in Wales in about 1970, and before I had understood much of it, it was the sheer physicality, and the combination of materiality and rhythmic movement, of its rendering of geology and prehistory that awed and excited me. This quality chimed in my mind with Thomas Hardy's sense of geological time, and with the temporal 'depth' of his 'past-marked' landscapes, with which I had been long familiar, though to Hardy the nonhuman is merely indifferent

---

[7] David Jones, *In Parenthesis* (London: Faber and Faber, 1937), p. 54. Hereafter referenced *IP* in text.

to the human, while to David Jones they are both forms of the one Creation. But of course, reading Hardy had followed long after my own early impressions of place, which were marked by what underlay it: sheer cliffs of inland chalk, stone hand-axes and mammoth bones, dredged from Southampton Water, and gravel and clay exposed under house foundations in the bombed city. The things I initially found in *The Anathemata* were similar to my first things, and they engendered a similar awe. Earlier I had responded to W. H Auden's northern landscapes, and to the earth poetry of T.S. Eliot's *East Coker*. It was in David Jones, however, and to a lesser extent Charles Olson, that I first found a poetry of fact, and a strong physical intimacy with the *making* of place. As far as I am aware, David Jones had little or no influence on my style of writing. What I do owe in part to him is confidence in my own poetic materials, or what I like to call *ground*, which is the ground of place shaped, and continually being reshaped, by interacting forces – geology and ecology, history and society and culture – and shot through with personal and family and ancestral experience. As living in Wales was making me more aware of my Englishness, and as a problematic identity not a simple 'rootedness', so it was David Jones's sense of insular things, rather than Charles Olson's American materials, which helped to show me the subject I loved and partly knew, and had to explore.

Reading David Jones, at the same time that I was getting to know something about modern Welsh poetry, in translation, helped to change my idea of the poet's function, which before I had vaguely associated with self-expression. The experience of living in Wales also strongly affected my sense of what is valuable in modern English and American and European poetry. My interest in Modernist writing was quickened, largely because I saw its formal and linguistic devices – parataxis and ellipsis, presentation and spacing of images, fragmentation and sequence – as affording 'openings', out of the self, and onto a cosmic order. At the same time, I became preoccupied with common ground, the ground of shared experience, and increasingly aware of how difficult it is to identify and express, particularly for an English poet today. The Welsh poet Gwenallt became a touchstone for me. Or, it would be more accurate to say, since I had almost no Welsh, an idea of Gwenallt did: the idea of him as a man rooted in the experience of his people, in industrial South Wales and also in a rural neighbourhood, and speaking *from* a society and a tradition.

The idea was not altogether false, I think, although at that time I had less sense of Gwenallt's intellectual and spiritual pilgrimage, from

Marxism to revolutionary Christianity. Something of what I came to admire in Gwenallt and other modern Welsh poets may be seen in Charles Reznikoff's idea of the poet, as described by Michael Heller in his book on the Objectivists:

> The poet, according to Reznikoff (perhaps in particular the Jewish poet of the People of the Book) stands always with history at his back. For such a poet, the work is not one of self-expression but one of a desire to speak for those voices lost or denied in time, for individuals caught up in historical forces beyond their control.[8]

As I was reacting against an English idea of the poet as a person with a special sensibility, and against the divisiveness of social class, so there was, no doubt, a compensatory element in my idea of the Welsh poet as a voice of the historical community. For the Welsh poet also, in Welsh and English, Heidegger's question (after Hölderlin) is a living reality: in a destitute time, what are poets for? When I think of writers such as Emyr Humphreys and Roland Mathias, Jean Earle and Ruth Bidgood and Tony Conran, however, all of them writing in English in Wales, I realize the extent to which the sense of community in the Welsh tradition, and of community of the living and the dead, informs their work.

The post-war English poems I most value have, for all their differences from each other and from the work of David Jones and other Welsh poets, something of the same quality of being at once personal and drawn from a life which the poet shares or has shared with others. During this period there has been an upsurge of English poetry associated with place: in Basil Bunting's *Briggflatts*, Geoffrey Hill's *Mercian Hymns*, Roy Fisher's *City*, and Donald Davie's *Essex Poems*; in Jack Clemo's Cornish poems, and Charles Tomlinson's poems set in Gloucestershire; in the work of C.H. Sisson, Michael Hamburger, Ted Hughes, Paul Hyland, Molly Holden, Kim Taplin, John Welch and other poets. The American poets Ronald Johnson and John Matthias have drawn on native resources in their seeing of English places, with a celebratory intensity that it would probably be impossible for an English poet, implicated in the complexities of the society, to match. For all the differences among these and other poets' uses of place, one point is, I think, generally valid. Having a sense of place works against alienation and a feeling of radical disconnection

---

[8] Michael Heller, *Conviction's Net of Branches* (Carbondale and Edwardsville, IL: Southern Illinois University Press, 1985), p. 68.

between the self and others; indeed, it provides the poet with a world 'between', in the sense Martin Buber defined in *Between Man and Man*: 'We do not find meaning lying in things nor do we put it into things, but between us and things it can happen'.

When I first read it, I was struck – even shocked – by a word in Seamus Heaney's 'Now and in England' (1977), later reprinted in *Preoccupations*, with the title 'Englands of the Mind'. Writing of three contemporary English poets – Ted Hughes, Geoffrey Hill and Philip Larkin – who were, he said, 'afflicted with a sense of history', Heaney claimed that 'Their very terrain is becoming consciously precious'.[9] It was the second of the two meanings of 'precious' – affected – and its possible relation to the first meaning – valuable – in this context, that struck me. Affectation is, after all, a charge that can be justly brought against modern English art and verse that uses place as an escape from the world, and therefore betrays the reality of place. Only consider the way in which Rupert Brooke's use of the words 'England' and 'English' in 'The Soldier' has made it impossible for later English poets to use the words without the utmost caution. Not that it is fair to blame Brooke for what was in the air in 1914: a kind of patriotic sentiment that would ultimately problematize *any* sense of an English identity.

To write about place is, as Heaney himself has demonstrated, to draw upon, and be drawn by, strong original attachments. There is more to be said about contemporary English poetry of place, however; and Heaney said some of it. After quoting Philip Larkin's 'Going, Going', Heaney continues:

> I think that sense of an ending has driven all three of these writers into a kind of piety towards their local origins, has made them look in, rather than up, to England. The loss of imperial power, the failure of economic nerve, the diminished influence of Britain inside Europe, all this has led to a new sense of the shires, a new valuing of the native English experience.[10]

This was something that needed to be said, and could be said, perhaps, only by a poet who was not English, but had an ironically detached yet

---

[9] Seamus Heaney, *Preoccupations: Selected Prose 1968–1978* (London: Faber and Faber, 1980), pp. 150–151.
[10] Ibid., p. 169.

sympathetic view of contemporary English poetry. Yet Heaney's argument is, in certain respects, limited. For one thing, it does not acknowledge the larger historical context of the subject, or the extent to which English poets of the First World War, especially Edward Thomas and Ivor Gurney, had experienced a painful tension between their love of England and their knowledge of the British State. Nor did recognition of such tension originate with the First World War, or even with Coleridge when, in 'Fears in Solitude' in 1798, he suffered in his mind the conflict between England's tyranny and 'the bonds of natural love' binding him to his 'Mother Isle'. For another thing, Heaney's concentration on three post-war English poets hardly suggests how a sense of place is implicated in the ontological 'homelessness' which has been widely felt in the secular modern world, and which lies at the heart of Heidegger's philosophy. Also, what may be deemed a parochial problem, if one is thinking exclusively about contemporary English poetry, is actually the experience of many different peoples, uprooted from their native lands and cultures by the cataclysms of twentieth-century history. It befits an English poet to keep a sense of proportion and not to make free with a word like 'exile' when reflecting upon his experience of social mobility or whatever reason he had for leaving 'home'. Yet it is necessary also to avoid using the kind of irony that constitutes a refusal to recognize in oneself fundamental human needs.

In seeing place, the poet may explore those needs. David Jones sought in *The Anathemata* to make a shape out of the very things of which he was himself made. Wordsworth, in the 1802 Preface to *Lyrical Ballads*, defined the poet as one who carried 'everywhere with him relationship and love'. The aims are complementary, and both are involved in poetry of place. What are 'the very things'? What are the relationships by which we live?

There is another question, which George Oppen asks in 'Blood from the Stone': 'What do we believe/To live with?' My discovery of the American Objectivists, and my reading of George Oppen and Charles Reznikoff in particular, were most intense during the period 1981-83, when I first returned to live in England for a time. I was then beginning to think of an analogy between a poetic form and a place, which I first formulated in my journal as follows:

> A large poem, in which the reader can move about, continually interested and frequently surprised by detail, as a place we explore has new features that we come upon at every turn, and we

simultaneously find ourselves in discovering the connections and order in what is initially a patternless maze, and are taken out of ourselves by the fascination of exploration and the enlightenment of discovery. So that in a generous space the spirit is freed.

The difficulty of what I wanted to attempt may be gauged by another journal entry, made during the same month, July 1981, after I had returned from an excursion to the great prehistoric stone circle at Avebury to news of the riots in Toxteth:

> What use an art of the common place when it can't in fact approach the actual common places – Toxteth or Brixton or Southall or even the area of Southampton where I used to live – but can only flourish on ancient deserted sites, or on signs of long-vanished cultures? I have no answer; nor can I accept the way of a Gary Snyder or a J.C. Powys which finds the real only in an order from which all but a few people in the West today are excluded...
>
> ...even as I write 'us', 'all of us', 'fellow countrymen', etc. I know the implication of sharing is willed, not felt and exists much more in the threat common to us all today – enforcing a negative brotherhood – than in genuine fellow feeling. Together in hopelessness; but how together in hope?

It was in the context of such thoughts and feelings that Oppen's question came to seem to me *the* question.

As I understand it, there is, in Reznikoff and Oppen, a sense of the value of public space, of the space that lies between human beings and between us and other creatures and things, and it is ultimately here, in this space, that meaning is to be sought. No poet could have been more concerned than George Oppen with sincerity of thought and feeling and clarity of seeing. The result for Oppen was a mental and spiritual discipline such as that we associate with Simone Weil, and a way of seeing as individual as Emily Dickinson's. Inevitably, therefore, Oppen experienced acute tension between his individual vision and his unity with humanity, and, because he did not slacken the tension, by escaping into either populism or a private imaginative world, he explored the possibility of common meaning in poetry as almost no other poet of our time has done.

The art of seeing, and seeing place, becomes critical in Oppen. There are, I think, affinities between the art of seeing practised by certain English writers – Richard Jefferies, John Ruskin, and Gerard Manley Hopkins in the nineteenth century – and the clarity of perception of the Objectivists. There is obviously a major difference between a Jefferies essay and a Reznikoff poem, in that one is focused upon nature and the other on the city. Yet there is in each a common loving quickness and care that lets the otherness of what is seen *be*. The tragedy inherent in the Jefferies way of seeing was its isolation of the see-er from humanity. Objectivist seeing, on the other hand, was profoundly human, and humane. Nevertheless, Oppen's 'Of Being Numerous', in which he explores the relationship between the one and the many, includes this painful recognition:

"Whether, as the intensity of seeing increases, one's distance
    from Them, the people, does not also increase"
I know, of course I know, I can enter no other place.

For Oppen, his 'place' is the question whether seeing intensely distances the poet from the people with whom he shares the world. There are other important questions about the poet's relationship with place, but this one about distance between the poet and others, within the very place itself, seems to me the most important. I am not writing this essay in the conviction that there is an answer. The only things that are certain about this subject are: that seeing place is never finished, and the poem of place must incorporate the difficulties of seeing it.

In 1981, whilst living in Winchester, I got to know something about the tradition of the Winchester School of Artists, which spanned the Anglo-Saxon and Norman periods. I became fascinated by the work of one artist in particular – the anonymous illuminator whom Walter Oakeshott in *The Artists of the Winchester Bible* (1945) called 'Master of the Leaping Figures', and who worked on the twelfth-century Winchester Bible.

The initial which opens IV Kings is a great example of this master's work. Here, in the roundel of the letter P, the prophet Elijah is depicted rebuking the messengers sent by the King of Samaria to Baalzebub; half way down the stalk of the letter Elijah ascends in the chariot of fire; his cloak falls below him, and at the bottom Elisha catches the cloak in his hand. So much prophetic action at different times dramatized in a small space! Colour accentuates the drama: red against dark blue; flame-like, different coloured vegetation, figures like flames; the holy Byzantine gold which forms the frame. It is a marvellously dynamic work, and perfectly controlled, inside and outside the frame of the initial. The figures leap with passion and vitality, and the design contains them.

In my poem 'Master of the Leaping Figures' I imagine the master working on this and other illuminations at a time when civil war has engulfed the city in flames:

> Under his hand the great book
> glows with lapis lazuli, red,
> gold, and in the smoke
> of fire-balls falling on the city.
>
> Outside, the torturer's art:
> figures hung up by the thumbs,
> jerking on a blackened ground.
> Devils fill the castles, and the people
> reel in a divided land, fleeing
> from the horsemen; peasants
> are forced from the fields
> to drag carts loaded with stone,
> and the crops rot.
> Men say openly that Christ
> and His saints sleep.
>
> Under his hand, they do not sleep.
> Here he is master,
> illuminating the Word in a little letter,
> painting in a tiny space
> the beginning and the end.
>
> Lines cut deep in time
> meet in his hand: from Rome,
> Byzantium, Ireland
> and the Viking north;
> from tracks hacked through woodland
> and seaways marked by wrecks;
> from monks of the Saxon minster,
> a ruin outside the workshop.

> It is not love of violence
> that leaps in the figures,
> but violent love:
> David gripping the lion's jaw;
> Moses clubbing the Egyptian,
> as a Saxon remembering his home
> might dream of smashing the skull
> of his conqueror;
> Christ thrusting the devil into Hell.
>
> All flame against the dark,
> like the prophet who is one
> fire with the horses of fire,
> blazing against the blue
> of a midsummer night-sky
> with a rim of gold;
> a man barely contained
> by the frame holding him
> who leaps in flesh of flame
> in a world on fire, burning
> in the mantle that he passes on.
> (*CL*, pp. 137–38)

Torture, also, is an art which deploys considerable ingenuity. But here, in the scriptorium, with war raging outside, the master wakes religious truth with his images. His work contains everything, the beginning and the end; even the Word, his Maker, is illuminated 'in a little letter'. Violent love leaps in his figures; he and his world blaze with the fire of a living tradition, which has descended to him from different times and places, and which he passes on.

That is my portrait of the medieval artist, and, like all such portraits, I now realize, it probably reveals more about its modern author. The master is anonymous, skilled, a craftsman working within a tradition; he serves a well-defined purpose; he renews an art which reveals truth, and passes it on. He is almost everything that a modern poet is not.

At the present-day School of Art in Winchester, I met the sculptor and painter Lee Grandjean. Later, in 1987, he would design the cover of my book of which 'Master of the Leaping Figures' is the title poem. It is a vivid design, with contained, dynamic rhythms: a modernist image, which corresponds to the medieval master's dance of energies. Subsequently Lee

Grandjean and I have worked together on a collaboration, *Their Silence a Language*, which involves sculpture and drawing, poetry and prose, and explores new relationships, new forms of participation between man and nature. In the written part of the work I return to the New Forest as my ground, but bring to it questions of meaning which I share with Grandjean, and which first helped to draw us together.

What we recognized in each other's work were, among other things, a similar love of the vital and significant image, and a similar search for values. Lee Grandjean combines a strong conviction of the necessity of the artist to respond to life in the present in his work, with a strong sense of tradition. When we first met, in 1981, he, too, was concerned with the predicament of the artist without a community. The artist seeks forms to express his own feelings, but how is he to make living images, in which we can share meaning and know our humanity, when there is no community to provide and validate the images? At that time, Grandjean had come to the end of a dominant mode of abstraction, which he found meaningless and had returned to the human figure as a source of imagery, and to the task of making images which both have sculptural integrity – the primary need, without which the work is vacuous – and belong in a world to which they 'speak'. So much I gathered from our conversations and from looking with Grandjean at the work he was making. Evidently, whatever the differences of emphasis in our ideas of community and place, we shared ideas and feelings about what is involved in the making of images, and about the problems of making images at the present time. Our subsequent work, independently and collaboratively, has, among other things, addressed and explored the problems. So much, at least, may be said, provided it is understood that talk about 'problems', like talk about 'issues' and 'themes' and the like, is an abstraction from what is actually felt, in the work that the sculptor or poet feels compelled to do.

Praise Awe Despair (1988) is one of Grandjean's painted reliefs. It is obviously a modern work of art, inconceivable without modernist experiments in painting and sculpture. It is, also, traditional: 'primitive', as much modern art is, but also having affinities with medieval illuminated manuscripts and stained glass. Like the Initial to the opening of IV Kings, *Praise Awe Despair* creates a symbolic landscape in which the same figure is depicted in different states of passion; the relief, too, is intensely dramatic and dynamic, and uses colour with emotional force. The colouring is not ornamental or descriptive, but accentuates sculptural form, contrasting the silvery blue figures with the brown of the tree image. The blue in the space between the branches echoes the paler colour of the figures, and thus intimates their affinities with the sky which the blue symbolizes, and their spirit which is integral with their material being. Praise, awe, despair are three states, three emotions or passions, of the one figure, and they form together a powerful sculptural object, with a dynamic rhythmic design. The relief is a work about the human condition, which it depicts both visually and by means of bodily images. Its appeal is to the imagination, which is rooted in our whole being.

    The following poem, 'Black on Gold', belongs to my collaboration with Lee Grandjean:

> He dreams he is a painter standing
> at his easel in an ill-lit attic painting
> studies in black and gold.
> A dead butterfly flutters in a breeze,
> dances at the window in a filthy web.
> Even when I was a boy (he thinks)
> walking with a rod in April among the trees
> I tasted filth. How free the mind?
> A man – but what (he asks) is man? –
> will do anything not to wake up.
> He dreams he is a sculptor hacking
> at the block that is himself.
> It is black, black as rainwater
> from the stump of the tree of knowledge.
> Let me let in the gold (he weeps)
> but the wood rots under his hand.
> He dreams he is a poet writing
> a poem about the shadow of a tree
> leaning over water, where sunlight
> touches the gravel bed with gold.
> He is losing his bony grip,
> the bank is eroding under him.
> Wild bees swarm in the hollow of his skull.
> He dreams he is a hunter chasing
> the beasts that seek him.
> On hands and knees, belly
> dragging in mud, icy skin,
> he follows where a black stream
> runs through bracken into the wood

> and a doe steps gracefully to the brink
> and bends her neck and drinks. (*CL*, pp. 186–87)

This is in part a dream poem. It draws on the instincts to paint and sculpt and write poetry, by which one might create a whole human image, instead of fragmentary states. It is about creativity, and it asks what 'man' is. It is also about the welling up of darkness, or depression, which is connected with the wrong use of knowledge. I have been conditioned to think of black and gold as opposites, the colour of death and the colour of life. But there is one respect, of special significance to me, in which the opposition is resolved – as perhaps in reality, behind the scenes, it always is. The New Forest streams are black and gold, when sunlight falls aslant opaque depths and touches the iron gravel. My father painted their light and dark, though he would not have used black or gold. They were among the streams which the house contained, and which it opened on. In a sense, the poem is about the struggle to make an artistic form that corresponds to a stream flowing, black on gold. It is about the rhythmic movement of life itself, which is not the opposite of death, and it is about the part colour plays in this. The poem is about mystery, but it is also about what Henry Vaughan, in the seventeenth century, wrote about in 'Affliction' (1):

> Beauty consists in colours: and that's best
> Which is not fixed, but flies, and flows…

'One is trying to make a shape'

I have been involved as a critic with David Jones's writings since 1970, but it is primarily as a poet that I have responded to them. It is inevitable, therefore, that in talking about what I as a poet have learnt from his writings, I shall have as much – or more – to say about my work as about his. For me, David Jones is the figure who towers over poetry in English in my lifetime, and his words in the preface to *The Anathemata*, 'one is trying to make a shape out of the very things of which one is oneself made' (*A*, 10), are the most succinct expression of what I understand the aim of poetry to be.

My first critical notice of David Jones appeared in 1970, in my first essay: a review-article of *The Lilting House*: An anthology of Anglo-Welsh poetry 1917–67. This anthology includes 'The Wall', 'The boast of Dai' (from *In Parenthesis*), and an extract from 'The Sleeping Lord'. I wrote, in a pompous tone, but motivated by respect for great poetry:

> Just as most young English poets would find their initial gratification at appearing in an anthology with Eliot soon turn to pain in the light of the contrast, so it must be beneficial (as such pain should be) for some of the younger poets in this book to share print with David Jones. *In Parenthesis* is, I think, one of the few great poems of the century; we shouldn't hesitate now to speak of it in the same breath as *The Waste Land* and other major works of modernism, and I admit that it gives me more pleasure than Eliot's early poems in two respects: in its generous humanity and in the scope and depth of the imagination shaping it. David Jones's learning can be valuable to us now, surely, by showing how the imagination immersed in history can give both depth and perspective to its interpretation of man's life in the present.[1]

I wrote this at a time when I was discovering David Jones's writings and it names qualities that I have continued to admire in them: the generous humanity, the scope and depth of the shaping imagination, 'immersed in history'. I went on to say, perhaps rashly: 'David Jones and R.S. Thomas

---
[1] Jeremy Hooker, 'Image and Argument', in Roland Mathias, ed., *The Anglo-Welsh Review*, Vol. 18, No. 42, p. 66.

do much to justify the claim made by another poet in this anthology [Keidrych Rees], that "the strength of the common man was always the strength of Wales". One can say of them, as Edmund Blunden has said of Hardy, that the feeling of their poetry is – in a true sense of the word – democratic'.

Responding to the generous humanity of David Jones's writings, I had misunderstood his politics; it has taken me a long time and an effort of readjustment to understand them. Even in 1980, I was bitterly disappointed to learn certain things from *Dai Greatcoat*. At that time, I wrote in my journal: "What has disturbed me most is his not being, as I thought, *in the common place*. I don't mean Wales or London, but simply in sympathetic touch with people from his original class… His friends in the years after 1918 seem all to have been 'upper' class; which unfortunately coincided with his hatred of the ersatz & the utile, which are associated mainly with people with whom he seems never to come into close contact, such as industrial workers and shopkeepers. In this respect, his attitudes are just another… version of the [Modernists'] boring and facile disdain for actual people, and idealisation of a mythic 'People'. Again, it is the reality of these 'islands' that is in question. How can it be truly represented when everything and everyone after 'The Break' – in effect, since the Industrial Revolution, and therefore almost everything we have and are now – are outside his love?"

The response may reveal my naivety: I had read *In Parenthesis* and some things in the other writings in the light of my own democratic socialist attitudes. I had found support from David Jones's example in my own 'poetry of place', in which I aimed at identifying and celebrating, 'common' experience, as opposed to expressing an alienated individualism.

A typical example of my poetry of the late 70s is 'On a Photograph of Southampton Docks' from *Solent Shore* (1978):

> Blinding silver on grey
> a suntrack points deep
> into this average morning.
> All is ready for work:
> launches at their moorings,
> small tubs off the pierhead,
> warehouses; and above all
> the cranes, these flying high
> or with pulleys dangling,

>   those far back, more spidery.
>   No, it's not their function
>   to please the eye.
>   Yet they do – more so
>   for the common goodness
>   of their function, for grace
>   extra to a working world
>   that neighbours sky and water,
>   drawing from all
>   some ordinary tribute;
>   for that reason too,
>   more beautiful, as they say:
>   like birds, like dancers. (*CL*, p. 83)

Here, I attempt to revalue words such as 'average', 'common' and 'ordinary' by associating them with the visionary and with depth. The emphasis is on 'the common goodness' of functional things, on 'grace/extra to a working world', and the value of the 'ordinary tribute'. I was writing about aspects of the world familiar to me since childhood, and in which I perceived both use and beauty, things which were valuable because shared. David Jones had helped me to see the possibilities of a poetry of place, together with the significance of my 'things' – things which, I had been shocked to feel, he disdained.

But this records a moment, in a sometimes troubled but in the main constructive relationship, through which I have learnt a great deal from David Jones. In the review-article I had referred to the value of his 'learning'. Subsequently his writings and their notes became part of my education. For example, I learnt from them a great deal about Wales, where I lived from 1965-84; about Welsh history and myth, and about the spirit of the land, as intimated for instance by the following brief quotations:

>   twine the wattles of mist, white-web a Gwydion-hedge
>   like fog on the bryniau
>   ('The Tutelar of the Place')

>   *

>   Small black horses
>   grass on the hunch of his shoulders
>   ('The Sleeping Lord')

>   *

> a prevailing sense of metamorphosis and mutability
>
> *
>
> The hedges of mist vanish or come again under the application of magic
>
> *
>
> It must be remembered that the *numina* of the hills see to the metamorphosis of whatever infiltrates those hills
> ('Wales and the Crown')

If I was changed by living for ten years in Welsh hill-country, 'under Mynydd Bach', it was partly because I saw the land and its aura under the influence of David Jones's vision.

The following is a panoramic view of the landscape in which I lived, as I described in a radio-poem, 'Englishman's Road', broadcast in 1980:

> Take a long view from Mynydd Bach: let your eye rise and fall with ridges that stone walls or bent thorns follow – green dragon backs, crested like petrified breakers; yet also the walls are always climbing or in flight.
>
> This is a country of vast spaces: it rolls with hidden hollows to the mountains of the north, against the sweep of sea –
>
>> preternatural grey,
>> the mountains of Llŷn
>> a chain of islands,
>> or blue as spirit flame,
>> or a lunula of beaten gold.
>
> Here the buzzard with broad wings spread draws a widening circle, ringing an intricate pattern of commons and enclosures, whitewashed farms and red-roofed barns.
>
> At night an irregular pattern of lights reflects the stars.

Here the western light is always changing, too quick for the eye though it notes

> grey mystery
> of April, haunted
> by the curlew's salty cry,
> or August
> floating the hills,
> or Winter
> with a hard whiteness
> hammering the ground.

And what the light changes is only a face – face of a work vaster and more laboured than the pyramids; but continuing. For this is settled country, its pattern absorbent, deeply ingrained, but unfinished; without the finality of a coiled fossil, though it too is a life wrought in rock. And here these English words play on a surface through which they cannot shine, to illumine its heart; they can possess the essence of this place no more than the narrow road under the Welsh mountain can translate its name.

> Lon Sais it is called,
> not Englishman's Road. (*CL*, pp. 132–33)

Rereading this passage, I am aware that David Jones's combinations of poetry and rhythmic prose in his poems encouraged me to develop the flexible style of 'Englishman's Road'. As far as I am able to judge, however, my use of language has little in common with the incarnational tradition of Gerard Manley Hopkins and James Joyce, to which David Jones belongs. In that respect my affinities are rather with naturalists and objectivists, with the nineteenth-century century nature writer, Richard Jefferies, whose essays I first read as a boy, and with American poetry in the tradition of William Carlos Williams. The 'barer' style of these writers may however be combined with use of words charged with a sense of history.

Stuart Piggott wrote of David Jones: 'As a poet should, he displays his word-hoard, but the words are radio-active with history'.[2] In respect of this 'radio-activity' David Jones has been influential. One thinks of Geoffrey

---

[2] Stuart Piggott, 'David Jones and the Past of Man', *Agenda*, David Jones Special Issue, Autumn–Winter 1973/4, p. 62.

Hill's *Mercian Hymns* (1971), and Seamus Heaney's *North* (1975), in both of which the presence of the past, in words, owes a palpable debt to David Jones. My poem 'Company', inspired by the New Forest, attempts to evoke the wood's religious and historical significance, and many layers of meaning: pagan, Christian, and literary. This is the third part of the poem:

> Figures emerge from the trees,
> stag-headed, wreathed with green leaves.
>
> Darkness covers the site –
> which light dissolves, opening
> cavernous depth.
>
> A sea wind gusts through the grove.
>
> The space fills with sunlight
> and shadows, whispering.
> Where, where?
> At the centre, the naked man,
> wearing the holly crown.
>
> In the trees
> forked bodies twist and writhe.
> Angels and beasts stare down.
>
> Ghost haunts ghost
> among the broken pillars,
> under the tattered canopy.
> The love song fades in the sigh of leaves.
>
> A god with arms outstretched
> bows down to the ground. (*CL*, pp. 204–205)

There are obvious stylistic differences between this and David Jones's 'To the woods of all the world is this potency – to move the bowels of us' and other evocations of woods as loved places, rich in cultural 'deposits', in *In Parenthesis*, and 'The Hunt'. I have no doubt, however, that I owe something to David Jones for confidence to attempt to render the presence of the past.

I hope I have shown what to me is the most important influence of David Jones's writings: their sense of poetic possibility. From the beginning, I found his writings exciting; rhythmically, linguistically, formally, and in subject. I will give two examples. First, the encounter with the "warden of stores" in Part 4 of *In Parenthesis*. Here, heightened prose simultaneously depicts an individual man, an aborigine, 'native to the place', and a representative never-dying soldier, Balaclava'd, 'greaved with mud', present at the raising of Stonehenge (he 'groped out from between two tottering corrugated uprights') (*IP*, pp. 89-91) and dug in on the Western Front. With its humour and kindness – a keyword in David Jones – the episode is redolent of humanity, in this moment and down the ages. As in our meeting with Shakespeare's Poor Tom, we come away from the meeting knowing more about ourselves, our kind.

The second example is the passage about the 'Master of the Venus' in 'Rite and Fore-Time' (*A*, pp. 59-60*)*, where the rhythmic and verbal excitement generates a sense of awe, as the poet brings us into the presence of the sacred. Sound-patterning and pacing are masterly. The rich and exotic words surprise, make connections, and, with references that may be obscure, point the reader to knowledge worth obtaining. A religious philosophy of creativity, divine and human, is concentrated in the images: 'man-hands god handled'; 'god-shape'; 'the fecund image of her'. As often happens in David Jones, awe is accompanied by tenderness. I believe the personal origin of this was familial: his love of his father and mother. In the poetry tenderness for male and female figures is devotional. This is a word that, in this context, would have probably embarrassed him, but it is applicable both in the Catholic sense of devotion to Jesus and the Virgin Mary, and in the sense of devotion to the fathering and mothering principles of creation, which is one of the strongest impulses in David Jones's writing.

In the passage about the 'Master of the Venus', Man is shown making himself from that which gave birth to him, ultimately Venus Genetrix, 'mother of us'. Is there a problem here for our gender-conscious and role-conscious time? Probably. But an artist can only make a shape that has integrity from the things he feels; and it is evident from such a passage that David Jones felt profoundly the mutual dependence of male and female in the act of creation, and the process of nurturing.

This leads me to make a general observation. Looking at David Jones's paintings and reading his writings one cannot doubt that he made his works from the whole of himself, including his sexuality and his 'childness'. I use this word instead of childishness or childlikeness, because it seems to me to fit better the following words of Coleridge, which apply to David Jones: 'To carry on the feelings of Childhood into the powers of Manhood; to combine the Child's sense of wonder and novelty with the Appearances which every day for perhaps forty years had rendered familiar ... this is the character and privilege of genius'.

David Jones enlarged my sense of the formal and spiritual possibilities of poetry. I found his experiments profoundly liberating from the dominant mainstream alternatives in Britain in the 1970s: the English ironic mode, represented by Philip Larkin in particular, and 'confessionalism', for which the major models were Robert Lowell and Sylvia Plath. I was at the same time learning to 'hear' Charles Olson and other Black Mountain poets, and was excited by Olson's formally innovative poetry of facts. But the influence of David Jones went deeper, because he opened a subject with which I could identify: the groundwork of a 'Brut's Albion' that most English poets ignore.

David Jones builds upon Modernism: the sense of history, the use of myth, the liberation from a narrow range of personal and social experience, the creation of forms hospitable to a wide range of 'materials' – in short the poetic revolution brought about in the early part of the century by writers such as Eliot and Pound and Joyce. His work has, too, a felt personal centre: in kindness, in awe, in devotion. And in suffering, in 'trapesing the night within, walking the inner labyrinth where also the night is, under the tortoise of the skull' ('The Wall'). I stand by what I wrote about David Jones in an essay in *Modern Painters*:

> no modern vision of the whole could carry conviction that does not have at its heart, as his does, an experience of maiming and brokenness.[3]

I would emphasise, however, that it is a vision of the whole, rooted in personal feeling, but transcending self-centred circumstances.

David Jones's example must have contributed to my idea of 'ground', which I developed through my poetry and criticism, from the early 70s, and summed up in a piece written a few years ago as 'a place with strong personal associations, but also charged with ancestral and social experience, together with the natural and historical processes that have made it. For me, knowledge of a ground is primarily felt, but I also seek to know the "materials" – geology, ecology, history, and so on – in depth, and with a view to factual accuracy'.

---

[3] Jeremy Hooker, 'Gathering All In', *Modern Painters*, Winter 1995, p. 64.

'Matrix' is an early example of my presentation of a ground. It is a prose poem, in which I evoke the landscape of the Cerne Abbas Giant, conceived not only as the hill-figure's immediate locality, but as the chalklands of southern England in their geological, prehistoric, and historical making, from their origins in the Cretaceous Sea through successive cultures to contemporary military occupation:

> A memorial of its origins, chalk in barns and churches moulders in rain and damp; petrified creatures swim in its depths.
>
> It is domestic, with the homeliness of an ancient hearth exposed to the weather, pale with the ash of countless primeval fires. Here the plough grates on an urnfield, the green plover stands with crest erect on a royal mound.
>
> Chalk is the moon's stone; the skeleton is native to its soil. It looks anaemic, but has submerged the type-sites of successive cultures. Stone, bronze, iron: all are assimilated to its nature; and the hill-forts follow its curves.
>
> These, surely, are the work of giants: temples re-dedicated to the sky god, spires fashioned for the lords of bowmen:
>
> Spoils of the worn idol, squat Venus of the mines.
>
> Druids leave their shops at the midsummer solstice; neophytes tread an antic measure to the antlered god. Men who trespass are soon absorbed, horns laid beside them in the ground. The burnt-out tank waits beside the barrow.
>
> The god is a graffito carved on the belly of the chalk, his savage gesture subdued by the stuff of his creation. He is taken up like a gaunt white doll by the round hills, wrapped around by the long pale hair of the fields.
>
> (CL, p. 45)

I realized later that an impulse behind the poem was the desire to present an image of aspects of England in depth. It was an impulse I shared with other post-war English poets (as Seamus Heaney has tellingly described in 'Englands of the Mind'), quickened in my case by the fact that I was living in Wales, conscious of a strongly affirmed Welshness among both ordinary Welsh-speakers and cultural nationalists. Living in daily contact with this spirit, and thinking about my home country, I was forced to be aware of Englishness as other, and as a problematic identity, and to consider what the Lady of the Pool calls 'our Engle-raum in this Brut's Albion' (*A*, p. 164).

One of the 'things' David Jones makes available to other poets is the Matter of Britain. This, however, at least for my generation, is inseparable from the truth of Heaney's observation: 'English poets are being forced to explore not just the matter of England, but what is the matter with England'.[4] The things of which one is oneself made include things of culture and nation. Making a shape of them entails exploring them, asking *what* one is made of. Complex and perhaps contradictory impulses are at work in David Jones's rendering of Britain: celebratory, as in the healing and reconstructive spirit which *The Anathemata* shares with other post-war literary works and cultural events, such as Jacquetta Hawkes's *A Land*, 1951, and the Festival of Britain. Darkly ambiguous, as in his readings of the robbery that is Empire. Despairing, even: 'We are all as uprooted as the nation of the Jews and that is why we weep when we remember Sion – the old local Sions with their variants of the form-creating human cultures. We are all of the diaspora now'.[5] His anguished tiring of 'the eyes of the mind' is palpable in 'A, a, a Domine Deus'.[6] But it is to David Jones's resistance to 'our placeless cosmopolis' that we owe his emplaced writings, which reveal 'what's under', and processes of cultural making, as well as the contemporary crisis of signification.

The poet 'must work within the limits of his love' (Preface, *A*, p. 24). Other poets will of course love and know other things than those which David Jones cherished. I am conscious that in some respects my sympathies, and therefore my world, are very different from his. This will

---

[4] Heaney, op cit., pp 150–69. I treat a similar subject, differing in some respects from Heaney, in an essay which focuses mainly on David Jones, Basil Bunting, and Geoffrey Hill in *The Presence of the Past*, pp. 9–32.
[5] David Jones, *The Dying Gaul* (London: Faber and Faber, 1978), p. 88.
[6] David Jones, *The Sleeping Lord and Other Fragments* (London: Faber and Faber, 1974). p. 9.

be reflected in my poetry of place. Its ambition, however, owes something to his example. For the most part, I write short poems, but usually in the form of sequences, some of them book-length. The poems are connected by, among other things, the place or ground they explore. Place, in fact, is a formal principle, as well as the matter of the poems:

> Entering a place that is new to us, or seeing a familiar place anew, we move from part to part, simultaneously perceiving individual persons and things and discovering their relationships, so that, with time, place reveals itself as particular identities belonging to a network, which continually extends with our perception, and beyond it. And by this process we find ourselves, not as observers only, but as inhabitants, citizens, neighbours, and locate ourselves in a space dense with meanings.

The achievement of the Jones long poem, combining poetry and prose, has been a major example behind my thinking about 'a poem that is like a place'. A major *modern* example, because it was David Jones's sense of connection and relationship that enabled the shaping of spacious and intricately detailed and connected forms, and links him to great poets in very different traditions –Langland, but also Wordsworth, for whom the poet carries 'every where with him relationship and love'. The hospitable form of the Jones poem – 'a space dense with meanings' – relates to what he loved and knew. Without some sense of a power greater than the self, I doubt that it is possible to write a poetry that transcends the limits of the ego, and makes, as David Jones does, a rich and generous space.

There are potential tensions and even conflicts in trying to be both poet and critic, as I have found in my work on David Jones. Tension last manifested itself acutely two years ago, when I reread his writings in their entirety, wrote a conference paper on 'David Jones and the Matter of Wales', and prepared to make the radio programme, *A Map of David Jones*, first broadcast in November 1995. I tried at the time to analyse the problem in my journal as follows.

"'It is the *humanity* that I love in David Jones's work: a humanity that expresses human being (as in his portrait of himself), and is manifested in friendship, in creatureliness – not just love of nature, but kinship with earth, animals, trees – a bond with all *in the flesh* – and in care for the living and the dead, in gratitude, in making. There is a unity in his work that stems from this quality. It has diverse manifestations in writings and paintings with or without human figures, but all of which embody the quality of his feeling.

This is what I have responded to in David Jones from the beginning: something that is more than the 'I feel' of romantic subjectivity; feeling embodied in rhythm, shape in words, image, verbal and visual 'thing'. And in subject: the things of the Island, from its geological making and prehistoric and historic artefacts and movements of people and cultural formations. Not the only England, the only Wales, but a deeper Britain, known and loved, than that of most other twentieth-century artists and writers. Patriotic feelings, yes; but a deeper humanity. Not a comprehensive vision, not a vision that responds to a multicultural society *in the present*, but realities of place during a period of narrow subjectivity in the arts, short views in politics, reduced humanity (failure to feel outside of the self or a narrow circle).

The source of unity in his art is feeling. But it seems to me now that in his ideas about culture and man-the-artist he sought an impossible *conceptual* unity. And I feel there's a consequent narrowing in his vision, in his focus on the Island as part of Catholic Europe. In a way, he never accepted the Reformation, even Britain after 1282, when, with the death of Llewellyn, the connection with the unity formed under the Romans was severed.

> Denied the vision of hope he could only see what lay behind – the smouldering ruins of man's history and a litter of broken things.[7]

So wrote Philip Hagreen of David Jones after Petra Gill had broken off their engagement. And there's *some* truth in it, I think, though it wasn't necessarily the broken engagement that caused the denial. Or say there's a logic, given David Jones's religious beliefs, in his denial of the post-Reformation world, of all that is not sacramental … What I feel, in part as a result of frustration born of trying to follow his thought, is that he sought an impossible conceptual unity, and that while his feeling gathers all in, at the level of idea, his vision fragments.

It is at this point, though, that I have to recognise the difference of our backgrounds, not just the fact that I don't share his dogma – though that is crucial – but that I was brought up in a different time, and another

---

[7] Quoted in Rene Hague, *Dai Greatcoat: a self-portrait of David Jones in his Letters* (London: Faber and Faber, 1980), p. 42.

social world. So that it isn't only an intellectual difference that separates us, but, in some instances, a love of different things. And as I immerse myself in this world, intent on not misreading or misrepresenting it, so it is my things, and the creative freedom I enjoy by virtue of being the person I am, with which I lose touch."

It was while making the radio programme, *A Map of David Jones,* that I regained, for the time being anyway, creative freedom, and especially in writing the poem dedicated to David Jones, parts of which were incorporated in the programme. I will conclude this essay with the penultimate part of the poem:

>At Capel, in love
>with the shape of things:
>
>Dai, in his army greatcoat,
>framed in a window, engraving.
>Or walking with his friend
>to unblock the stream
>and free the waters.
>
>Rhythm echoes rhythm
>for the hunter of forms –
>hill-shapes, trees,
>hart's-tongue fern,
>the horses that return
>without riders –
>the men betrayed to death.
>
>Falling waters loose,
>bind and loose,
>shaping the ways of change.
>
>And mist – mist crumbles rock.
>Cloud packs hunt the hills.
>
>Clouds, and mist, and something
>that is neither,
>a story of change woven
>around the things that change.

That the dead men lie down
in the shattered wood,
shed their skins like snakes,
crawl back to the womb that bore them.
                    (*CL*, pp. 293–94)

Ceridwen's Daughters:
Welsh Women Poets and the Uses of Tradition

Hilary Llewellyn-Williams's 'The Tree Calendar'[1] is a cycle of thirteen poems based on an ancient Celtic calendar which Robert Graves described in *The White Goddess*. The poems reaffirm 'the widespread ancient belief that trees and language (especially writing) were mystically linked,' and relate some images of the calendar to the poet's 'own experience, during the course of a year (1985)'. 'Alder/Fearn' (p. 16) begins: 'Bwlchwernen: the alder pass', juxtaposing Welsh and English words, the old and the new languages, in the Welsh countryside which is the poems' setting. In a way that is characteristic of many Anglo-Welsh poems, by women and by men, place-name and image evoke the *presence* both of nature and of the past in the landscape. The place has a visionary quality; it is where life and death coexist:

> Water shines from the fields.
> A brimful river sweeps
> roots of alder, leaving
> the rolled corpse of a lamb
> to bob in the shallows.

The poem continues to recall, at Easter, 'the outlawed story retold/ of an old resurrection'. It is the story of 'a grain reborn as a child', of Taliesin, 'a wizard of poets'. From this story Hilary Llewellyn-Williams gains knowledge:

> Now I visit my alder stream
> in a double life, knowing
>
> that nothing's been lost. A raven
> croaks *Brân* overhead:
> banished westward, but still
> surviving.

---

[1] All quotations from Hilary Llewellyn-Williams work will be from *The Tree Calendar* (Bridgend: Poetry Wales Press, 1987). Page numbers will be given in the text.

Brân, the Welsh for crow or raven, is also the giant figure in *The Mabinogion* who may be the source for the Fisher King. Hilary Llewellyn-Williams calls him 'the British god of eloquence'. Oracular powers link him to Taliesin, whom Robert Graves calls Brân's 'spiritual son'. In 'Alder/Fearn', then, and in 'The Tree Calendar' as a whole, the Welsh landscape and its creatures are charged with the magic power of an ancient poetry, which has been banished to the west. The surviving knowledge is the potency of 'resurrection', by virtue of which 'nothing's been lost'.

Poets in Wales, in both languages, frequently identify memory with the landscape, as indicated by book titles such as *The Stones Remember* and *The Land Remembers*. The memory may be a personal possession or, in part, imaginative fabrication, but its ground is cultural memory, which survives in the native language of a long-settled people. The difference with which Hilary Llewellyn-Williams uses the banished, but surviving knowledge is that she identifies as a woman and a poet with the mythic awareness of the ancient poetry, and with the power of natural resurrection. With the backing of a Welsh poetic tradition, she adopts a shamanistic role, and her journey is from one level of reality to another, from a constricted, violent, mechanistic modern world to a level at which she is of one skin with nature, waiting, as she says in 'Elder/Ruis', 'for a birth/that will change everything: the earth/born over and over' (p. 29). There are dangers here, in the gap between an idea of nature and the culture to which, whether she likes it or not, the poet belongs, and between that idea and the common conditions of life in the Welsh countryside. Indeed, the weakness of 'The Tree Calendar' is that the poet's considerable book-learning about shamanism, Celtic myth, the *I-Ching* and so on, sometimes shows. Its main strengths, however, are the realization of mythic consciousness in terms of sensuous and imaginative experience, rooted in the landscape, and the poet's use of her sexuality as a poetic energy – a way of knowing, and a way of shaping experience. Ultimately, her capacity to imagine resurrection stems from her inwardness with the process of giving birth.

> As the days shorten, holly's power grows:
> ripening power, the birth power, power
> from behind the eyes, dream power, spear-
> leaved and bitter-barked and full of berries.
>
> Holly saplings under graveyard yews
> like prongs of resurrection, spring
> from the shadows. The yews red-fleshed

and folded secretly, gave birth to them.
('Holly/Tinne', p. 21)

In this kind of new nature poetry, in which we are a long way from the male mode of perceiving nature from the outside, we are also far from the idea expressed by Praxis, in Fay Weldon's novel, that:

> Nature does not know best, or if it does, it is on the man's side. Nature gives us painful periods, leucorrhoea, polyps, thrush, placenta praevia, headaches, cancer and in the end death. It seems to me that we must fight nature tooth and claw.[2]

Kim Taplin, by contrast, writes in *Tongues in Trees* of 'the woman's privilege and right to identify with the earth'.[3] On this subject there is a vital difference of opinion in feminist thinking, which I have to take note of here, though this is not the place to consider it extensively. In her 1990 Preface to *The Death of Nature*, Carolyn Merchant observes the production by feminist scholars during the 1980s of 'an explosion of books on ancient goddesses that became the basis for a renewed earth-rooted spirituality'. She goes on to speak of 'an inherent contradiction' in the 'celebrations of the connection between women and nature':

> If women overtly identify with nature and both are devalued in modern Western culture, don't such efforts work against women's prospects for their own liberation? Is not the conflation of women and nature a form of essentialism? Are not women admitting that by virtue of their own reproductive biology they are in fact closer to nature than men and that indeed their social role is that of caretaker?[4]

These are real questions, but it doesn't beg them, I think, to say that someone has to take care of the earth, and it had better be men and women. Male ideas of a 'female principle', and male exploitation of some women's identification with the earth, do not obviate the need of all of us, men and women, to identify more closely with nature, and to learn from those who have already done so. Such identification need not be

---

[2] Fay Weldon, *Praxis* (London: Coronet, 1980), p. 147.
[3] Kim Taplin, *Tongues in Trees* (Bideford: Green Books, 1989), p. 209.
[4] Carolyn Merchant, *The Death of Nature* (San Francisco, CA: Harper & Row, 1990), p. xvi.

sentimental or escapist, either. Nor need it mean loss of identity in a passive acceptance of or merging with natural processes, including death. On the contrary, a woman poet identifying with nature may speak with her unique personal accents, and with emotional directness – a quality often ascribed to woman's poetry by women themselves. Like many women poets today, Hilary Llewellyn-Williams is writing about personal and human survival, which means knowing and using her power as a woman, and about survival of the earth in face of the misuse of mechanical power, which is mainly in the hands of men. The concern among women writers is worldwide. My argument is that for Welsh women poets, influenced by aspects of Welsh culture and poetic tradition, the concern has particular emphases, and opportunities of expression. Before examining these further, however, it is necessary to meet another objection.

In my view, the most significant literary event of the last thirty years or so – an event that is far from being only literary in importance – has been the release of energy in women's writing, and the shaping of new forms and apprehensions of reality that has ensued. The release has been marked, in part, by anger. As Adrienne Rich said, in an essay written during the Vietnam War, 'today, much poetry by women – and prose for that matter – is charged with anger. I think we need to go through that anger'.[5] The anger is both personal – in poems about fathers, husbands, lovers – and focuses upon the all-pervasive and fundamentally destructive use of male power, which now threatens the survival of the earth. Rich rejects what she calls 'the myth of the masculine artist and thinker', that the artist or thinker needs 'to become unavailable to others, to become a devouring ego'. She does however claim there is an irreconcilable conflict for a woman between writing and fulfilling traditional female roles:

> But to be a female human being trying to fulfil traditional female functions in a traditional way *is* in direct conflict with the subversive function of the imagination. The word traditional is important here. There must be ways, and we will be finding out more and more about them, in which the energy of creation and the energy of relation can be united.[6]

As an American, Rich belongs to a society with strong roots in a particular concept of individual freedom. As well as the intention to undermine male

---

[5] Adrienne Rich, *On Lies, Secrets and Silence* (London: Virago, 1980), p. 48.
[6] Ibid., p. 43.

myths and structures, it is this individualism, perhaps, together with a residual romanticism, that lead her to identify the role of the imagination as 'subversion'. Subversion is not the main function of the imagination in all cultures. The word 'traditional' can be used with a difference, to define the life of an ancient culture continuing into the present, fraught with internal tensions, and subject to external pressures, but with a distinct sense of cultural identity, and ways of thinking and making that can be adapted to present needs. In such a culture the imagination will be subversive mainly in the sense that it opposes the forces threatening to undermine the culture itself. Thus, in Wales, the primary function of the imagination is cohesive, and the poetry of praise and commemoration reinforces common bonds. This does not mean the Welsh women poets, too, do not need to find ways 'in which the energy of creation and the energy of relation can be united'. It means, rather, that the ways lie ready to hand – to their hands that will shape them to their ends – within Welsh poetic tradition.

From the sixth century A.D. until the second half of the twentieth century, the traditions of Welsh-language poetry have been almost exclusively in the keeping of male poets – the great exception is the hymn-writer Ann Griffiths in the late 18th century. With few exceptions, such as Lynette Roberts, few Welsh women poets writing in English came to prominence until the 1980s, when, among others, Gillian Clarke, Christine Evans, Hilary Llewellyn-Williams and Sheenagh Pugh established their reputations. This is no more than we would expect in a society in which, through prince or minister, trade union leader, MP, or head of household, the main public offices have been held by men. Yet Welsh poetic traditions have, from early on, offered an alternative to the celebration of male power. The duality is nicely encapsulated in the figure of Taliesin: the sixth-century poet of a warrior tribe, who founded the Welsh tradition of praise poetry, and the figure of romance and myth, associated with oracular powers, and first heard of in the ninth century. Emyr Humphreys explains that the 'charismatic name' of the heroic poet became attached to the magical hero:

> This second Taliesin quickly overshadowed the original figure because he was a popular representation in the Welsh world of a characteristic hero figure of Celtic myth, the poet-prophet who enjoys a complex relationship with a sequence of levels of existence of which the physical world that surrounds and sustains us is only one numinous manifestation. Because he lives in folk memory, Taliesin carries with him something of the powers of

the gods and spirits of the shape-shifting Celtic pantheon.[7]

Taliesin, the sixth-century poet, praised and commemorated the generosity and courage of his warring lords, and is known as father of the oldest surviving Welsh poetic tradition. Taliesin, the folk-hero, belongs to a different world, another order of reality. He is an elemental and a Protean figure, most famous for the boasts in which he claims to have been present in different forms at many times and in many places since the creation of the world. He is a shape-shifter, capable of metamorphosis, and metempsychosis, and associated with the elements and processes of nature. He has the magical gift of becoming other. He is, of course, male. But he draws his original power from Ceridwen, the great mother. In the folk tale the boy who will become Taliesin steals from Ceridwen's cauldron the magical drops which confer inspiration. She pursues him: he escapes as a hare, she chases him in the form of a greyhound; he turns himself into a fish, she changes herself into an otter; he becomes a bird, she becomes a hawk. At last he transforms himself into a grain in a pile of wheat, and she changes into a hen and swallows him. Nine months later he is born as her beautiful child; she casts him adrift in a coracle; he is found by a courtier, Elphin, and named Taliesin from his radiant brow. This is Taliesin of 'The Tree Calendar', 'a wizard of poets', gifted with the power of resurrection. He is more than a son of woman; he is a poet by virtue of his theft of inspiration from the goddess, and therefore his magical power of imagination has its source in the feminine principle. Caitlin Matthews sees Ceridwen as 'his initiator, forcing him to deeper levels of understanding until he reaches the primal essence of life itself, here symbolised by a grain of wheat'.[8] Ceridwen's cauldron is both 'the Fountain of Wisdom and the womb of life', and Taliesin is 'one of the last great seer-poets', with roots close to the shaman's.

Taliesin, a man in possession of the power of the mother, might have been invented for the twentieth century. No doubt we have re-invented him according to our needs. Thus, a number of male writers, including Robert Graves, John Cowper Powys, Charles Williams, Vernon Watkins and David Jones, have reconstructed Taliesin for their own poetic purposes. Broadly speaking, as he appears in the work of twentieth-century male poets, Taliesin stands for imaginative and emotional enlargement,

---

[7] Emyr Humphreys, *The Taliesin Tradition*, pp. 48–9.
[8] Caitlin Matthews, *Mabon and the Mysteries of Britain* (London: Arkana, 1987), p. 118.

escape from a time-bound existence, and for empathy that dissolves the boundaries of the ego. In recent years, as I have set out to show, the spirit of Taliesin is present in the work of a number of Welsh women poets. That spirit is above all a co-inherence of openness and integrity, a way of the poet being herself yet becoming other. Poetry informed by the spirit is an art of survival in dangerous circumstances.

In speaking of the poetic traditions available to the Welsh woman poet, we have to speak of a confluence of different streams, or of crosscurrents, some of which are also available to her English and American contemporaries, and some of which are not. Praise, celebration, commemoration: these are poetic functions descending to her from the first bard; functions which Welsh poets during more than a thousand years have adapted to the conditions of their changing society, from the hierarchical order of the princes to a democracy imbued with liberal and socialist ideas. There is also the homelier tradition of the *bardd gwlad* or folk poet, whom Saunders Lewis described as:

> a craftsman or farmer who followed his occupation in the area where he was born, who knew all the people in the neighbourhood and who could trace their family connections, who also knew the dialect of his native heath, and every story, event and omen, and who used the traditional social gift of poetry to console a bereaved family, to contribute to the jollifications at a wedding feast, or to record a contretemps with lightly malicious satire.[9]

Can a Welsh woman poet also be a folk poet in this sense, once she has won the freedom to write? Or does the struggle for freedom alienate 'the traditional social gift of poetry'? Hilary Llewellyn-Williams, Gillian Clarke, Ruth Bidgood, Christine Evans and Jean Earle are all, to different degrees, settled in Welsh communities, which they care for. There is however inevitably an ambivalence in their relationship with the community, which they can hardly be said to speak to and for, after the manner of the folk poet. The audience for a poet writing in English in Wales is, by and large, a literary audience, a scattered audience of individuals with special interests. Wherein then is the situation different from that in England? It is the *idea* of the *bardd gwlad* that is still powerful for some English-language poets in Wales, an idea reinforced by the example of a poet like Idris Davies,

---

[9] Quoted in W. Rhys Nicholas, *The Folk Poets* (Cardiff: University of Wales Press, 1978), p. 2.

who, for a time at least, could be felt to be the voice of the people. Nor is it only an idea. There is a special poignancy about Ruth Bidgood's mid-Wales landscapes, which are largely empty of the living, and in which she speaks for the dead; hers is, as it were, a poetry haunted by a lost function, in whose absence it has gained another. There is, I think, a general truth here for Anglo-Welsh poetry, in which personal lyricism echoes against the silence of lost community. Nor is this the whole story. In Jean Earle's poems, for example, the personal voice is informed by communal experience.

That the Welsh woman poet is a latecomer to the public functions of an ancient civilization is shown poignantly and wittily by the genealogy with which Gillian Clarke concludes 'Cofiant':

> Daughter of Penri Williams, wireless engineer of Carmarthenshire
>   and Ceinwen Evans of Denbighshire
> son of Williams Williams, railwayman and Annie of
> Carmarthenshire
> son of Daniel Williams, railwayman of Llangynog and Sara
> son of Thomas Williams, Baptist minister and Mary son of Thomas
>   Williams, smallholder of Nefyn and Jennet of Pystyll
> son of William Williams, farmer of Crugan, Llanbedrog
> son of Williams Jones, farmer of Crugan
> son of John Williams, farmer and lawyer of Crugan
> son of William and Mary[10]

and so on, 'son of' for another twenty-two generations, back to the age of the princes and of myth. Only 'daughter of' in the present generation, and in the person of the poet herself, the first woman of the family with the freedom to write such a poem. Yet it is a *Cofiant,* a biography of an actual historical family, and rich with details of place and occupation. Its self-consciously feminist perspective makes it a poem which could not have been written by a *bardd gwlad* – a 'poet who lived amongst his people and composed the poetry of civilisation and habitation' (Saunders Lewis) – yet the desire to voice a rooted civilisation – a neighbourhood with established, common values – is strong in Gillian Clarke's poetry.

In an early poem, 'Dyddgu replies to Dafydd', Gillian Clarke took the part of the great mediaeval Welsh poet Dafydd ap Gwilym's lover. It is a poem of joyful sexuality, which affirms a healthy, heathen spirit in the woman as lover:

---

[10] Gillian Clarke, *Letting in the Rumour* (Manchester: Carcanet Press, 1989), p.79.

> Original sin I whitened from your
> mind, my colours influenced
> your flesh, as sun on the floor
> and warm furniture of a church.

But Dyddgu also shows restiveness at the role she plays, waiting, becoming anxious, fearing 'desire's alteration'. Love is not enough: men can move on, women cannot:

> The feet of young men beat, somewhere far off
> on the mountain. I would women
> had roads to tread in winter
> and other lovers waiting.[11]

Finally, Dyddgu settles for patience. Gillian Clarke, however, has continued to make poems out of the tension between a powerful attraction to a traditional way of life, which demands women's subservience, and the desire to escape to freedom. Thus, 'Letter from a Far Country' includes images of imprisonment associated both with the social and creative restrictions upon women in a patriarchal society and with domestic satisfaction:

> The gulls grieve at our contentment.
> It is a masculine question.
> 'Where' they call 'are your great works?'
> They slip their fetters and fly up
> to laugh at land-locked women.
> Their cries are cruel as greedy babies.[12]

But, despite the acknowledgement of being locked in and fettered, at the end of the poem the letter of farewell goes unposted and the woman-poet, by implication, returns to her role of family keeper and minder and comforter. This is partly because 'Letter From a Far Country' celebrates motherhood, as well as showing the limitations it imposes upon the woman as an independent creative being, and partly because of the poet's ambivalent attitude towards traditional Welsh rural society, domain of the forefathers and their subservient if strong-spirited womenfolk.

---

[11] Gillian Clarke, *The Sundial* (Llandysul: Gwasg Gomer, 1978), pp. 20–21.
[12] Gillian Clarke, *Letter from a Far Country* (Manchester: Carcanet Press, 1982), p. 11.

I do not mean to suggest that Gillian Clarke and other Welsh women poets do not feel and express the anger of which Adrienne Rich writes – 'female anger and this furious awareness of the Man's power over her'. I mean to say, rather, that, especially in 'Letter from a Far Country', at least some of the anger has been drawn off by England perceived as destroyer of Welsh culture and the Welsh language, while traditional Welsh rural society is, for all its patriarchal structure, nevertheless an object of love. That is to say, the society is identified with the Welsh language and with neighbourly values as well as with hardship and patriarchal fetters. Adrienne Rich's terms translate only with difficulty into the Welsh situation, in which the imagination serves the interests of community, and it is still possible for a woman poet to identify both the energy of creation and the energy of relation with traditional values. Gillian Clarke has a strong sense of sisterhood; it is one of the most notable features of her work. As a feeling and as a theme, it is relatively new in Welsh poetry, whose male tradition has emphasised brotherhood, but its potential for female subversion of male power is restricted by the equally strong feeling that the Welsh people are a family, which also pervades Gillian Clarke's poetry.

The title of Ruth Bidgood's book *Kindred* underlines the theme. Ruth Bidgood's rural mid-Wales is a country of "the haunted present". As she finds in the landscape 'the mystery/That complements precision',[13] so her clear-sighted images and descriptions evoke the mystery of a past that is somehow still alive. She adopts the function of the poet as rememberer on behalf of the household or community:

> I bring a thought into this day's light
> of Esther and Gwen, paupers:
> Rhys and Thomas, shepherds: John Jones,
> miner of copper and lead:
> who lived here and are not remembered,
> whose valley is re-translated
> by holiday bathers across the river,
> lying sun-punched: by me…[14]

But Esther and Gwen and the others are remembered, of course: the poem names and commemorates them. Moreover, Ruth Bidgood 'translates' their valley into her language. She speaks of herself, guiltily, together

---

[13] Ruth Bidgood, *The Given Time* (Swansea: Christopher Davies, 1972), p. 18.
[14] Ruth Bidgood, *Kindred* (Bridgend: Poetry Wales Press, 1986), p. 32.

with the holidaymakers, as one by whom their 'valley is re-translated'. In effect, however, her English-language poetry carries over the values of the now departed Welsh-speaking community, and makes them present. Her awareness is not mythic, like Hilary Llewellyn-Williams's; in 'Llyn y Fan Fach', for example, the parched landscape by the lake is haunted by the *absence* of 'the lady of legend', who left her human family to go back into 'the shadowed water'. Ruth Bidgood's awareness is historical and religious. I spoke earlier of the relative 'emptiness' of her landscapes, and of her poetry being haunted by a lost function, and, indeed, in characteristic poems we find her alone in a landscape which has partially reverted to the wild, hearing 'voices' of nature, and 'voices' of the dead. I would like to qualify the earlier observation, however, by saying that, again and again in her poems, she brings life out of death. In 'Red', for example:

> Small and still, the hedgehog crouched
> in the shining road. He had accomplished
> little of that sluggish perilous crossing.
> His prickly-proofed coat had availed him nothing.
> In five miles of autumn from hamlet to village
> his was the finest red, soft berries of blood
> springing from nostrils and little jaws.
> He was still warm. He would harden soon
> in that meek posture, with two paws
> at his face, as if helping death
> to darken his eyes. Quiet and blind
> he crouched in the sun. Exultant there sang
> for a while, till it darkened and dulled,
> loud as October leaves, the splendid red.[15]

This is, I think, one of Ruth Bidgood's finest poems; a quiet but vivid poem, which thrills with vibrancy. There is a pathos about the dead creature; the exultant colour sings against the darkening and dulling that threaten to overwhelm it. The poem carries no obvious message of a hope that avails against death. Yet, with its imagery of blood, and of crouching and fruiting, shining and singing, with their subtle pagan and Christian associations, it intimates the possibility of regeneration. At any rate, it is a poem about death that is charged with the energies of life and renewal.

---

[15] Ruth Bidgood, *The Print of Miracle* (Llandysul: Gwasg Gomer, 1978), p. 40.

Helen McNeil, in her book about Emily Dickinson, defines what she calls 'imagery of the humble object' and places it in a religious context:

> Such images are at the heart of Protestant meditative and poetic tradition, from early emblem books through the English and American poets of the seventeenth century, such as George Herbert, Anne Bradstreet and Edward Taylor. The poet is himself or herself a humble object, and the poem uses the imagery of everyday and domestic life to bring the experience of faith and doubt into a realistic context.[16]

There is no reason, of course, why Welsh women poets should not encounter such imagery in Emily Dickinson's poems, or Elizabeth Bishop's, or in the work of any or all of the other poets Helen McNeil names. It is also important to note, however, without necessarily making much of the Welsh connections of the Metaphysical poets, that the Welsh women writers inherit a strong native Puritan tradition, which thinks in terms of parables and apprehends the revelatory nature of domestic and natural objects. 'Red' is a poem with this tradition behind it; indeed, the way of seeing influenced, but not restricted, by Puritan values is characteristic of Ruth Bidgood, and of Jean Earle too. Helen McNeil says that, 'when used by women, …the humble object served to enhance received cultural attitudes'. No doubt this is true, but the way of seeing also draws upon the revolutionary potential within Christianity, which subverts all worldly powers, exalts the lowly, and converges with pagan impulses to affirm that all created things are sacred. This was the vision that energised the new English poetry in the early period of the French Revolution, and exalted the common world of man and beast. The power of the democratic spirit within Welsh society – the spirit of brotherhood and sisterhood – owes a great deal to the Nonconformist release and channelling of the same revolutionary potential.

Jean Earle begins one poem:

> Every day, something is given –[17]

---

[16] Helen McNeil, *Emily Dickinson* (London: Virago, 1986), pp. 165–66.
[17] Jean Earle, 'Every Day', *Selected Poems* (Bridgend: Seren, 1989), p. 29. All subsequent quotations from Jean Earle's poems are from this book; page numbers are given in the text.

In another, 'Visiting Light', she looks at roofs:

> Here broods a latent poetry
> Nobody reads.
> The weed that has managed flowers,
> Pinched in a crack,
> Lays its thin shadow down
> In the afternoons; as a new mother will,
> In the room below.
>
> Jackdaws are in these chimneys,
> Their difficult lives
> Reflect our own... (p. 167)

The conviction, here explicit, of the kinship between human beings and the rest of creation informs Jean Earle's poetry as a whole. In 'The Dancing Stone' (p. 36), for instance, she observes, in old glass, an older way of looking, different from that which man the predator casts on other creatures. The medieval etcher, who has depicted the Holy Family among farmyard beasts, saw 'Kinship of man with animals, their shapes incurved/One with mansoul'. The gentleness of this vision of 'a yearning group' is palpable; 'and yet', the poet asks, prompted by her realism, 'perhaps next day/The butcher came?"' 'No answer comes – now or at any time.' What all creatures share, however, is, in the words of 'The Picture of the Tiger Hunt' (p. 103), 'the last appeal' –'Towards light'.

If Jean Earle's vision is like any male poet's, it is like Wordsworth's – she has 'a seed of honesty' from his garden, and her poetry merits the symbolic implication. She too celebrates 'common' life – only she is closer than Wordsworth was to its grittier and harsher manifestations. Looking at people, she sees their whole lives, as when in 'Escape to Felingano"' she sees an old woman: 'child, girl, wife, mother of sons/ And slow widow' (p. 71). Her poetry as a whole shows that she sees as the child she herself was, but also sees that child's 'naïve' vision with her grown-up understanding. Her humane perception is a quality which has, in the words of 'A Neighbour's House', 'To do with looking at what life is, /Together' (p. 125). Jean Earle's poetry, therefore, is far from being an expression of the egotistical sublime. She is however aware that people also share the condition of being each one alone. Thus, her respect for the other, and for what cannot be known about him or her, complements her empathy. Her poetry knows the 'dark' we all inhabit, and the 'light' that visits us, coming and going. As I have said, she shares her care for the particular and generally overlooked life-history, or everyday object, with other poets, women and men, but the strength of her democratic feeling belongs to a Welsh tradition, which in her case is rooted in the social experience of South Wales, where she has spent part of her life.

In 'Visiting Light', Jean Earle describes herself cleaning her doorstep:

> Rubbing with bluestone in the old way.
> My scour against the world's indifference
> To important symbols – the common roof,
> Likeness of patterns.

The act of scrubbing a step is hardly subversive of women's traditional role! Yet, for Jean Earle, the humble task is a means of vision, and what she sees – the likeness between human beings and other creatures, common patterns, kinship – subverts the categories and structures and relations of a male-dominated society. Her unsentimental tenderness towards all life makes her react with horror and anger to man's vileness towards nature in his pursuit of material gain. Her later poetry, in particular, is charged with a sense of shared threat, of global catastrophe, due to man's worship at the altars of technology and of money. It is a threat to all life engineered by human beings, compared to whom insects show wise care for their kind. In 'Peter, Dreaming' (pp. 146-47), a poem about a child's nightmare of global annihilation, she describes the beauty of a wasp nest, each hexagon 'a home/Perfect for wasps', *The whole geared to the future of the grubs*', and asks:

> Where's the dynamic force of world-parents,
> Dedicated hordes
> Organised fiercely as wasps
> To save Peter?

It is true, as Carolyn Merchant suggests, that women's identification with nature *can* work against their prospects of liberation, and indeed, is likely to, I would say, if it lends itself to male exploitation. But it can also, as, for instance, Jean Earle's poems show, empower resistance to human destructiveness and folly.

One of Taliesin's great gifts is empathy, by which I mean to designate, not reverence for the other which comes from awareness of difference, as in Martin Buber's philosophy of 'I and Thou', but the imaginative capacity to *become* the other. Some of the most remarkable poems in Christian Evans's *Cometary Phases* show this capacity. 'Whale Dream', for example:

> In a dream I loosed my voice
> into the echoing vault of the ocean
> knowing once it would have stirred an answer
> half a world away among the ice.
>
> Slowed and strengthened to cetacean pulse
> I swam in the womb of the world
> and the stars were a whalespine above me
> charged focuses that sang my bearings
>
> and I could read the streams with all the skin
> of my glistening long body…[18]

The poetic technique shown here contrasts interestingly with Gary Snyder's in his equally powerful, but quite different, 'Mother Earth: Her Whales'. Evans 'looses' her voice and it flows, responding like a whale's body to ocean pressures and movements. Flow is as important to Snyder, who says 'Each living being is a swirl in the flow',[19] but his poem builds its world with images and historical facts, after the method of Pound's *Cantos*, and with something of the passion for *data* in *Moby-Dick*. Ultimately, 'Mother Earth: Her Whales' is about man's misuse of language, with which he categorises and justifies his exploitation of nature. 'Whale Dream', also, is concerned with language:

> But my singing was a memory of how
> nursed deep within the waves' turmoil
> in the still heart of flowing
> we wove our patterns of shared song

---

[18] Christine Evans, *Cometary Phases* (Bridgend: Seren, 1989), p. 29. All subsequent quotations from Christine Evans's poems are from this book; page numbers are given in the text.
[19] Gary Snyder, *Turtle Island* (New York, NY: New Directions, 1974), Introductory Note.

> in a language kinder than words
> loops and swirls of sense that make words seem
> small closed hooks
> to button meaning, keep it closed.

In the 'language kinder than words' *'To sing is to join/the song of the universe'*. The imaginative achievement of the poem is to convince us that the poet has slipped the hooks that button meaning and become one with the whale through the sisterhood of creatures. The identification – the sense that the poet knows what it feels like to be in the skin of the whale – is more convincing in that she does not claim it, but recognises her human limitations: 'half of me knew I was a woman/dreaming a whale; for the rest I seemed/a cetacean's fear of being human'. 'Whale Dream' and 'Mother Earth: Her Whales' are new nature poems, poems of the modern ecological awareness, whatever they may owe to older traditions. It would be hazardous to generalise from them, but I shall risk it nevertheless. Snyder's poem is that of an impassioned observer: a man who sees the wonder of nature and the grotesque horror of man's destructiveness; by and large, the western tradition of nature poetry, dominated by men, is an art of seeing. Evans's poem, on the other hand, has, imaginatively, a skin-to-skin relationship with its subject, from the inside. This is not to say that women poets cannot see, and men poets cannot put off their egos and identify with the life of their subjects. It is to say that the latter is rare, and ecological survival requires it.

In 'Cometary Phases', Christine Evans recalls

> that night I dreamed
> a world where my companions and I
> drifted like medusae on the updrafts
> pulsing with the colours of shared thought
> through cumulus that had the lapis glow
> of neutrons or of oboe notes
> and we sang to the sister races
> to the whales on the blue-white world
> and other singers under older suns (p. 93)

And she recalls that she woke,

> a deaf forked
> creature or a chrysalis

> that's glimpsed the shimmer of the wings
> we've sacrificed
> in the million years it has been taking
> to grow the hand, to learn
> its itch. (93)

Thus, she sees evolution as a sacrificial process, in which companionship and 'shared thought' and singing to 'the sister races' have been lost in producing that violent and possessive thing, the human hand. Such a dream is an agonized response to a destructiveness that has grown with the human organism. But it is a manifestation of hope too – an instance of a new poetic language, which, in linking the human voice to the song of a kinder creation, also expresses our capacity to care for the nature we are part of. In this respect, Christine Evans, along with other women poets in Wales and elsewhere, is responding to the theft of women's 'power of naming', described by Mary Daly, as a result of which 'inadequate words have been taken as adequate'.[20] Her empathy produces a liberation of language and of consciousness.

It is significant that in 'Whale Dream' and in the passage from 'Cometary Phases' Christine Evans achieves imaginative release through a dream. This is, of course, a traditional technique, by which the poet transcends the limitations of daytime logic and gains access to the power of magical transformation which exists in the mind's underlife. It enables Christine Evans to escape from the bounds of superficial personal experience, of the ego at its narrowest, though, as Virginia Woolf and others have claimed, the female self is in any case more porous than the male to other existences. The escape is into life – 'the womb of the world': life experienced biologically, through the rhythms and processes by which the woman participates in nature, and apprehended imaginatively. The at-oneness with nature is realized by a strong poetic intelligence – it is not a vague wallowing in the amniotic fluid. There is poetic justice in the way in which Hilary Llewelyn-Williams and Gillian Clarke, as well as Christine Evans, re-appropriate this gift, which Taliesin stole from Ceridwen, and adapt it to their contemporary needs, substituting a sense of relationship within creation for the competitiveness and isolation and executive power associated with the male model of reality. Christine Evans and Jean Earle, in particular, are poets who respond to the new physical sciences. In the words of Louise B. Young, they are aware that

---

[20] Mary Daly, *Beyond God the Father* (London: Women's Press, 1986), p. 8.

'The discovery that everything is related to everything else is one of the most important insights of our time'. Young well describes the new vision of the earth, to which the poets I have discussed are responding:

> Over and above the living communities, the working partnerships, the symbiotic marriages, we are beginning to recognize the outlines of an even larger organization of matter. It is a system in which we, too, take part, though we never dreamt of its existence until just a few decades ago when we broke free from the force that had bound us for millions of years to the earth's surface. For the first time in human experience we could look back and see our planet whole. Set against the fluid blackness of space, we saw a luminous bubble of matter, variegated with moving patterns of light and shadow, with the delicate shadings of life. It looked as fragile and vital as a diatom floating in the darkness of the night sea.[21]

The new nature poetry is largely, but not exclusively, a poetry by women, and it is a poetry which shares the vision of Gaia, but also apprehends the 'system in which we, too, take part' from the inside. That inwardness or participation, which has been exploited in patriarchal society to keep women subservient, is now a gift which all human beings need to develop if the species is to survive.

It would be foolish to imply that the Welsh women poets discussed in this essay have nothing in common with their male counterparts, and have not been influenced by them, or by poets writing outside Wales. Gillian Clarke owes something to both Ted Hughes and Seamus Heaney, and Ruth Bidgood to Edward Thomas. Gillian Clarke, in turn, originally influenced both Hilary Llewellyn-Williams and Christine Evans, who also seems to owe a debt to Gary Snyder, though she transforms the influence in her use of it, as I have shown above. The ideas of Peter Redgrove and Penelope Shuttle have points of contact with thinking about nature and imagination discussed here. Lines of influence and of communication are open both into and out of Wales, though, sadly, there is little evidence that the achievement of Welsh poets, whether writing in Welsh or in English, is known outside Wales. What I have discussed are possibilities available to Welsh women poets, possibilities inherent in certain Welsh literary and cultural traditions, and offering alternatives to the influences

---

[21] Louis B. Young, *The Unfinished Universe* (Oxford: Oxford University Press, 1993), pp. 112–13.

of Anglo-American culture. I have argued that traditions survive within Welsh culture which not only support a sense of Welsh identity, but from which the world as a whole could benefit. Broadly speaking, the traditions are: a sense of the value of community, or common life, embracing the living and the dead; identification with nature; recognition of kinship between human beings and the rest of creation; the Protean capacity of the imagination to become another; the arts of praise, celebration, commemoration. Drawing upon these traditions, the work of Welsh women poets is important both to their Welsh identity and to their sense of themselves as women, and also serves the aim of what Louise B. Young calls seeing the planet whole. I have not meant to suggest that these are their only traditions, or only possibilities, or that one can often perceive *direct* connections between contemporary writing and poetry of the past, as distinct from creative adaptations or transformations of traditional means to meet present needs. Nevertheless, it is demonstrable, I believe, that the poetry I have considered draws sustenance from ancient imaginative powers, such as those associated with the figure of Taliesin; powers banished westward, but still surviving in Wales.

Heartlands: On Some Poems by Ruth Bidgood and Christopher Meredith

The heartlands of Ruth Bidgood and Christopher Meredith are Welsh territories. Bidgood's Abergwesyn, North Breconshire, is the location of what Matthew Jarvis calls her 'mid-Wales epic'.[1] Tredegar and its surroundings, the Brecon Beacons and the Black Mountains and southern Marches, provide the groundwork for much of Meredith's poetry and fiction. The Welsh language, however, has been eroded and largely replaced by English in the poets' territories. Social and cultural changes, together with language loss, raise profound issues of meaning.[2] The heartland is riven with tensions and divisions. Paradoxically, it is, in effect, an edge, or frontier between past and present, and Welsh and English influences.

Professor Prys-Thomas in Christopher Meredith's novel *Shifts* 'said that the town – our town, he said – was on many frontiers … the frontier of rural and industrial; the frontier of farmland and desert; the frontier of moorland and dense forest, and others he produced almost casually, huge ideas'.[3] A poet on 'the frontier' will know the 'huge ideas' experientially, confusedly, and attempt to find or construct order. Heartland as frontier raises the question of what it means to call Wales home.

Christopher Meredith's fictional medieval Welsh poet Griffri, in the novel of that title, has a well-defined official function: 'Keeper of memory. Lister of the dead'.[4]

This suggests a role within a secure social order. But what Griffri lives through is chaos, which throws memory into confusion. Song, he says, 'can tell us what we are.'[5] This is a fine definition of poetry in any age. It becomes an especially challenging definition when *what we are* becomes a question.

---

[1] Matthew Jarvis, *Ruth Bidgood* (Cardiff, Writers of Wales: University of Wales Press, 2012), p. 130.
[2] M. Wynn Thomas describes the larger context of modern Anglophone Welsh writing as the 'transition of twentieth-century Wales from a predominantly religious to a predominantly secular culture', *In the Shadow of the Pulpit* (Cardiff: University of Wales Press, 2010), p. 8.
[3] Christopher Meredith, *Shifts* (Bridgend: Seren, 1988), p. 135.
[4] Christopher Meredith, *Griffri* (Bridgend: Seren, 1994), p. 146.
[5] Ibid., p. 9.

From the nineteen sixties until the present, Ruth Bidgood has been writing about landscapes in mid-Wales. She has observed the afforestation of a large area of Breconshire, and the eventual felling of the trees. She has witnessed the remains of an older way of life, often in the ruins of houses and farms which for centuries had been sites of an indigenous Welsh culture and pattern of work. She registers what has been lost, the lives, the traditional occupations, the buildings, and the culture. But she is not only an elegiac poet. She celebrates the life of the past, and at visionary moments glimpses its continuing presence in the landscape. As an historian, she knows the changing story of her area in time. She is also a poet of spiritual intensity; whose poetry is a form of personal 'grounding'. At the same time, she acknowledges herself to be a 'latecomer' to an area where other people have belonged. The word 'home' has social and cultural implications but also takes on a metaphysical resonance in her poetry.

There are affinities between Ruth Bidgood's exploration of the border between past and present, and between belonging and being an incomer in her Breconshire landscape and Christopher Meredith's exploration of the meanings of his Welsh 'frontier'. There are differences, too, which are partly generational, and partly due to the poets' different landscapes, rural in Bidgood's case, but with afforestation on an 'industrial' scale, and partly rural and partly post-industrial in Meredith's. The following two short poems will help to indicate these differences and affinities.

Ruth Bidgood's 'Links' is from her poem-sequence 'Riding the Flood' subtitled '(a memory sequence)':

> Some have said that by the pillar
> where Becket was struck down,
> they felt not pain but derangement
> of nerve-ends, a distant echo of blows,
> enervation like blood-loss.
>   And I
> in a windbitten valley have laid my hand
> on stone of old walls, and felt a held life,
> all the remembering there is
> of what was made in that starved place,
> a barely accessible material memory
> woken with a touch.[6]

---

[6] Ruth Bidgood, *Symbols of Plenty*: Selected Longer Poems (Norwich: Canterbury Press, 2006), p. 48.

Imagination here is intimately connected to remembering, feeling a life 'held' by 'what was made in that starved place'. The poet herself is a maker; she works with 'material memory/woken with a touch'. The poem dissolves clichés that might attach to 'starved place'. It does not deny poverty but wakes the mind to the human home-making capacity.

'Earth air' is a poem from Christopher Meredith's *Air Histories*:

> This piece of earth's a billowing pavilion
> you never quite peg down.
> Odd corners have a stone church hammered in –
> Patricio, Cwmiou, Cwmdu, Capel y Ffin.
> But their grip's uncertain.
>
>   One day the earth will wake and stretch and sigh
>   and each church will pop its button
>   and she'll fly.[7]

'This piece of earth' is specific. As the place names indicate, it is a piece of the Black Mountains. The landscape is imaged as elusive and unstable, 'peg down' suggesting something that might blow away. The words also suggest understood, held in the mind, kept firm. One can see how a view of the Black Mountain, especially an actual or imagined aerial view, might suggest a huge tent about to blow away, 'a billowing pavilion'. The place names call to mind a deeply settled, historical landscape. 'But their grip's uncertain.' The poet strikes a humorously apocalyptic note, each church popping its button like a tent peg. The humour is integral to a serious vision, as in all Meredith's work. Human constructions hold earth in place, but earth – the force of nature – is prior, and will endure after humans have gone. Air also importantly incorporates the sense of melody, presenting the poet as a singer, a musical pattern maker. The title *Air Histories* thus introduces a maker, one who makes a song from the histories – however overwhelming – that make him.

At the centre of Ruth Bidgood's 'Hawthorn at Digiff', from *Kindred*, is a house in a landscape, a derelict 'house full of hawthorn'. The landscape too is semi-derelict. The feeling generated by the tree growing 'in the midst' of the house is ominous, but qualified. The tree's 'doomy sweetness', a sensation attached to the house, determines a tone 'of doom and celebration'. It seems as if the tree of evil omen has won; but the

---

[7] Christopher Meredith, *Air Histories* (Bridgend: Seren, 2013), p. 56.

tree itself is dying. Has it brought death into the house? The poet brings something else, 'a thought into this day's light

> of Esther and Gwen, paupers:
> Rhys and Thomas, shepherds: John Jones,
> miner of copper and lead:
> who lived here and are not remembered,

But the former inhabitants are remembered. The poet and consequently the poem's readers remember them.

Ruth Bidgood places herself as an incomer: she is an observer of the life of the valley, and she is also a participant. Christopher Meredith, though a native of Tredegar, also, in the words of an early poem, 'Prisoners', places himself as 'onlooker and participant'.[8] This is crucial to both poets' work. In 'Hawthorn at Digiff', Ruth Bidgood describes herself as one who 're-translates the valley'. Translation implies change of language as well as occupation. The poem is about the house and the people memory restores to it. It is also, perhaps in part unconsciously, certainly very modestly, about the poet and her art. It indicates where she stands in relation to the place. Like Roland Mathias in his Wales, Ruth Bidgood stands outside but looking in, passionately engaged with the life she sees.[9] 'Hawthorn at Digiff' manifests the poet's 'touch', both literal and metaphorical, as she touches the 'cankered flowers' gently. She observes the 'held life', celebrates it, mourns its passing, but does not claim to belong. The poem restores the place to the people who made it. The poet is able to do this because she is, in more than one sense, a kind of borderer.

Christopher Meredith's 'Borderland'[10] is a villanelle, a form that calls attention to artifice, verbal pattern-making, and simultaneously orders precariousness, as the reader thinks: will the poet make it, will he complete the form? The villanelle incorporates edginess, and 'borderland' is about edge, both geographical and linguistic. Meredith introduces the poem with a note: '*Ffin* is the Welsh for *border*. It *occurs inside* diffiniad which *means* definition, *and in* Capel y-Ffin, *a place in the Black Mountains*'. His

---

[8] Christopher Meredith, *Snaring Heaven* (Bridgend: Seren, 1990), p. 63.
[9] Roland Mathias described himself as standing outside 'the house' of his Welsh inheritance. In their humility, as local historians who sometimes, in 'found' poems, give voices to people from the past, and as poets who honour and celebrate the dead, there are spiritual as well as poetic affinities between Ruth Bidgood and Roland Mathias.
[10] *Air Histories*, p. 8.

characteristic wit operates *within* as well as between words. The edges of the poem are edges between earth and sky, rock and building material, is and is not. Edges are within words too; they are 'where meanings happen'. These Black Mountains are places of transformation, where the material becomes spirit, the skylark's muscle turns to 'art/ful song', stone becomes human. Equally, the made becomes unmade – 'self here blurs into annihilation. /Larkfall, earthfall, skyfall, manfall '. This borderland is also a poetics: 'edges are where meanings happen'.

A sense of the numinous, which attaches to the Black Mountains and places such as Capel-y-Ffin, is not absent from Christopher Meredith's poems. It is however more marked in Ruth Bidgood's poems of mid-Wales. In 'All Souls' the time, the weather, and the place combine to engender a feeling of awe, and the sky sliding back creates a sense of revelation. 'A conversation of lights' includes dead farms. But what on All Souls' night is dead?

> Light at Tymawr above me, muted by trees,
> is all the voice Brongwesyn has,
> that once called clearly enough
> into the upper valley's night.
> From the hill Clyn ahead
> Glangwesyn's lively shout of light
> celebrates old Nant Henfron, will not let
> Cenfaes and Blaennant be voiceless.[11]

Ruth Bidgood has been criticised, stupidly, for using place-names in her poems. But it isn't only that the names have an inherent poetry; they are redolent of 'held life', and constitute neighbourhood, community that embraces the dead. Observing this is the poet's function: 'I am a latecomer, but offer/speech to the speechless'. As with Roland Mathias, this function is now best served by a poet who fears to trespass, who does not claim to belong, but whose very 'distance' – in time and across languages – enables commemoration and celebration. Memory, that is not only personal memory, is a passion in Ruth Bidgood's poetry. At once powerfully emotional and moral, recollection in her poems speaks for the dead, and continues a 'conversation' between living and dead, in her mid-Wales landscapes.

---

[11] Ruth Bidgood, *The Print of Miracle* (Llandysul: Gwasg Gomer, 1978), p. 12.

Belonging to a place is no easy assumption, but a qualified experience in Ruth Bidgood and Christopher Meredith's poems. In 'On Hay Bridge'[12] is a quite early Meredith poem, which may in consequence be especially revealing of where the poet stands. At the centre of the poem is a salmon, 'a yard long, dark slate/blotched with sour milk'. The observing poet finds himself in his time in relation to the salmon, which is at once actual and mythical, calling to mind the salmon of Llyn Llyw, the oldest of all creatures, in *Kilhwch and Olwen*. Myth, though, is seen here in historical terms: 'Gerallt saw her eight hundred journeys back'. The landscape, as in R. S. Thomas's 'Welsh Landscape', recalls a violent history - homesteads set on fire, Norman castles replacing Welsh 'wooden towers': the history, in fact, of *Griffri*. As that novel concerns a fictional medieval Welsh poet, so 'On Hay Bridge' reflects on the identity and function of the poet in the present. Meredith thinks of an actual medieval poet, a local man, Bedo Brwynllys,[13] who 'sang sweet and politic of loving girls'. He had a nice line in imagery (girls' 'eyebrows curved/like rainbows or like squirrels' tails') while his country was under the heel of conquerors. The author of this modern poem doesn't want to be like him, forgotten, and 'politic', complicit in his nation's betrayal. Christopher Meredith is emphatically a political poet: a Welsh poet concerned with betrayal or complicity and good faith, and with questions of how to act and how to be.

The salmon represents, among other things, continuity of being, what Jack in *Shifts* calls 'the fucking biological imperative'.[14] It is, thus, a female salmon. The life-giving salmon belongs. But what of the poet? Is he to be complicit with a history of Welsh defeat, of losing 'less by retreat', of stories of martyrdom and emotional song 'to warm an evening perhaps', a history that works to make the Welsh homeless in their own homeland, as twentieth-century Welsh-language poets and philosophers have felt? Against this fate he wishes for the salmon's strength 'to inch against what pushes me from home'. A poem such as 'On Hay Bridge', compacted with difficult feeling, warns against any simple notion of Christopher Meredith as a poet of belonging, at the same time as it signs him a Welsh poet who draws powerfully upon the historical life of a particular area of Wales and faces the question of identity in the present.

---

[12] *Snaring Heaven*, pp. 25–26.
[13] Bedo Brwynllys (fl. 1460) was a poet remembered mainly for his love poems. Christopher Meredith lived at Bronllys in the period 1984–87.
[14] 'The old salmon leaping up the river' Jack said. 'You know. The fucking biological imperative.' *Shifts*, p. 75.

Both Christopher Meredith and Ruth Bidgood invoke continuities. These, however, are often troubled, to be suffered, worked for, imagined, and not simply celebrated. Continuity, as a number of her poems emphatically testify, has metaphysical implications in Ruth Bidgood's work. As 'Hoofprints' says:

> In the rock of our days
> is hidden the print of miracle.[15]

'Hidden' is a key word. For religious and secular poets alike, Welsh landscapes are imbued with religious feeling, whether for ancient Celtic religion, or Anglicanism and alchemy, or Catholicism, or the faith of the chapels. The latter is a shaping element in Ruth Bidgood's 'To the Fish Traps'.[16]

Beginning with a journey, a difficult ascent on 'savage twists' and an imagined fall, with heat giving way to 'the river's cool', the poem enacts meaning, bringing out what is hidden in the landscape. This is, in fact, a landscape of the nonconformist mind. Words of Howell Harries, the Methodist revivalist, echo loudly here, where he 'preached glory, love and fire, /and "Glory!" his hearers shouted back'. Fish traps for collecting eggs of salmon and sea-trout represent the biological imperative, and also, of course, have a Christian symbolism. Here, though, spiritual principle and material process are held in tension:

> Tower and ruined house
> confront each other over an acre of grass;
> two thought-shapes over years of change.
> Past the stones of Cwmdu,
> beyond forests grown, forests felled,
> stretch the *blaenau*:
>   through it all
> a living homeness, like blood, like breath.

Forests planted by man come and go below the *blaenau* – uplands where rivers rise, the Welsh word representing an older stratum, bedrock. In the closing line the keyword 'home' is the word that haunts the ruined houses

---

[15] *The Print of Miracle*, p. 11.
[16] Ruth Bidgood, *Above the Forests* (Blaenau Ffestiniog: Cinnamon Press, 2012), p. 46.

in Ruth Bidgood's poems: 'through it all/a living homeness, like blood, like breath'. 'Homeness' lives in a conflicted historical landscape, where religious meaning – salvation and damnation in Howell Harries's terms – and spirituality oppose but also interact with material process, life force and human making. Life is thus held in the poem, 'like blood, like breath'.

'To the Fish Traps' with its landscape below the *blaenau* and its Methodist history is decidedly a Welsh poem. It could also be interpreted as a metaphysical poem that modernises the incarnational, embodying a fraught relationship between matter and spirit. By contrast, Christopher Meredith's take on religious history is humorous and sceptical, as we see in 'The churches'.[17] The beginning – 'We live in low places/or on mountaintops. /Don't expect us to aspire.' – implicitly identifies the speaker as Welsh. The landscape of shale, mud and stone is viscerally material. But this is Christopher Meredith's Wales as edge-land, place of transformation, 'where meanings happen'. It is a poem that simultaneously affirms identity and precariousness:

> We fasten in hinterlands
> or cling to edges
> in the turn of light round cloud
> where hill slithers into cliff
> where mountain arches into air
> where snouts of land
> push into sea
> that turns to light
> and light that liquefies.

Metamorphosis, protean shape-shifting, is also a strategy for survival, as in the tale of Taliesin. 'The churches' has also a kind of transcendental elementalism that may remind us of scenes in Christopher Meredith's latest novel, *The Book of Idiots*, involving parachute jump and gliding, activities at once dangerous, exhilarating and affording a sense of beauty. The poem, however, brings us down to fundamentals: 'But at the base all's earth.' On this foundation churches are like the popping pegs of 'Earth air', and it is 'old lonely life' that 'endures'. For all its material reality, though, Wales, like the poem, is hard to pin down.

Elusiveness characterises lyric poetry, which is poetry of the individual mind and sensibility, and necessarily subjective, however much it draws

---

[17] *Air Histories*, p. 19.

on the reality of the outer world. It is consequently a form of art that best catches the living moment, and has special relevance to the following words of Boris Pasternak:

> Although the artist is of course mortal like everyone else, the joy of existence experienced by him is immortal and can be experienced by other people centuries later, since his work allows them to come close to the living, personal form of his original sensations.[18]

Of course, it is not only 'the joy of existence' that speaks to us across the ages, nor has the poet, from the time of Inanna of Sumer, always been a man!

Ruth Bidgood's 'Butterflies at Wellfield'[19] conveys a sense of life in time, both historical time and the time of personal memory. Again, it is an empty house that is a magnet for Bidgood's imagination. And for the poet it is words that catch memory, 'butterfly' calling up 'Wellfield, for many childhood years/the empty house next door'. But what does it mean? The house's meaning is elusive, like the shrub in Edward Thomas's 'Old Man'. It was 'a puzzle and provocation' to the poet and her friends as children, and it remains enigmatic for her in age: a solid 'big house' remembered in its setting, but as elusive as butterflies in the meadows. 'Wellfield', a name of profound symbolic significance, combining source and field, means something that cannot be caught. What the poem delivers is a movement of the poet's mind, its mysterious processing of dream and trance, image and word. It is a poem of her mind working with memory, the 'well' and 'field' sources of her imagination.

By contrast, Christopher Meredith's 'My mother missed the beautiful and doomed'[20] is a poem rich with specific social and historical detail. One may glimpse Meredith the novelist in recording scenes from his mother's service as a maid in a big house, in, for example, the Foreign Secretary 'his collar of vermiculated astrakhan/flawed with sparkling rain', and in his response to another novelist – 'Where Waugh, hot for some pious ormolu/dreamed Brideshead' – and in the poem's subtle narrative. Its sharp satirical edge frames controlled anger. But there's more than anger

---

[18] Quoted from Pasternak's *Essay in Autobiography* in Jon Stallworthy and Peter France, *Boris Pasternak; Selected Poems* (London: Allen Lane, 1983), p. 20.
[19] *Above the Forests*, p. 38.
[20] Christopher Meredith, *The Meaning of Flight* (Bridgend: Seren, 2005), pp. 38–39.

in the poem, which – given that the subject is the poet's mother – has a remarkable objectivity.

Meredith shows the effects of national and world history in a life, the personal part reacting against but being shaped by social circumstance. The basic situation is simple: 'my mother' looking at a photograph of the House in which, as a young woman, she served as a maid. The poem lays time on time, process on process, the time of her smoking a cigarette and the historical time of her service. Both processes are destructive, the smoking being like an internalisation of the history in which the House is implicated: coal mining, armament production, the Spanish Civil War. Intimate personal tragedy and mass catastrophe are conjoined: 'her two dead children, /two atom bombs ago'. The woman suffers condescension and sexual insult but the poem doesn't offer easy judgement by portraying, simply, a working-class victim of upper-class manipulation. The emphasis, rather, as in 'On Hay Bridge', is on complicity.

> Unwilled complicity can hurt so much.
> She clutches at the deaths of millions.
>
> 'A skivvy all my life' she says
> and strikes another match.

Christopher Meredith's poems are strong in social awareness, as poetry and fiction from a working-class background tend to be. The perspective, however, is that of one who is at once 'onlooker and participant', and who deploys his sources with acute intelligence, drawing on the language of social realism but subverting or transcending it in the interest of larger human truth. In 'Colour',[21] another poem concerning a family member, Meredith describes his grandmother's lived experience as being 'incomprehensible' despite or because lived in historical time, 'a war and a strike and another war ago', in a place central to the crisis of the age: 'when Armageddon stood at the turn of the hill/in Troedrhiwgwair'. The truth of the poem counters the lie of a photograph:

> you simplified in monochrome,
> the pinny and the big forearms
> grotesque as some comedian in drag,
> hands stiffened to arthritic paddles,
> two shadows masking pale blue eyes.

---

[21] *The Meaning of Flight*, p. 18.

The living fact of a loved person, concentrated in the colour of the eyes, escapes all clichés, whether photographic, linguistic or dramatic, and especially the cliché of 'colourful' character. Life escapes the naturalistic writer, as Virginia Woolf said,[22] and as Christopher Meredith's poems show, like hanggliders at the conclusion of 'Colour' 'signalling *we live, we live*'.

Photographs recur in poems in Ruth Bidgood's *Above the Forests*, a motif foregrounded in the first poem in the book, 'The Copy'. As in her early poem 'Little of Distinction' the poet finds in overlooked objects and scenes 'the mystery/That complements precision', so, in 'The Copy', 'An unremarkable photograph/ [was] born of a wish to record/even the less distinctive/dips and summits on the fringe/of a happy afternoon'. Recording 'little of distinction' – small 'things' in which life inheres – is what Ruth Bidgood does so movingly in the spirit of the tradition in which, broadly speaking, she writes. That is the tradition of the nature poets, John Clare and Thomas Hardy, and above all Edward Thomas. Her poetry over the years has grown in psychological subtlety, and through distrust of what can be seen and shown and said, in a deepening sense of duality – 'dips and summits', shadow and laughter – and life's mixture and elusiveness. Her poetry is lucid but recognises that it isn't only lucidity and clarity that illuminate. Here, in 'The Copy', 'a botched anomalous image' reveals 'the strangeness here' – something suggesting mixed light and dark, happiness and sadness, life and death, but refusing summary. Prose may analyse and summarize and engage in abstract speculation; lyric poetry of this order does not. Its domain is 'strangeness', and its favoured terrain edges and margins and borders.

Christopher Meredith's sense of edge, at once geographically specific and metaphorical, destabilizes summarising, prosaic vision – a clichéd idea of industrial or post-industrial south Wales. 'The slurry pond',[23] depicting his childhood landscape, is as actual as Wordsworth's Lake District, to which it refers:

> A ruined city lay around *us*
>   in our infancy
> – the pumping station, railless sidings,
>   workings of an age
> we didn't realise was not quite dead.

---

[22] See Virginia Woolf's 1923 essay 'Mr Bennett and Mrs Brown'.
[23] *Air Histories*, p. 26.

This place has a special geology underlying a dying industry and is 'a place of edges' – elemental ('coal surfacing, becoming air'), disease ('shadow on a lung'), and time ('a border/broken backed across a war'). The human cost of industry might suggest a protest poem. But this is nothing so simple. The opening words could not be more emotionally accepting, even possessive: 'My heartland'. The allusion to Wordsworth's 'Intimations of Immortality' ode ('Heaven lies about us in our infancy') isn't only ironic. Nor is that to the Garden of Eden: 'Quarries and cliffs, moor and shaletip/ all were the garden of our/innocence'. 'Us' and 'our' are not loosely general, but communitarian, denoting the children of the place. The poem is in the spirit that Glyn Jones defined as that of the dragon with two tongues, the Welsh poet writing in English: 'not a man apart, a freak, but rather an accepted part of the social fabric with an important function to perform'.[24] But while this (the quip about 'freak' apart) is a useful definition, it is also a potentially misleading one, suggesting the sort of belonging that can result in nostalgia and complacency. 'The slurry pond' is far from being either. Beginning with 'heartland' it concludes with 'its mud heart sucked you down', expressing the danger, the deathliness, of this place. But the poet is not 'sucked down'. The place is 'heartland', loved home terrain, but seen with detachment that prevents mere immersion. Though it ends with an image of death, the poem confirms life specific to the place.

Writing in English from Wales since the First World War centres on ideas of home, exile, homecoming, and of belonging and not belonging. It is understandable why this should be so in a country so racked by social changes, with communities and landscapes devastated, and with the threat to the Welsh language and the culture it sustains. Ruth Bidgood's poems, for the most part, spring from a landscape apparently out of earshot of the forces that have made and unmade and are remaking Christopher Meredith's terrain in and around Tredegar. Her poetry, however, is fully awake to change in rural Breconshire, to ecological damage, including forestation and deforestation, ruin of communities, and what is ostensibly more elusive, changes of ways of life with spiritual consequences.

'Homecoming'[25] is a poem that defines Ruth Bidgood's great theme of home through negatives. It describes the disappointment of people seeking out 'the family farm', place of their forebears, and finding 'nothing to see/ only a shelf of hill'. Powerful historical attachments, such as pope and

---

[24] Glyn Jones, *The Dragon Has Two Tongues*, Revised edition, ed. Tony Brown (Cardiff: University of Wales Press, 2001), p. 127.
[25] *Above the Forests*, p. 43.

conqueror feel for their native ground, 'didn't work for them'. Expectations based upon such hierarchical figures are absurd in this context, as they should see. The poem we begin to realise is partly a poem about false expectations. Partly, because it also shows what belonging means.

> Here, they found nothing to recognise,
> nothing to claim them, nothing
> to belong to. There seemed no point
> in staying to hear wind in the grass,
> watch cloud skim the hill, let the eye
> follow an ancient path down to the stream.
>
> Nursing bafflement, dissatisfaction,
> they turned away, with no notion
> that with footfall after footfall
> over generations, their brief
> dismissive tread would be part for ever
> of the ground of home.

What the visitors to their ancestral 'home' want is nostalgic and unrealistic, even anti-human – 'the shell/in which the secret, vulnerable/family-creature had lurked'. But human beings are not snails or limpets, creatures that secure themselves with a shell, obviating the need to act, which entails work and suffering. Ironically, the visitors have no notion that the visit resulting in dissatisfaction defines their relationship to 'the ground of home'.

What, then, does home as the poem defines it mean? It means enduring elemental conditions through time. Above all it means not the passive life of snail or limpet but making, work, the human endeavour that made the 'ancient path' and keeps it open. The diction is simple but, as often in Ruth Bidgood's poems, takes on symbolic weight and depth. 'Ancient path down to the stream' represents a way of life ('path') and the source ('stream') that is both life-flow and source of life.

The juxtaposition of two poets with such evident differences also draws attention to what they have in common. Both have a strong historical sense. Ruth Bidgood is a distinguished local historian with a book about Abergwesyn, *Parishes of the Buzzard*, and numerous articles to her credit. She is a remembrancer; she offers 'speech to the nameless', sometimes restoring their speech in 'found' poems. Acutely aware of change and transience in her mid-Wales, she observes 'held life' in ruins and materials and words, honouring the lives of actual people.

Christopher Meredith has evidently made a close study of the history of the region in which he grew up. His first novel, *Shifts*, signals the link between a sense of history and identity, with Keith, as Kirsti Bohata says, 'a keen amateur local historian, trying to make sense of his present through his past'.[26] Keith knows history is 'not something you can escape from'.[27] History 'included everything'. Towards the end of the novel Keith is carrying around a Welsh dictionary, with which he is 'trying to translate some grave inscriptions'. In the novel we are aware of something missing – the Welsh language and its culture: a dimension that could give meaning to the characters' lives. In an interview Christopher Meredith said; 'learning Welsh is one of the most important things I've ever done'.[28] Looking at the salmon from Hay Bridge, aware of what 'pushes me from home', he sees the salmon in terms of his Welsh historical sense as a symbol of Welsh continuity.

But Meredith's Gwent is an area of instability, where 'we ... cling to edges' and the Black Mountains are 'a billowing pavilion' with 'each church', traditional container of meaning, ready to 'pop its button'. His work lends itself to discussion in postcolonialist terms, as in Kirsti Bohata's *Postcolonialism Revisited*. Discussions of the novels *Shifts* and *Griffri* by Bohata and Dafydd Johnston emphasise his Welsh borderland as central to Welsh experience, especially in light of the erosion of the language.

In 1894 O. M. Edwards, observing 'something like a literary awakening among English-speaking Welshmen', noted 'a strong desire for a literature that will be English in language but Welsh in spirit'.[29] In *The Dragon Has Two Tongues*, in 1968, Glyn Jones defined this spirit as communitarian. 'It seems to me that the basic Welsh conception of the poet even today ... is ... of a sort of craftsman, well integrated in the community of which he is a product.'[30] Edwards and Jones assumed that the Welsh poet is a man; since the 1970s women have written some of the best Anglophone Welsh poetry.

---

[26] Kirsti Bohata, *Postcolonialism Revisited* (Cardiff: University of Wales Press, 2004), p. 124.
[27] *Shifts*, p. 210.
[28] Sheenagh Pugh, 'Good God! There's writing on both sides of that paper! – Interview with Christopher Meredith', http://sheenaghpugh.livejournal.com/68450.html
[29] Quoted in *The Dragon Has Two Tongues*, p. 200, n. 24.
[30] *The Dragon Has Two Tongues*, p. 121.

Ruth Bidgood and Christopher Meredith are both poets of place. On the basis of Glyn Jones's idea of the Welsh poet, we might consider their places in terms of the Welsh concept of *bro*. This, Ned Thomas argues, has become 'a term of social rather than physical geography, an area with subjectively perceived borders, and perhaps embracing people as much as land'. It 'comes with a structure of feeling … a good deal warmer than does the overused word "community" which tries too hard to achieve the intimacy that comes naturally with the word *bro*.'[31] Like Glyn Jones's definition, this sense of place presses us to think of the Welsh poet as one who belongs.

At worst, this is a concept of the poet that robs him or her of individuality, and denies poetry as an art of personal exploration. Ruth Bidgood and Christopher Meredith are both passionately engaged with a heartland, 'a living homeness, like blood, like breath'. It would be sentimental and untrue, however, to describe them as 'well integrated' in the communities of which they are products. Both are at once onlookers and participants. Ruth Bidgood observes social and environmental change in mid Wales. Her voice is a voice of resistance which works to remember lives that the changing community is prone to forget. Dafydd Johnston's description of *Griffri*, 'as an attempt to repossess Gwent's Welsh past and to reclaim it as an integral part of Wales',[32] is equally applicable to Meredith's poetry. His border is at once personal heartland and central to the condition of Wales. Like his country, he has to work against forces pushing him from home. This work has included learning the Welsh language. With the two languages integral to his sense of history, and in the confusion of social and cultural change, he knows his place as an edge 'where meanings happen'. Neither poet offers the craft of one 'well integrated in the community'. Both are lyric poets, and poets of relationship, who express the livingness – the strangeness – of experience. By exploring *what* they are, poets with heartlands on several 'frontiers', they help us to know what we are.

---

[31] Ned Thomas, 'Bro', *Planet* 207, August 2012, pp. 82 – 83.
[32] Dafydd Johnston, 'Making History in Two Languages: William Owen Roberts's *Y Pla* and Christopher Meredith's *Griffri*', *Welsh Writing in English: A Yearbook of Critical Essays*, Vol. 3, 1997, p. 123.

The Tree of Life: Explorations of an Image

1

Near where I live in Somerset, there is a Norman church on which the tympanum over the North door is carved with a Tree of Life.[1] Two beasts stand one on either side of the Tree, which they appear to be devouring. Evidently nature inspired the sculptor – as well it might, considering that the church had been built in a clearing within an ancient royal forest, which the Britons had called *Coit Maur*, 'Great Wood'. It must have been an awesome, dangerous place, dense with trees and alive with beasts, and closer to the wildwood that established itself after the last Ice Age than any subsequent phase of our cultural landscape. It is equally evident that the sculptor derived his motif from a forest of symbols. The Tree of Life is an ancient symbol, known to us from Old Europe of the fourth millennium BC, from early Mesopotamia, and from elsewhere in the Neolithic world. To the mediaeval sculptor carving the motif on the Somerset church it may have signified conflict between the powers of light and the powers of darkness, between Life and Death. But the Tree would also have symbolised for him the Cross, and thus the victory of Life *through* Death and Resurrection. In that respect, the Tree on the church has something fundamental in common with manifestations of the Tree in other cultures, for although the motif is fertile of many different meanings, it is always in some sense the axis of a world-view, connecting nature and the supernatural, and relating the creative and destructive forces on which life depends.

My intention here is to look at some examples of trees in British art and poetry, mainly of the past two hundred years. I begin with the Norman sculptor's Tree of Life because it is, for me, a touchstone of the real image, and because I want to bear in mind that the universal symbol is also an historical phenomenon, which expresses particular beliefs and needs. Thus, when, in 1799, William Blake wrote, 'The tree which moves some to tears of joy is in the Eyes of others only a Green thing which stands in the way,' he was engaged in a fundamental conflict in his society between vision and scientific analysis, imagination and utility, creation and destruction. He affirmed that 'This World is a World of Imagination

---

[1] At the time of writing, I was living at Buckland Dinham, near Frome in Somerset. The church is at Lullington.

& Vision,' but his reshaping of traditional symbols was necessarily individual, and opposed to the mechanistic principles re-making the world in his time.

In the previous century, some 150 years before Blake wrote, 'As a man is, so he sees,' a shoemaker's son had looked through the gates of Hereford and seen the earth as if on the first day of Creation:

> The Gates were at first the End of the World, The Green Trees when I saw them first through one of the Gates Transported and Ravished me; their Sweetness and unusual Beauty made my Heart to leap, and almost mad with Extasie, they were such strange and Wonderful Things.

Thomas Traherne's ecstatic vision of nature was indeed a vision of God's Creation. Its later visual equivalent might be a painting from Samuel Palmer's Shoreham years, say *Pastoral with a Horsechestnut*, 1831-32, or Stanley Spencer's *The May Tree*, 1932-33. These seem to burgeon effortlessly with God's plenitude, although they are, of course, skilfully composed. Nevertheless, it is significant that Traherne's vision, which prefigures the Romantic apprehension of nature charged with the supernatural, should be a child's.

There is nothing inevitably childish about an adult seeing with the eyes of a child. In the context of a worldview that produces division within the individual psyche and between us and the world at every level, it may be a means of integration, connecting adult and child and restoring the artist to participation in nature. C. R. Leslie, in his *Memoirs of the Life of John Constable*, wrote that he had seen Constable 'admire a fine tree with an ecstasy of delight like that with which he would catch up a beautiful child in his arms'. Such an impulse is not to be ascribed primarily to a taste for the Picturesque. Both Gainsborough and Constable saw nature not only through the eyes of Dutch landscape painters, but under the deep-rooted impressions of their boyhoods. *Cornard Wood*, c.1748 is rightly known as *Gainsborough's Forest*. The painting, which he began while still at school, images a world in which human beings, at work and at leisure, animals and trees, all have an equivalent, harmonious life. Perhaps the world only appears thus to a child who feels part of things. Later, often as a background to portraits of the gentry, Gainsborough painted the landowners' England, turning his early vision either to pastoral or into an attribute of social position. Constable retained his early impressions.

"I should paint my own places best," he wrote; "painting is with me but another name for feeling, and I associate 'my careless boyhood' with all that lies on the banks of the Stour; those scenes made me a painter, and I am grateful." He combined scientific observations of nature with feeling, through which the man remained in touch with the boy. Empathy is a fruit of participation in nature. Constable's trees are not only closely observed, but have integral being, and 'grow' in place. He did not make a distinction between nature and the supernatural. Thus, in *Salisbury Cathedral from the Bishop's Grounds,* 1823, for example, the trees are not pillars and the spire is not the echo of a tree, as they are in paintings by Caspar David Friedrich, but both have an equivalent life. As it was with Constable, so it was with Wordsworth and John Clare: the boy was immersed in nature, and what he felt the man learnt to see. But all, in different degrees, experienced strain, for the revolutions in industry and agriculture were pulling apart the world they would hold together in images of wholeness. For all three, the problematic term, which should connect the self and others, and man and nature, was community.

In the last decades of the nineteenth century, agricultural depression and the decline of the rural population stimulated the back-to-the-land movement. But as the utilitarian exploitation of the land had increased, and as the traditional connection between religion and nature had ceased to be a common experience, so the capacity of nature to provide a symbolic language had diminished. With a confidence that would later seem astonishing, Wordsworth had written

> One impulse from a vernal wood
> May teach you more of man;
> Of moral evil and of good
> Than all the sages can.

But what Wordsworth's successor, Thomas Hardy, the greatest Victorian imaginative writer about nature, found in the woods was evidence of the defects of natural law – the struggle for existence between species and individuals, maiming, disease, death. Hardy derived his life-long love of nature from growing up in the country, but the love was gradually overshadowed by an *idea* drawn from contemporary science.

Edward Thomas is another poet who, in the period before and during the First World War, looks back nostalgically to the child's unselfconscious oneness with nature, and experiences the diminished capacity of nature to sustain the man's spirit. 'The Chalk Pit', typically a poem of divided consciousness, concludes

> imperfect friends, we men
> And trees since time began; and nevertheless
> Between us still we breed a mystery.

But 'mystery', for Thomas, is a word that has lost its religious potency, and in consequence he often turns back on himself, and cannot find in nature a larger reality that he is part of. That is, indeed, a strength of his poetry, in which he honestly confronts his dis-ease and separateness, but his pre-war prose is often tainted by the fanciful myth-making to which English pastoral is especially prone. Particularly for writers and artists before the First World War, 'mystery' tended to mean a literary form of enchantment, compounded of nostalgia for childhood and an imaginary past and 'haunted' country places.

Paul Nash's early perception of Wittenham Clumps, which would be a focus of his mature vision, was in this fey spirit. He described, in 1911, 'grey hallowed hills crowned by old old trees, Pan-ish places down by the river wonderful to think on, full of strange enchantment ... a beautiful legendary country haunted by old Gods long forgotten'. A few years later, in paintings of which the best known is *We are Making a New World*, 1918, he was imaging trench landscapes composed of mounds of mud, craters and naked, shattered trees. These are indeed places haunted by death, with a 'presence' that prefigures that of his post-war images of Wittenham Clumps. Indeed, the rhythms and arrangement of the forms of mounds and trees in the trench landscapes foreshadow both the composition and symbolism of the latter. I would make a distinction between the works in which Nash continued to call up 'enchantment', such as his 'Monster Field' studies, and the paintings, like *Landscape of the Vernal Equinox*, 1943-44, in which he fully realised his poetic vision, and which are genuinely mysterious. The latter combine, through colour, images and forms, corresponding opposites: light and dark, earth-rootedness and flight, past and present, life and death. They are personal landscapes, which both realise the spirit of place and compose a modern version of the Tree of Life, rooted among the dead, charged with the power of resurrection.

'Wounded trees and wounded men,' were, for David Jones, 'very much an abiding image' of the First World War. The descriptions of the battleground in *In Parenthesis* (1937) make connections between them, not at the level of physical resemblance alone, but in terms of the kinship between men and trees that is richly depicted in religion and myth. David Jones's first mental breakdown, in 1932, ended a period of intensive painting, in which he had attempted to realise his vision of the whole, 'contained' in the paintings as the 'little thing, the quantity of an hazelnut,' which Christ showed to Julian of Norwich, contained 'all that is made'.[2] Following another breakdown, in 1946, David Jones made a series of drawings of trees in the garden of the nursing home, or at his boarding house nearby. Each tree in the series is instinct with sap and thrusting wood, and so are the trees in the painting with which the series culminates, *Vexilla Regis*, 1947. This is a great work of fluid symbolism, in which 'many confluent ideas are involved in a single image'.[3] Here, trees from a suburban garden have become, under the form of paint, the 'trees' on Calvary, standing in a landscape which bears the signs which, for David Jones, related human history and the whole creation to the Incarnation, Crucifixion and Resurrection. Nowhere else, perhaps, either in painting or writing, did he come closer to containing his vision of the whole in one space. For him, as for the Norman sculptor, the Tree of the Cross was the Tree of Life. The symbol, however, was not ready to hand in his culture, but had to be renewed, with great effort, in face of the destruction of religious and natural signs. For the same reason, *Vexilla Regis*, and the work of modern religious artists generally, may be admired for its composition, but without our realising all that it means.

2

Jean Giono's *The Man Who Planted Trees* was first published, under another title, in 1954. Its first publication in Britain, in a paperback edition with wood engravings by Michael McCurdy, in 1989, is a sign of the times. The story concerns an imaginary shepherd, Elzéard Bouffier, who, during a period spanning the two world wars, single-handedly reafforests a barren area of Provence. A vast improvement in the quality of human life in the area is a consequence of the ecological change his tree planting brings about. Like R. S. Thomas's Iago Prytherch, in 'A Peasant', Bouffier is 'a winner of wars/Enduring like a tree under the

---

[2] See David Jones, *The Dying Gaul and Other Writings* (London: Faber and Faber, 1978), p. 142.
[3] *Dai Greatcoat: A Self-Portrait of David Jones in His Letters*, p. 151.

curious stars'. Unlike Prytherch, he is one whose care for nature makes civilisation possible.

Common Ground, directed by Angela King and Susan Clifford, would surely endorse Bouffier as a hero for our time. Like Bouffier planting the wasteland with seedlings, they have either commissioned or published or supported most of the recent books and pamphlets, projects and art exhibitions, concerned with trees. They are continuing a tradition, which might be described as the practical side of the Romantic movement, but with an urgency necessitated by the greater threat to the earth today. Coleridge described Wordsworth's object in his poems in the *Lyrical Ballads* as 'to give the charm of novelty to things of every day and to excite a feeling analogous to the supernatural, by awakening the mind's attention from the lethargy of custom, and directing it to the loveliness and the wonders of the world before us'. Constable associated himself with Shakespeare who, he said, 'could make everything poetical', and claimed, 'I should paint my own places best'. Common Ground works in the same spirit, 'to encourage new ways of looking at the world, to excite people into remembering the richness of the commonplace and the value of the everyday'.[4]

Angela King and Susan Clifford have edited *Trees Be Company*, an anthology of poetry about trees. This book nicely complements Kim Taplin's *Tongues in Trees*, which is subtitled 'Studies in Literature & Ecology', and is illustrated with sensitive drawings by Laurie Clark. Kim Taplin reads with 'an ecological eye', and is concerned with poetry's affirmation of 'the underlying unity between the natural and the spiritual worlds'.[5] She is polemical, but also considers a range of writers, from Keats to Frances Horovitz, and is attentive to what each has to say.

According to Kim Taplin, Frances Horovitz 'uses the woman's privilege and right to identify with the earth'.[6] I find the words arresting, partly because they confirm what I have observed in some recent poetry by women, in Hilary Llewellyn-Williams's *The Tree Calendar*, for example, and in books by Christine Evans, Jean Earle and Gillian Clarke, to name only poets from Wales. That 'Women are often better able than men to feel what is happening to the earth,'[7] is, however, a looser statement.

---

[4] 'About Common Ground', *Trees Be Company*, ed. Angela King & Susan Clifford (Bristol: Bristol Classical Press, 1989), p. xi.
[5] *Tongues in Trees*, p. 19.
[6] Ibid., p. 209.
[7] Ibid., p. 21.

The war poetry of David Jones, Wilfred Owen and Isaac Rosenberg has provided us with our most powerful images of the destruction of nature as well as men, and with some of our most sensitive images of the kinship between humankind and nature. One of the finest modern poems in *Trees Be Company* is Thom Gunn's 'The Cherry Tree', in which the poet identifies with the tree giving birth to her fruit, 'to lose them into the world'.[8] Certainly, women have reason to know that, in Stevie Smith's words, 'Nature is sick at man' ('Alone in the Woods', *TBC*, p. 4). But of course, anyone of either sex might know that. It was Gerard Manley Hopkins who, in 'Binsey Poplars' (*TBC*, p. 19) realised that country is as 'tender' as the eye with which we see (or do not see) her, and thus offered us an idea of our mutual vulnerability appropriate to our time.

The medieval sculptor carved the Tree of Life on the church as the trees about him were being felled, and their wood put to a variety of uses: so poets have developed a metaphorical and symbolic language of trees as the woods have served our everyday and historical purposes, and in relation to them. Our sense of time, both historical and cyclical, is intimately bound up with trees. William Cowper, in 'Yardley Oak', one of the greatest of all poems about trees, wrote:

> Time was, when, settling on thy leaf, a fly
> Could shake thee to the root – and time has been
> When tempests could not. At thy firmest age
> Thou hadst within thy bole solid contents
> That might have ribb'd the sides or plank'd the deck
> Of some flagg'd admiral… (*TBC*, p. 113)

He was not an idolater of trees, he belonged spiritually to the age before the Romantics revived tree-worship but he saw in the oak a 'survivor', 'a shatter'd veteran', and admired its strength and endurance. Naturally, poets see in trees the qualities they would like to have. In his early 'The Tree' (*TBC*, p. 130), Ezra Pound identifies with a tree, knowing the truth of the fables of Daphne and of Baucis and Philemon, the truth, that is, of metamorphosis, which was the poetic function he wished to exercise. Pound's approach was Classical; he looked to his time for a new Renaissance, which would recover lost meanings. Ted Hughes, on the other hand, is an expressionist, who wrings from his tree meanings applicable

---

[8] *Trees Be Company*, p. 30. All further quotations from poems in this essay will be from this anthology, hereafter referenced *TBC* and given in the text.

to a century of death-camps and police states. Interrogated by wind, 'tortured by huge scaldings of light', the tree 'tries to confess'. It survives only by absolute resignation, dumbly letting 'what happens to it happen' ('A Tree', *TBC*, pp. 129-30). As the title of the anthology, taken from a poem by William Barnes, suggests, however, it is for their 'company' that poets since Cowper have most valued trees. Duke Senior in *As You like it* contrasts the forest of Arden favourably with the court, but Shakespeare makes it clear that the court is, ultimately, where courtiers belong. It is the Romantics who seek among trees what they do not find among their own kind. Or the rooted tree may be a symbol of community. Blake shows his innocents, young and old, gathered together under the oak on 'the Echoing Green'. For Clare, the elm beside his cottage was integral to his religion of hearth and home. For Ruth Fainlight, today, trees are 'our mute companions'. They are witnesses, huge mild

> beings who suffer the consequence
> of sharing our planet and cannot move
> away from any evil we
> subject them to, whose silent
> absolution hides the scars of our sins,
> who always forgive – yet still assume
> the attributes of judges, not victims. (*TBC*, pp. 138-9)

Trees may not always be able to 'forgive'. But the poem does provide, I think, an apt celebration of trees for the present.

Other real images, by artists, appeared in the South Bank Centre exhibition, 'The Tree of Life: New Images of an Ancient Symbol', which was proposed by Common Ground. The exhibition as a whole left me with mixed feelings, however. I found in it some arresting, and some beautiful, works, by, among others, Stephen Cox and Garry Fabian Miller, John Hubbard, Terry Setch, Ken Kiff and Andrzej Jackowski. It is not surprising that, in modern conditions, the works should be notable for their individualism and variety, and therefore fail to provide an overall coherence and cumulative impact. More critically, I felt the concepts described in the Introduction to the exhibition were, too often, in excess of what was actually realised in the works, and that, generally, a great deal of book-knowledge of the tree-symbol in myth and religion was being drawn on, while only a few artists were working from deep, first-hand knowledge of trees, or were compelled by the motif, as distinct from fulfilling a commission to make a painting or a sculpture on a theme. It would be more rewarding, I felt, to look at a body of work that manifested that knowledge, or explored the motif – by David Nash, say, or Lee Grandjean, or Andy Goldsworthy.

This feeling was subsequently confirmed by Andy Goldsworthy's exhibition 'Leaves' at the Natural History Museum. Goldsworthy has what Common Ground values most, the ability 'to focus our attention on the ordinary and to transport us to the extraordinary, to reawaken a sense of wonder in the everyday'.[9] He approaches nature with respect; indeed, he manifests the new piety towards nature that is abroad among a number of artists and poets, and finds its most eloquent philosophical expression in the writings of Wendell Berry. It is a piety which, in Goldsworthy's work, has a light touch, and does not exclude humour. He has learnt from his materials. 'The sycamore has taught me most,' he writes. 'The biggest lesson being that so much can be found in something common and ordinary.'[10] By using the 'architecture' of the leaf he realises 'forms that grow from the leaf': imaginary forms, and forms that echo other natural forms – cone, snake, trilobite, for example – and suggest life's primordial shape-making. The titles of the works refer to both material and place.

The book of the exhibition contains a clear scientific exposition by the exhibition organiser, Paul Nesbitt, of the nature of leaves. 'Now is a time,' Nesbitt concludes, 'when creative artists and scientists are needed more than ever, to remind us of our immersion in the natural world and to deepen our understanding of it.'[11] Wordsworth and Constable would have approved the sentiment. The science which was transforming the world in their time had its ultimate source in Bacon's philosophy, which maintained that 'knowledge is power', and in the idea (ascribed to Bacon) of putting nature to the rack to wring out the answers to our questions. Constable, in particular, shared with Gilbert White the habit of close observation, which might be described as the positive side of the Baconian heritage. The scientific attitude that followed Wordsworth's time, and derived from a reading of Darwin, perceived nature as a battleground, on which victory depended upon pitiless self-interest, ingenuity, and the exercise of power. The principal message of modern science, on the other hand, seems to be that we exist on earth together with all living and

---

[9] Foreword by Common Ground, Andy Goldsworthy, *Leaves* (London: Common Ground, 1989), p. 7.
[10] *Leaves*, p. 18.
[11] Ibid., p. 16.

inanimate things by virtue of a subtle web of interrelationships, and our choice is between knowing ourselves part of the web, and conducting ourselves accordingly or ripping it apart, and in consequence destroying ourselves and possibly the earth as well. There are poets and artists at work now who know themselves immersed in nature in this sense, and who seek to reconcile art and nature, and art and science. As always, the tree, as organism and as symbol, is at the centre of creative activity.

American Visions of England: Ronald Johnson and John Matthias

Post-imperial England, in a state of decline, has proved a problem for English poets with a strong sense of the native land and traditions. Philip Larkin laments the loss of a once-hallowed culture, as he foresees 'England gone, /The shadows, the meadows, the lanes, /The guildhalls, the carved choirs'.[1] Geoffrey Hill's patriotic feeling is embroiled with his dissection of a prevalent English nostalgia, coupled with loss of historical memory. In *The Triumph of Love*, he describes England as 'a nation/with so many memorials but no memory'.[2] For a fresher vision, without the strains of entanglement in the politics of decline, it is interesting to turn to two poems by American poets inspired by their experience of England and Wales.

Ronald Johnson's *The Book of the Green Man* was first published in 1967. It is a response to Johnson's visit to England and Wales in autumn 1962. The visit lasted for about a year, during which he made excursions, with his fellow American poet, Jonathan Williams, to parts of Britain rich in literary and artistic associations. John Matthias's 'An East Anglian Diptych: Ley Lines, Rivers', published with two other long poems in *A Gathering of Ways*, in 1991, has a narrower geographical focus, but draws upon a longer experience of living in England. In the 1970s and mid 80s Matthias and his wife had spent long periods in Suffolk and Cambridge. In consequence, his English 'poem of place' carries strong personal feeling. As Matthias wrote: "in many ways 'An East Anglian Diptych' ... is a farewell to the part of England I knew and loved".[3]

Christopher Middleton's eloquent endorsement to the English edition of *The Book of the Green Man* includes the following words: Johnson 'presents an image of England, or, to be precise, of sundry English scenes, with a vividness and a strangeness beyond the reach of any English poet'. When Middleton goes on to say that this image of England is 'unknown ... since the days of Blake, Calvert and Palmer', we may recall Geoffrey Grigson's claim that: 'Everybody – except the English perhaps – knows

---

[1] 'Going, Going', Philip Larkin, *Collected Poems* (London: Faber and Faber, 1990), p. 190.
[2] Geoffrey Hill, *The Triumph of Love* (London: Penguin Books, 1999), p. 40.
[3] John Matthias, *At Large* (Bristol: Shearsman Books, 2016), p. 365.

that England is a mysterious country, inhabited by a mysterious people'.[4] Vivid and strange are epithets we may apply to the mysterious country that Johnson and Matthias, in their different ways, reveal.

In *The Book of the Green Man* Ronald Johnson, standing by Wordsworth's grave in Grasmere Churchyard, says

> I wish
> to make something circular,
> seasonal, out
>
> of this 'wheel' of
> mountains
> – some
> flowering thing in its
> cycle – an image of our footsteps
>
> planted in homage
>
> over each ridge
>
> & valley. (*BGM*, pp. 17–18)

His poem is that of a man walking in England and Wales, imaging what he sees and feels with bodily immediacy, and paying homage to the land. His excursions take him to many places rich in literary and artistic associations, such as Samuel Palmer's Shoreham and Alexander Pope's Twickenham. At the same time, he is a maker, and the seasonal circularity of the poem contains other patterns connecting the poem and its visionary materials to the landscape. The maze, with its rich metaphorical associations, is a recurring image. Johnson's homage includes extensive references to, and quotations from, native writers, painters and musicians, such as Francis Kilvert and Henry Vaughan, Constable and

---

[4] Edwin Smith and Geoffrey Grigson, *England* (London: Thames and Hudson, 1957), p. 5. Johnson draws upon Grigson's writings as a source for his poem, and says: 'one should read *all* of Grigson; his books are seminal and essential'. *The Book of the Green Man* (London: Longmans, 1967), p. 85. Subsequent quotations from this book will be designated *BGM* and included in the text. A new edition, with an Afterword by Ross Hair, was published by Uniformbooks in 2015.

Palmer, and Frederick Delius. While open to these English and Welsh influences, Johnson works in the spirit of Thoreau, finding in 'old books … a certain fertility, an Ohio soil, as if they were making a humus for new literatures to spring in' (*BGM*, p. 83). The newness of Johnson's poem brings formal and stylistic methods indebted to Ezra Pound and William Carlos Williams to his English subject matter.

The freshness of *The Book of the Green Man* owes much to Johnson's sensuous responses to the places through which he walks, and to natural sounds, such as birdsong. The poem is quick with living detail. At the same time, the poet both perceivers patterns in nature and the landscape and constructs a patterned verse. He sees, and makes, 'connections':

> – between an earth, sentient with moles,
> & the owl's
> radiant eyes –
>
> fine as a web drawn
> by spiders,
>
> close as the grain of oak…
>
> from earth, to mistletoe, ivy & lichen, to owl's-
> wing, to thunder, to lightning, to earth – & back
> 			(*BGM*, p. 27).

The poetry is vibrant with energies; colours, movements, sounds, and scents, all work together. Particular connections embody a vision of the universal. In revealing this Johnson is responding to an English, and Celtic, visionary tradition, both drawing on it, and finding it in the landscape. He invokes 'the Wye itself/to cut these pages', and the river's 'Celtic loops & interlacements' take the view 'to Kilvert – Vaughan' (*BGM*, p. 32). In Grasmere Churchyard, where Wordsworth is buried, he perceives 'a blinding/darkness'. The image recalls Henry Vaughan's 'The Night': 'There is in God (some say)/A deep, but dazzling darkness'. Later, at 'Bredwardine, where Kilvert lies buried', he invokes Henry Vaughan again, quoting 'The Retreate':

> Where from his grave, 'bright
>
> shootes':
>
> daffodil, primrose, snow-drop, white violet (*BGM*, p. 37)

A common vision connecting the Romantic poet, Wordsworth, with the Metaphysical poet, Vaughan, and the Victorian diarist, Kilvert, finds its embodiment in the wild flowers of April. As he invokes Vaughan again, we see how for Johnson poetry and place form together a vision of the universe:

> *Silex Scintillans*
> these mountains –
>
> the Black & Brecon Beacons
>
> – a deep but dazzling darkness. Beckoning…
>
> dissolving,
>
> to white cloud,
>
> & swan, & clod.
>
> Everything,
>
> one river running… (*BGM*, pp. 42-43)

The myth of the Green Man operates as a structuring principle in the poem. The figure connects the poet to the natural world, in which he participates, and joins the British myth to the spirit of Walt Whitman, who, in 'Song of Myself', affirmed his sense of himself as a universal natural being: 'I find I incorporate gneiss, coal, long-threaded moss,/ fruit, grains, esculent root,/ And am stucco'd with quadrupeds & birds all over' (quoted in *BGM*, p. 38).

John Matthias's 'An East Anglian Diptych: Ley Lines, Rivers' has a similar earthiness to Whitman's lines. It opens with materials, times, and seasons:

> ...& *flint by salt by clay*
> *by sunrise and by sunset*
> *and at equinox, by equinox,*
>
> these routes, these
> lines were drawn, are drawn,
> (force by source of sun)[5]

The ellipses indicate that the poem begins with process. The process is material; it derives from human making – prehistoric industries that made routes for transport of necessities from place to place. The ultimate source of living processes is the sun. The poem's dedication, '*In Memoriam/Robert Duncan and David Jones*', invokes makers with a sense of the sacred, who treat life in terms of human artefacture, cultural history, and myth. Matthias works in a similar spirit, and in this poem his guiding myth derives from T. C. Lethbridge's *Gogmagog*, which describes the archaeologist's controversial claim to have unearthed 'buried' gods and goddesses belonging to an ancient Celtic religion on Wandelbury Iron-Age camp in the Gogmagog Hills near Cambridge. From the point of view of the poem, the controversies surrounding Lethbridge's excavations and claims are not important. What is important is the fact that Lethbridge was a dowser; and his prototype was the Dodman, 'prehistoric surveyor who aligned the paths and tracks' (*GW*, p. 117). In invoking this figure, and in drawing upon Lethbridge's work and ideas, Matthias is engaging in a form of poetic archaeology, that uncovers the potency of a buried England.

Matthias delights in materials, their forms, and textures, and uses. In this poem, the principal materials are earth and water. He has, also, a strong feeling for the strange materiality of words, which corresponds to his awareness of historical processes, with their continuities and changes. His *pietas* towards his subject is reminiscent of Jones and Duncan, of whom he has written: 'Duncan's signs, his anathemata, signify a range of

---

[5] John Matthias, *A Gathering of Ways* (Athens, OH: Swallow Press/Ohio University Press, 1991), p.3. Further quotations from this book will be included in the text, and designated *GW*. The three sections of *A Gathering of Ways* appear as separate poems in Matthias's *Collected Longer Poems* (Bristol: Shearsman Books, 2012).

beings, powers, and energies that exist before, after, below, above, or to the side of David Jones' eucharistic center'.[6] As the poet journeys through space and time, from prehistory to the present, he is attentive to human occupations and the historical nature of language:

> The carter thakketh his hors
>
> upon the croupe and jumps up in his wagon.
> He's off to town. The men who work the maltings
> and the bargemen line up for their pay.
>
> The bird that flies above them angling toward
> the Orford Ness they call a *mavis*;
> by the time it reaches sprawling spider-webs
>
> of early-warning radar nets it's lost its name,
> and anyone at Chantry Point
> looking with binoculars for avocets or curlews
>
> would only see, if it passed by, a thrush (*GW*, pp. 16–17).

Matthias's fascination with history coincides with his love of East Anglian places, one manifestation of which is his cherishing of place names. Thus, in 'Rivers', the second movement of the poem, he traces the course of the river Alde, known as Fromus in earlier times, from its beginning at Framlingham, through a number of named places rich in commerce and historical conflict, to the coast. This section ends:

> Scratchings on the nave in Parham church
>
> show navigable reaches: ships of little draft
> came all the way from Normandy past
> Orford, Sloughden, Iken, down this stream
>
> that flows
> into a pipe below a petrol station
>
> now (*GW*, p. 14)

---

[6] John Matthias, 'Robert Duncan and David Jones', *At Large*, p. 246.

The isolation of 'now' is significant. The word occurs at the beginning of the poem, and recurs. As well as emphasising the present, it signifies the present moment, in a many-layered landscape, freighted with the past.

If Wordsworth, Henry Vaughan, and Samuel Palmer were Ronald Johnson's guiding spirits in *The Book of the Green Man*, John Matthias's presiding geniuses are Edward Thomas and John Constable. He renders the poet and the painter as parallel figures. Thomas enters the poem principally as author of *The Icknield Way*, the last prose book Thomas published before going to fight in the First World War. This track is the chief ley line followed in the poem.

> Home, returned on leave, exhausted,
> bored by prose he's published only months before
> and talking with a friend who'll ask:
> *And what are you fighting for over there?*
>
> he'll pick a pinch of earth up off the path
> they're walking and say: *This!*
> *For this,* he'll say.
> *This This This*
> *For*
>
>   *this* (*GW*, p. 6)

With this emphasis, Thomas is associated with earth, the fundamental substance of place. It is specific, English earth, which Thomas gave as his answer to the question 'what are you fighting for?' This is what 'home' means. Matthias gives the word '*this*' a parallel importance to the word, '*now*', thus underlining the particularity of his vision in the poem, which emphasises the importance of time and place, and the creative work, in every sense, that connects them. As for Duncan and Jones, the word is a sign, and as a sign it is sacred. Following Lethbridge, Matthias invokes gods and goddesses: 'Gog (the sun/Bel/Baal/Belenus/Helith, etc.), Magog (the moon/Meg/Magg/Epona, etc), and Wandil (darkness/the East Anglian devil/the giant with a sword, etc.)' (*GW*, p. 118). In the poem, these are best understood as underlying powers, energies, forces of creation and conflict. The powers are shaping forces in the landscape, and active in the lives of Thomas and Constable, in their struggles and achievements. Thus, Constable's answer to the question '*And what are you drawing landscapes for out here?'* is the same as Thomas's: *'For this'*. With this answer, as much as with Matthias's invocation of gods and goddesses, we know that his East-Anglian material, like the material of Duncan and Jones, is sacred matter.

It is clear that *The Book of the Green Man* and 'An East Anglian Diptych: Ley Lines, Rivers' are both about places and things the poets love. Both are wonderfully particular. Johnson and Matthias relish their places, in which they have lived, studying them, feeling the ground under their feet, and savouring the poetry of place on their tongues. In style and form the two poems are quite different. Johnson depends more upon space, silence between words, intimation, suggestion, and allusion. Matthias is more playful, as in the fun he has with 'gog' words, and more concerned with fact, the historical making of place, and materials and their uses. What both poems have in common is a celebration of native British places and traditions that, on this scale, and without irony, is extremely rare in post-war British poetry. The American poets are free to embrace the magic and mystery that they find in the native tradition. They bring modernist innovations, mainly, but not exclusively American, to writing about their English and Welsh subjects. They are open to the sacred, which most of their English contemporaries have abandoned. They release energies from the *materia poetica* of a land from which its native poets, embarrassed by ideas of 'vision', have cautiously turned away.

To Fit a Late Time:
A Reading of Five American Poets

The idea or feeling that we are situated 'late' in time is a potent one, especially for poets who are heirs to the modernist tradition, and who seek to find or reconstruct a common world among the ruins of civilisation. John Matthias, in an essay on Robert Duncan and David Jones, quotes Jones's view that, 'Normally...the flowers for the muse's garland would be gathered from the ancestral burial-mound'.[1] Matthias notes the implication, 'that we live in abnormal times, that we come very late indeed into the world of our ancestors'. Consciousness of 'lateness', in one sense or another, is shared by the poets with whom I am concerned in this essay.

I shall base what I have say on readings of new books, or books published quite recently, by five American poets whose earlier work was represented in the anthology of that title published by Carcanet in 1979: Robert Hass, John Matthias, James McMichael, John Peck, and Robert Pinsky. One reason for grouping the poets in the anthology was that they had been students of Yvor Winters at Stanford. Michael Schmidt, in his Introduction, says that if they 'share a debt to Winters, it must be as much a moral as a poetic debt', and claims that 'all five poets evince one element of Wintersian discipline'.[2] This is 'sanity'; in the words of John Matthias, 'sanity at work in poetry even where emotion is nearly intolerable'.

It is not my intention to pigeonhole the five poets by discussing them exclusively in the light of their debt to Winters or to claim that comparing them is an adequate way of doing justice to their individual talents. All are highly ambitious poets, and each is marked by a high degree of poetic intelligence. But the latter is a link as well as a distinguishing feature, as it manifests their alertness to the situation of poetry in the late twentieth century.

In his anti-romantic stance, Winter's idea of 'spiritual control', in the poem and in the poet, belongs with his idea of 'a common moral territory', or tradition which communicates absolute truths, as distinct

---

[1] John Matthias, *Reading Old Friends* (Albany, NY: State University of New York Press, 1992), p. 122. The quotation from David Jones (Matthias, p. 109) is from Preface to *The Anathemata*, p. 25.
[2] Michael Schmidt, Introduction, *Five American Poets* (Manchester: Carcanet Press, 1979), pp. ix–x.

from the confusions of romantic notions of 'truth' to private feelings. Winters praises Thomas Hardy, for example, as a poet who stood firmly on this territory. In Hardy's poetry, 'one feels behind each word the history of the word and the generations of men who embodied that history; Hardy gets somehow at the wealth of the race'.[3] But what can the poet who does not scorn tradition do if he believes 'the wealth of the race' has been squandered or spent? In other words, on what will the poet who, transcending the limited aims of self-expression, seeks 'a common moral territory', ground himself in a time of social and cultural disintegration?

'Lateness', as it affects the American poets with whose work I am concerned, is not an abstraction but an experience produced by particular social and historical circumstances. Robert Hass, reviewing a book by James McMichael, describes how the post-Second World War generation, to which the five American poets belong, 'watched the planning and the confidence and the technical inventiveness turn, with what seemed to the young unbelievable callousness and efficiency and fury, on Vietnam'. Planning was something 'the Vietnamese did not fit and the American young who were supposed to fight the war did not fit'. In consequence 'a generation of American writers has come to look at the central mechanisms of American life with a deep, stunned, curious detachment'.[4] 'Fitting', or not fitting, in more than one sense, is another term of my enquiry in this essay.

Not fitting enforces detachment, not just from American society but from the West as it is today; detachment which shows in different ways in all the books on which this essay is based. In John Peck's *Selva Morale*, for example, the poet continues to develop his essentially *hermetic* poetry. Peck's poems are often perplexing, at times infuriatingly difficult, but they have, too, a jagged and sometimes beautiful 'singing' quality. This relates closely to his art of self-transcendence, by which he locates himself in nature and in culture. For, as he has written, 'Song is both finder and preserver. To sing is to find oneself among others while confirming and conserving oneself in the performance of exchange'.[5]

Above all, Peck is a poet who models his imagination on Hermes, the flying man, who, crossing between worlds, looks down on the living

---

[3] Yvor Winters, 'The Morality of Poetry', *In Defense of Reason* (Chicago, IL: The Swallow Press, 1947), p. 28.
[4] Robert Hass, *Twentieth Century Pleasures* (New York, NY: The Ecco Press, 1984), pp. 170–71.
[5] John Peck, 'Note', *A Colander of Modern Poetry*, *P. N. Review* 100, p. 97.

and the dead, and sees energies patterned in matter, and connections between forms of natural and human making. His 'gaze' is that of 'the crane or heron, the whole round/its field, from shore aeons up through black new',[6] a gaze which encompasses creative processes in time as well as the 'things' they make, in space, and is alert to the unknown 'new'. It is necessarily a complex vision, exciting and baffling by turns. Peck, however, states his political position unambiguously in the haiku of 'Spring-through-Fall Epistle to Hakuin':

> Speech trails in tatters,
> letter shapes decay, because
> Justice wears gashes.
>
> Armored privacy
> regards it, garrisoned
> property sees it, not.
>
> From Ike through earth-death,
> fall of empires, plague, the same
> fast cars and slow towns.
>
> (p. *SM*, 43)

It is a politics, highly critical of the loss of a responsible public domain in the West, which recalls George Oppen's. Peck's affinities as a poet, however, are rather with poets who include history, and whose vision of the past is ordered by a sense of spiritual reality, such as Ezra Pound, and David Jones and Robert Duncan. The range of cultural references in *Selva Morale* is enormous, and is not confined to the West, but extends to Sufi, Buddhist and other traditions. Complementary ideas working in the poems include Jung's idea of 'the larger personality' and Charles Williams's idea of exchange: 'the great co-inherence of all life'.[7]

This is a poetry, in the words of 'Early Summer Evening, Kanton Zurich', made 'on the edge/of terminal awareness' (*SM*, p. 34). Terminal, not in the sense of 'confessional' extremism, with its emphasis on the isolated self, but in the sense of a new way of seeing the interconnectedness

---

[6] John Peck, 'Tobelwacht', *Selva Morale* (Manchester: Carcanet Press, 1995), p. 39, hereafter referenced SM in the text.

[7] Charles Williams, 'The Way of Exchange', *The Image of the City and Other Essays*, selected by Anne Ridler (London: Oxford University Press, 1958), p. 153.

of all things, based on Jungian psychology and the new sciences, and drawing upon ancient uses of the imagination, such as alchemy. Peck combines an awareness of life as a patterning and exchange of energies with a sense of his responsibilities as a citizen, thus uniting expansion of consciousness with Wintersian discipline, though he draws on 'magical' sources which Winters, defender of reason, would surely not have approved of. Thus, in 'Book of Life', Peck writes:

> A scarf it was, existence, that fell over my throat.
> Web-soft yet inseparable, a harness woven
> from seed-piths, tourniquet of seasons.
> Then my hands found it, open at the last page:
>
> *He was born in a small city...*
> (*SM*, p. 29)

Peck's sense of 'law', however, his celebration of 'Field and floor of the living that does not belong to us' ('On that high plateau', *SM*, p. 79), is reconcilable with Winters's absolutism.

If the image of the poet that comes to mind in reading John Peck is that of Hermes, the flying man, who sees the making of Europe from a great height (and also explores it in depth), the image of the poet that springs from reading Robert Pinsky's *The Want Bone* (1990) is that of a poet whose mind turns often to a particular place – Long Branch, the ocean resort in New Jersey where he grew up – but bringing with it foundational ideas from his Jewish inheritance and other world religions. Pinsky has recorded, in *Poetry and the World*, that many of his favourite poetic works 'involve a bridge or space between the worldly and the spiritual'.[8] Pinsky's blue guitar, so to speak, is a dead shark's mouthbones: 'A scalded toothless harp, uncrushed, unstrung. /The joined arcs made the shape of birth and craving'. This is 'the want bone' of the title poem, which begins: 'The tongue of the waves tolled in the earth's bell'.[9] From the local and particular, the shore at Long Branch, therefore, Pinsky conjures a music of cosmogonic desire.

In 'The Hearts', 'The legendary muscle that wants and grieves, /The organ of attachment', is described as 'clinging in stubborn colonies//Like

---

[8] Robert Pinsky, *Poetry and the World* (New York, NY: The Ecco Press, 1988), p. 3.
[9] Robert Pinsky, *The Want Bone* (New York, NY: The Ecco Press, 1990), p. 14, hereafter referenced *WB* in the text.

pulpy shore-life battened on a jetty' (*WB*, p. 10). The power of Pinsky as a philosophical poet who explores the tension between the worldly and the spiritual, and ultimately builds a bridge between them, is evident in the following passage from this poem, in which he both uses images and inquires into processes of image-making:

>   In the beginning God drenched
>
> The emptiness with images: the potter
> Crosslegged at his wheel in Benares market
> Making mud cups, another cup each second
>
> Tapering up between his fingers, one more
> To sell the tea-seller at a penny a dozen,
> And tea a penny a cup. The customers smash
>
> The empties, and waves of traffic grind the shards
> To mud for new cups, in turn; and I keep one here
> Next to me: holding it awhile from out of the cloud
>
> Of dust that rises from the shattered pieces,
> The risen dust alive with fire, then settled
> And soaked and whirling again on the wheel that turns
>
> And looks on the world as on another cloud,
> On everything the heart can grasp and throw away
> As a passing cloud, with even Enlightenment
>
> Itself another image…
>   (*WB*, pp.11-12)

From the shore-life of Long Branch to Benares market the poem moves with apparent effortlessness, metaphor sprung from the world of childhood carrying thought to far reaches – in the way of American pragmatism which we find in William Carlos Williams, and in Whitman. It is a way Pinsky develops with a sophistication which does not lose touch with the sheer physicality of places and things.

Pinsky has, nevertheless, a large measure of detachment. Great figures of myth and history move through his poems – Jesus and Mary and

Daniel, Tristram and Isolt, Hindu gods – and enact philosophical and religious dramas fundamental to human life. All serve his poetry of ideas, his concern with the worldly and the spiritual, and with our decayed public domain. In 'Immortal Longings', the one and the many come together, in an airplane, floating 'separately in our seats//Like the cells or atoms of one/ Creature, needs/And states of a shuddering god'. Under this creature, city lights are 'the glittering/Zodiac of intentions' (*WB*, p. 41). Thus, Pinsky shows our world, driven by desires that both join and separate us, as a reversal of the ancient idea of the Heavens determining events on earth. It takes a poet detached from his society and its intentions, indeed a poet to whom all ideas and needs are transparent, to be able to see in this way.

Oddly, while reading Pinsky, I thought not only of Whitman but of Whitman's father, the carpenter, building houses in Brooklyn. For Pinsky, for all his view of universal metaphysics, is very much an American poet, with an appetite for making, and an immense curiosity about how things (including philosophies and religions) work. He sees 'lovers' who 'love the boardwalk, the games of chance/And the cheap bright treats, booths and indifferent surf,/The old conspiracy of gain and pleasure//Flowering in the mind greedily to build the world/And break it'; he explores 'the mysteries, Love and Work, we have made/And that make us willing to die for them' ('What Why When How Who', *WB,* p. 44). Pinsky is a poet who diagnoses the ideological making of America, as do Hass and McMichael, with a sharpness of perception consequent upon their enforced detachment from the society which they know from the inside.

In the title poem of *Human Wishes* (1989), Robert Hass quotes the Upanishads, 'Man is altogether desire'.[10] It is a theme that he shares with Pinsky. And it bears upon the nature of identity, and the relation between self and others: concerns which, with the decay of a public domain in the West, preoccupy all the poets whose work I am considering here. Writing, in *Twentieth Century Pleasures*, of the haiku poet, Hass remarks that 'a deep identification with natural process is the root of polytheism'. This, he says, may provoke a contrary impulse, which he describes as 'the monotheist rage for unity'. His argument is evidently germane to his own poetry, in which he celebrates diversity, and seeks a unifying oneness: 'There is a natural polytheism to the life of art, and it is fuelled often by this monotheist rage'.[11]

---

[10] Robert Hass, *Human Wishes* (New York, NY: The Ecco Press, 1989), p. 23, hereafter referenced *HW* in the text.
[11] *Twentieth Century Pleasures*, pp. 297–98.

Human Wishes consists in part of prose poems, in which Hass develops what he has described as 'stories', or 'incidents that might be stories', in which 'there is always a moment, different for different memories, when the image, the set of relationships that seem actually to reveal something about life, forms'.[12] In his 'stories' he displays, at times, an unsettling fiction-making omniscience. In 'Quartet', for instance: 'Four people, the women with soft breasts, the men with soft, ropy external genitals' (*HW*, p. 31). But if omniscience is one mode, with which Hass may also glimpse 'many visions/intersecting at what we call the crystal/of a common world, all the growing and shearing, /all the violent breaks' ('Santa Barbara Road', *HW*, p. 53), he also frequently writes of relationships as a participant. It is as a family man, in particular, that Hass writes, sometimes humorously, and with a likeable vulnerability. The following extract from 'Santa Barbara Road' is a good example:

> Leif comes home from the last day of his sophomore year.
> I am sitting on the stoop by our half-dug,
> still-imagined kitchen porch, reading
> Han Dynasty rhyme-prose. He puts a hand on my shoulder,
> grown to exactly my height and still growing.
> 'Dad', he says, 'I'm not taking any more
> of this tyrannical bullshit.' I read to him
> from Chia Ya: *The great man is without bent,*
> *a million changes are as one to him.*
> He says: 'And another thing, don't lay
> your Buddhist trips on me.' (*HW*, p. 57)

Californian Robert Hass celebrates natural profusion and diversity, 'the abundance/the world gives; the more-than-you-bargained-for/ surprise of it' ('On Squaw Peak', *HW*, p. 83). He seeks to find and reveal 'identity, that word which implies that a lot of different things are the same thing'.[13]. It is an aim that requires a degree of abstraction, of mental detachment from the world of phenomena, but also participation: direct knowledge that 'there is one desire/touching the many things, and it is continuous' ('Natural Theology', *HW*, p. 73). His political awareness, his knowledge of suffering, and his refusal to 'fit' the 'armoured privacy', the self-isolating ideology of American society, are not less than those of

---

[12] Ibid., p. 272.
[13] *Twentieth Century Pleasures*, p. 57.

his contemporaries, but, more than in their work, the pleasure principle asserts itself in his poetry, which affirms 'the blessedness of gathering and the blessing of dispersal' ('Spring Rain', *HW*, p. 8).

Anyone reading the opening lines of James McMichael's *Each in a Place Apart* – 'At school I was a/squad-leader. I'd gotten enough votes.' – could be forgiven for expecting his poetry, with its vernacular speech rhythms and diction, to be the polar opposite of the complex and sometimes difficult poetry of Peck and Pinsky. Stylistically, it is. But, as well as being, in Frank Bidart's words, quoted on the back cover of the book, 'a narrative about the genesis and dissolution of his second marriage', McMichael's book-length poem is also an extremely intelligent exploration of male-female relationships in contemporary American society, and especially of the disjunction – the bad 'fit' – of a man's desire and a woman's needs.

Place or setting is the site of the fissure – hence the book's title: the fact of each being apart in a place questions whether it is the same place, and indeed what 'place' in modern America is. McMichael begins his exploration with his childhood and adolescence, emphasising a passion for fishing, seen in sexual terms. Of fish in a mountain lake, he writes: 'The water touched their noses, it touched their sides. Hungry, /beautiful and secret, they held to the beryl half-light, / the sunken boulders opaline and faint'.[14] This becomes as it were the woman's element – 'place' of desire, beauty and mystery – in which the man seeks a kind of total immersion: 'A highway runs the/length of the peninsula. The suburbs overlap. /She lived in one of them and took around with her/her setting' – which 'promised it would yield the longed-for' (*EPA*, p. 7).

Bearing in mind that any synopsis of the poem is bound to be cruder, psychologically and politically, than the poem itself, I would say that McMichael conducts a modern analysis of the idea of man as an island, who seeks to lose his isolation in the being of the longed-for female: an idea that makes of desire the 'longing' that fatally distances him from the woman's needs. Analysis is a cold word, however, and this is far from being a cold poem. It is, on the contrary, poignant and moving, and the more so in that the method of narration enables the reliving of particular moments, at the same time as the poet reveals awareness of what he did not see at the time. It is consequently a poem which, like the best work of McMichael's contemporaries, refuses to sacrifice understanding to feeling

---

[14] James McMichael, *Each in a Place Apart* (Chicago, IL and London: The University of Chicago Press, 1994), p. 3, hereafter referenced *EPA* in the text.

and emotion, but wins understanding from felt experience, in a way that would not, surely, have been alien to Winters.

Describing the river running through 'her places', McMichael writes:

> Tracts of barley and the bright coarse grasses fit
> irregularly along it over the floodplain,
> the mouths of its feeder-creeks hidden in green flags,
> a single cream- white camas spearing
> up through the ferns to the tip of its tall sheaf.
> I've been restless for her... (*EPA*, p. 41)

Here again is a landscape seen closely by the man, but with sexual hunger and unease. Barley and grass 'fit' the river but his vision, saturated with desire, fails to 'fit' the woman's needs. Later, he is able to say:

> Over the years, we'd taken our
> bodies along in company to certain places. In
> front of me a little, to the left, she'd answered 'Yes' to
> 'Two for dinner?' I wasn't thinking, at the time, how I
> fit into what she cared about: she fit for me. It comes
> back to me now because I have to change it, I'd
> gotten it wrong. (*EPA*, p. 60)

Robert Hass has argued that Yvor Winters, in his poetry, 'never solved for himself the problem of getting from image to discourse in the language of his time'.[15] McMichael, however, has solved it, as also have, in different ways, Pinsky and Peck and Hass himself, in their philosophical poems. Only consider the meanings of this one word, 'fit', which McMichael uses imagistically, as in the description of the river landscape, but also as a means of moral discovery, through its sense of fittingness, propriety.

And property. For this is what *Each in a Place Apart* is about: an idea of woman, and an idea of place, as a man's property. It is an idea that is bound up with the poet's writing, which he understands as part of the process of alienation: 'The rest of the time is/mine, the time my writing takes becoming/proper to me, another of my properties, like my/cold hands' (*EPA*, p. 52). The perception is a saving one, for in *this* poem, the act of writing is a means to understanding and to a moral decision: 'I have to change it/I'd gotten it wrong'.

---

[15] *Twentieth Century Pleasures*, p. 148.

John Matthias's new books, unlike those of his contemporaries which I have discussed above, are collections which represent the whole of his work to date: *Beltane at Aphelion*, his collected longer poems, and *Swimming at Midnight*, his selected shorter poems. There are important points of connection between his work and theirs: formally and stylistically, in his assimilation of methods from diverse modern poets, Auden, as well as Pound and Charles Olson, Robert Duncan and David Jones; thematically in his preoccupation with place in an increasingly placeless culture, and his search for a tradition upon which to ground himself.

Like his contemporaries, too, Matthias's awareness of poetic tradition reaches outside the English-speaking world, and far back behind modern literature. Thus, as he tells us in *Reading Old Friends* (1992), it was Wordsworth who led him, exhausted by political activism, in the 1960s, to seek 'a place of my own' – which he found at his wife's home in Suffolk. In light of what I have said above about the analysis of the relationship, in male perception, between woman and place in McMichael's long poem, it might be thought that Matthias's quest represents a form of escapism. What makes it rather the opposite of this, however, are his sense of history, and his steady awareness of himself as an outsider. There is in consequence a 'scribal' Matthias, a Matthias intent on gathering evidence, and reading signs, with scribal fidelity to original meaning. There is also, however, a playful Matthias, a poet capable of inventiveness and self-mockery, and aware that play is a profound form of human creativity. In broad terms, this duality means that reading his work in collected form brings one into contact with a poetry rich in facts, a poetry of names and places, and with a comic and at times tragic personal spirit.

In 'An East Anglian Diptych', Matthias recalls men working at Aldeburgh maltings in the nineteenth century:

> The bird that flies above them angling toward
> the Orford Ness they call a *mavis*;
> by the time it reaches sprawling spider-webs
>
> of early-warning radar nets it's lost its name,
> and anyone at Chantry Point
> looking with binoculars for avocets or curlews
>
> would only see, if it passed by, a thrush.[16]

---

[16] John Matthias, *Beltane at Aphelion*: Longer Poems (Athens, OH: Swallow Press, Ohio University Press, 1995), p. 124.

Use of bird flight here, to reveal history shaping a landscape, is comparable to a method of John Peck, and has a source in the shared detachment of a generation whose cultural overview is inseparable from their sense of 'lateness'. What is especially characteristic of Matthias, however, is his sense of a changing relationship between names and things. This, together with the forms of human making which cause change, is a theme of Matthias's major long poems, 'An East Anglian Diptych', 'Facts from an Apocryphal Midwest', and 'A Compostela Diptych', in which, as the titles indicate, Matthias 'sings' cultural landscapes in England, North America, and Western Europe respectively.

The care of Matthias's poetic 'gatherings' reveals what has been traditionally regarded as a feminine element in his sensibility. Indeed, all five American poets show themselves to be men of their generation both in their awareness (and avoidance) of masculinist aggression, and their willingness to risk tenderness. The latter is particularly notable in Matthias and in Hass. In one of his finest shorter poems (it is in fact quite long), 'Poem for Cynouai', Matthias says of some watercolour paintings:

> How luminous their rendering of a world
> we both believe in
> and can sometimes share: –
> where names are properties of things
> they name, where stones
> are animate and wilful, trees
> cry out in storms, and compulsive
> repetition of the efficacious formulae
> will get us each his way.[17]

As in poems by Hass, there is a vulnerability here, which is a poetic strength. It is evidently rooted in love – for his daughter, but also for the kind of world in which Matthias strives to 'place' himself. His art of naming springs from this, and his inclinations to praise and celebration and prayer. In a new poem (the last in *Swimming at Midnight*), 'Dedication to a Cycle of Poems on the Pilgrim Routes to Santiago de Compostela', he addresses his daughter:

---

[17] John Matthias, *Swimming at Midnight: Selected Shorter Poems* (Athens, OH: Swallow Press, Ohio University Press, 1995), p. 82.

> You had to show the saint your poor
> tormented frail human body. You had to drag it there
> driven by your guilt or your desire.
>
> The journey's so entirely strange I cannot fathom it.
> And yet this map, this prayer:
> That she will somehow get to Compostela,
>
> take that how you may, & that I will be allowed to follow.
> And that Santiago, call him what you like,
> Son of Thunder, Good Saint Jacques, The Fisherman,
>
> Or whoever really lies there –
> hermit, heretic, shaman healer with no name –
> will somehow make us whole.[18]

It is appropriate, I think, to bring this essay to a conclusion with this plea for wholeness.

Detachment, whether enforced or chosen, provides the poet with an overview, a way of seeing that may lead to a kind of poetic 'mapping'. Thus, Matthias and Peck figure movements of history, processes of making, Hass and Pinsky delineate desire as the force that constructs and destroys the human world, McMichael diagnoses the working out in terms of personal experience and relationships of an acquisitive and atomized society. And for each poet his way of seeing is not separate from desire, but an expression of need; not an escape from the consequences of loss of 'a common moral territory' and the resulting abnormality of a late time, but an attempt to meet the loss. A map that is also a prayer is, therefore, a fitting image for what all of them attempt. It would be wrong to ascribe any orthodox religious position to Matthias and his four fellow American poets, but the generous inclusiveness of his lines ('hermit, heretic, shaman healer') expresses a spirit common to them all, while religious in the broad sense of a concern with wholeness is certainly what they are. It is a concern which, as I have attempted to show, springs from a desire to locate 'common moral territory', but in a situation late in time, a time of ends (but with possibilities of new beginning), in which shared values – in fact, the grounds of civilization – are hard to find.

---

[18] Ibid., pp. 153–54.

Building with Images:
'Jerusalem the Golden' and 'Of Being Numerous'

Charles Reznikoff's 'Jerusalem the Golden' was first published in 1934, and George Oppen's 'Of Being Numerous' in 1968. Both are poems of New York, which use imagist techniques to construct capacious structures. Ezra Pound, who described images as 'the fundamental building blocks of poetry', was the primary stylistic influence upon these two 'objectivist' poets - a word whose primary meaning is 'the objectification of the poem, the making an object of the poem'. The idea of building a poem applies with special relevance to poems of the city. We should be aware, however, that while the imagist movement, which began shortly before the First World War, was developed especially in relation to urban experience, the Oriental influence upon it, particularly through the haiku, drew upon nature and opened the mind to the universe. The 'built' structure of poems such as 'Jerusalem the Golden' and 'Of Being Numerous' may be likened by analogy to collage and mosaic, forms that arrange fragments within an encompassing structure. The analogy is suggestive, but becomes misleading if we think of it as mechanical, or based upon a predetermined order. Pound's 'all poetic language is the language of exploration'[1] is a truer guide to what we find in these poems, which are processes of thought and perception, not poems made to a fixed plan.

Reznikoff and Oppen were friends, and Oppen looked up to the older man with great respect. They were also both Jewish Americans, and their Hebrew inheritance influenced their poetry, but in widely different degrees. It is scarcely an exaggeration to say that Reznikoff's poetry helped Oppen to survive as a man and a poet. One image that meant a great deal to Oppen comprises section 69 of 'Jerusalem the Golden':

> Among the heaps of brick and plaster lies
> a girder, still itself among the rubbish.[2]

---

[1] Ezra Pound, *Gaudier-Brzeska* (Hessle: The Marvell Press, 1960), p. 88.
[2] 'Jerusalem the Golden', *Poems 1918–1936, Volume 1 of the Complete Poems of Charles Reznikoff*, ed. Seamus Cooney (Santa Barbara, CA: Black Sparrow Press, 1976). All quotations from 'Jerusalem the Golden' will be from this edition, and will be designated by section numbers in the text.

He would often misquote these lines, substituting 'rubble' for 'rubbish'. It was a significant slip: rubbish represents a general sense of waste, while rubble refers mainly to demolished buildings. George and Mary Oppen were communist activists in the 1930s, working among the poor of the tenements. 'A girder, still itself' conveys a sense of unbendable integrity, and may also be seen as an image of survival among the debris of a wrecked social dream. Oppen shared with Reznikoff a conviction of the value of 'little' words naming universal particulars. In an interview, he said: 'The small and common words that build Reznikoff's tremendous poems will be with me, I think, in my last moments: these common words, the common scenes that build a universe'.[3]

In the first two sections of 'Jerusalem the Golden' Reznikoff presents himself – the speaker of the poem – as both a Hebrew who has 'married the speech of strangers' and a 'barbarian' who has slowly learned to read Greek. He invokes, first, Shulamite, and, secondly, 'blue-eyed Athena'. He thus indicates that he will make free, if problematic, use of both Biblical and Greek mythological resources. He also introduces the presence of the female into the poem. Particular women and the idea of woman as guiding spirit are prominent in the work of both Reznikoff and Oppen, and the latter indicates how much his work owes to his wife, Mary, so that it is virtually a conversation with her. In this respect, both poets break with the strand in imagism represented by T. E. Hulme's emphasis upon 'virile thought' and what Oppen described as 'Pound's ego system, Pound's organization of the world around a character, a kind of masculine energy'.[4] The original imagists were reacting against Victorian sentimentality and rhetoric, and espoused a linguistic 'hardness' associated with a male point of view. As inheritors of imagism, Oppen and Reznikoff are equally concrete in their use of language, but they show no fear of the feeling traditionally ascribed to women. On the contrary, they bring to the world of urban experience a humanizing quality of tenderness. In 'Jerusalem the Golden' the latter may be seen in, for example, the image of 'crushed earthworms/stretched and stretching on the wet sidewalk' (8), and it touches the perception of human and natural life throughout.

The Oriental influence upon imagism, through the haiku and Pound's *Cathay*, enters Reznikoff's work mainly in the spirit of 'a Chinese poet of

---

[3] Quoted in Stephen Fredman, *A Menorah For Athena* (Chicago, IL and London: The University of Chicago Press, 2001), p. 145.
[4] Interview with George Oppen, *The Contemporary Writer* (Madison, WI: The University of Wisconsin Press, 1972), p. 183.

the eleventh century', who wrote; 'Poetry presents the thing in order to convey the feeling. It should be precise about the thing and reticent about the feeling'.[5] This belief corresponded to Reznikoff's law school training, which emphasised the importance of evidence and undesirability of opinion. Reznikoff shows us 'things', or scenes, that have moved him, and as he has been moved, so are we, the readers. His is a poetry of the observing mind and heart, but this does not mean that 'Jerusalem the Golden' has a narrow range. It is, in fact, a capacious poem, in which short sections, including one-liners, appear in proximity to lengthy passages. Some of the latter quote, or adapt, prophetic voices, such as Ezekiel, and Jeremiah, and Karl Marx. Sections 54 to 62 celebrate a love relationship and lament its ending, with imagery from the Song of Songs playing against experience of life in the modern city. In and behind the contemporary scene we are aware of the American and Hebrew ideal (Dream, Heavenly City) that is tarnished and betrayed in the subways and on the sidewalks but continues to exist in human hope, and as a God's eye view. Overall, it is Reznikoff's sympathy that creates a compassionate vision.

Reznikoff's critics discuss his relationship as a Jew with his American material. Paul Auster says that: 'Neither fully assimilated nor fully unassimilated, Reznikoff occupies the unstable middle ground between two worlds and is never able to claim either one as his own. Nevertheless, and no doubt precisely because of this ambiguity, it is an extremely fertile ground'.[6] While this is true, we may also reflect that Reznikoff was not a poet who would 'claim' a world in any circumstances. Stephen Fredman, in his fine study of Reznikoff 'and the Jewish dilemmas of Objectivist Poetry', *A Menorah for Athena*, writes suggestively of the poet's 'betweenness', which Fredman describes as 'the modern Jewish condition'.[7] As a poet 'between' Jewish and American, Hebrew and Yiddish, Hebrew and English, Reznikoff occupied a position of creative linguistic and social tensions. As a habitual walker and wanderer about the city, he came to know New York intimately. As a stranger, he responded keenly to the strangeness of the city, which he saw as both ordinary and mythic, and profane and sacred.

---

[5] Reznikoff quotes the epigraph to A. C. Graham's *Poets of the Late T'ang*, in Interview, The Contemporary Writer, p. 206.
[6] Paul Auster, 'The Decisive Moment', in Milton Hindus, ed., *Charles Reznikoff Man and Poet* (Orono, ME: The National Poetry Foundation, 1984), p. 156.
[7] Stephen Fredman, *A Menorah for Athena* (Chicago, IL and London: The University of Chicago Press, 2001), p. 12.

His images combining the everyday and the fabulous both amuse and enlighten. For instance:

> This smoky winter morning –
> do not despise the green jewel shining among the twigs
> because it is a traffic light. (48)

'Do not despise' are words that go to the heart of Reznikoff's New York. He sees squalor as well as beauty, but he does not despise anything. 'Betweenness' also defines a situation between the materiality of the city and a religious perspective. Rachel Blau DuPlessis and Peter Quartermain, in their Introduction to *The Objectivist Nexus*, speak suggestively of Reznikoff's 'angelic subjectivity' in *Testimony*. Unlike this later work, 'Jerusalem the Golden' is not 'an implacable record' expressing the 'ferocious vocation of recording angel'.[8] It is, however, a work that may be seen as 'made in the spirit of reporting to God'. But here we must exercise caution. 'Jerusalem the Golden' is not a poem of orthodox religious vision. It is open to both Biblical and pagan perspectives, and combines mythic and romantic elements, in invocations of the moon, for example. It is a notably individual, even idiosyncratic, work, which, for all Reznikoff's detachment, shows his mind and heart. This is as evident in a marvellous one-line section called 'August' – 'The trees have worn their leaves shabby' (29) – as in the longer, more complex sections. Reznikoff's sympathies are equally with the eighteenth-century scholar and mystic, Moshe Chaim Luzzatto, the young man trying 'to listen to what the angels say' (78), and Karl Marx, to whose revolutionary vision he gives the final section of the poem. 'Jerusalem the Golden' is a poem in which spirit penetrates the world of the city, as prophetic voices break into the poet's meditative wanderings. It may be tempting to think that Reznikoff is being ironic when he writes: 'Rooted among roofs, their smoke among the clouds, /factory chimneys – our cedars of Lebanon' (40). But ironic contrast between an ideal of perfection, the heavenly city, and New York as it exists is not his way. He sees the contemporary city built with steel and cement, and sewers emptying into the river, without illusion, but he feels it, too, as his human habitat, in which there is no sharp dividing line between natural and urban beauty. His seeing fluctuates with his feeling, so that he can say:

---

[8] Rachel Blau DuPlessis and Peter Quartermain, eds., *The Objectivist Nexus* (Tuscaloosa, AL and London: The University of Alabama Press, 1999), p. 16.

> Feast, you who cross the bridge
> this cold twilight
> on these honeycombs of light, the buildings of Manhattan. (46)

We are familiar with an urban poetry influenced by T. S. Eliot in which London Tube or New York subway is a symbol of spiritual darkness, and imagery of 'men and bits of paper' represents ultimate human dereliction. Reznikoff's contrasting vision is well represented by section 10 of 'Jerusalem the Golden':

> These days the papers in the street
> leap into the air or burst across the lawns –
> not a scrap but has the breath of life:

'Jerusalem the Golden' portrays the contemporary life of New York realistically with a wealth of concrete images and vivid scenes. With no diminution of realism, the language of the poem is charged with imagery belonging to pagan myth and the Hebrew Scriptures. Images of the moon and trees and water recur with the impact of sacred presences. Reznikoff himself is a presence, a man among other men and women; a human being who is an organism, like the trees:

> Now that black ground and bushes –
> saplings, trees,
> each twig and limb – are suddenly white with snow,
> and earth becomes brighter than the sky,
>
> that intricate shrub
> of nerves, veins, arteries –
> myself – uncurls
> its knotted leaves
> to the shining air. (52)

To refer back to Paul Auster's words, Reznikoff does not claim 'the fertile ground' of New York as his own, not only because of his 'betweenness' as a Jewish American, a stranger in the city, but also because of his humility in face of the sacred. Human life does not 'belong' entirely to humankind. Darkness and light, rain, trees and flowers, river and sea, speak of other powers. With human beings, there are always other stories. Charles Reznikoff must have been a tricky man to interview. For, almost invariably, he would answer a question by telling a story, and avoiding generalizations and abstract terms. This is how Reznikoff sees New York: as a place of stories, or scenes; and it is these with which he builds his poem. He regards what he sees with fellow feeling, but does not pretend to know. Stephen Fredman quotes Spinoza: 'Whatever is, is in God, and nothing can be or be conceived without God'.[9] Reznikoff's interpretation of this, Fredman says, 'marks the ultimate expression of the sanctity of the ordinary'. The last voices we hear in the poem are the voices of Spinoza and Marx. The section called 'Spinoza' begins:

> He is the stars
> multitudinous as the drops of rain,
> and the worm at our feet,
> leaving only a blot on the stone;
> except God there is nothing.

The image of the worm is reminiscent of William Blake, who perceived God 'in the lowliest effects as well as in the highest causes, for he is become a worm that he may nourish the weak'. There is another perspective beyond that of any human being including the poet, though he may make, or find, images that intimate it. He is a creature among the other creatures, including worms; he is not master or possessor of what he sees.

If Charles Reznikoff's Hebrew inheritance helped to make him at home in New York, a stranger familiar with the strangeness of the city, George Oppen's sense of Jewish identity was more problematic. As he said, 'I am myself quite a number of Jews, despite my lack of Yiddish and all'.[10] He shared with Reznikoff what he called 'nearly a sense of awe, simply to feel that the thing is there and that it's quite something to see. It's an awareness of the world, a lyric reaction to the world'.[11] Burton Hatlen speculates 'on the possibility that a distinctly Jewish religious vision emerges from time to time in the writing of some of the objectivist poets'. Hatlen hears 'some distinctively Jewish overtones in the insistence of the Objectivists that the world is not only real but also Other – and inherently numinous'. As an example, he cites words from Oppen's poem 'World, World –':

---

[9] *A Menorah for Athena*, p. 66.
[10] Rachel Blau DuPlessis, ed., *Selected Letters of George Oppen* (Durham, NC: Duke University Press, 1990), p. 128.
[11] Interview with George Oppen, *The Contemporary Writer*, p. 177.

> The self is no mystery, the mystery is
> That there is something for us to stand on.

Hatlen interprets Oppen as saying 'We stand on/in the presence of mystery'.[12] To this I would add that the 'us' is deeply significant. 'World, World' – concludes:

> We want to be here
>
> The act of being, the act of being
> More than oneself.[13]

From this we see that Oppen's concern with 'the act of being' is at once ontological and socio-political, and involves the relationship between the one and the many, the single person and humanity.

A major difference between Oppen and Reznikoff is that Oppen, inspired by the thought of Kierkegaard and Heidegger, was an existentialist. Unlike Reznikoff, he does not tell stories in interviews, but thinks intensely, and sometimes agonizes about issues of ethics and aesthetics, and especially the relationship between words and reality. He is a poet concerned above all with what enables meaning in a sense of shared reality. After his 25 years silence, following exile to Mexico in order to avoid the McCarthy persecution of Leftists, the first poem he wrote, 'Blood from the Stone', asks:

> What do we believe
> To live with? Answer
> Not invent – just answer – all
> That verse attempts.
> That we can somehow add each to each other?[14]

In desperate times, poetry, for Oppen, is crucially a question of belief, and belief 'to live with', belief shared with other human beings.

A phrase that insistently comes to my mind in reading 'Of Being Numerous' is H. G. Wells' 'mind at the end of its tether'. It is a poem

---

[12] Burton Hatlen, 'A Poetics of Marginality and Resistance: The Objectivist Poets in Context', *The Objectivist Nexus*, p. 45.
[13] George Oppen, *New Collected Poems*, p. 159.
[14] *New Collected Poems*, p. 52.

whose intensity is at once desperate and visionary. In an interview, Oppen was asked about the meaning of 'objectivist', which described the movement with which he and Reznikoff and Louis Zukofsky had been first associated in the 1930s. 'What I felt I was doing, ' he said, 'was beginning from imagism as a position of honesty'. He shared with Zukofsky 'the attempt to construct meaning from the imagist technique of poetry – from the imagist intensity of vision'.[15] In the 1960s, in writing 'Of Being Numerous', Oppen was as much tormented by 'intensity of vision' as enlightened by it. Reasons for this are not hard to seek in an America traumatized by war and race riots, a society deeply divided, in which most intellectuals felt alienated, and poetry and the other arts took a turn to extreme subjectivity. Oppen was keenly aware of the plight of the disaffected young faced with the madness of their society, and the prospect of being drafted to fight in Vietnam. Close to the heart of 'Of Being Numerous' is a question posed to Oppen by a student – Rachel Blau (later Rachel Blau DuPlessis) – and his response to it:

> 'Whether, as the intensity of seeing increases, one's distance
>   from Them, the people, does not also increase'
> I know, of course I know, I can enter no other place [16]

'Place', in this sense, threatens to be a New York, an America, in which the poet is isolated 'from Them, the people', and in which his vision becomes, like Crusoe's on his island, 'the bright light of shipwreck'(9). Instead of being one of humanity, and one with humanity, the poet risks becoming 'the absolute singular'. The poem Oppen builds with his 'imagist intensity of vision' risks sharing in the solipsism of an atomised, late capitalist society:

> Hollow, available, you could enter any building,
> You could look from any window
> One might wave to himself
> From the top of the Empire State Building – (11)

'Of Being Numerous' at once diagnoses the predicament of an extreme individualism, that would reduce poetry to what Martin Buber defined

---

[15] Interview with George Oppen, *The Contemporary Writer*, p. 173.
[16] 'Of Being Numerous' 9, *New Collected Poems*, p.167. Subsequent references to this poem will be given by section number in the text.

as 'the life of monologue', and resists it.

The tragic possibility with which Oppen struggles in this, his most philosophical poem, fraught with existential *angst*, requires to be understood in the light of George and Mary Oppen's' original political and artistic hopes and ideals, when the young couple set out, in 1927, to travel in America and discover their 'roots'. In her autobiographical *Meaning A Life* Mary Oppen describes their aim:

> We were in search of an esthetic within which to live, and we were looking for it in our own American roots, in our own country. We had learned at college that poetry was being written in our own times, and that in order for us to write it was not necessary for us to ground ourselves in the academic; the grounds we needed was the roads we were travelling. As we were new, so we had new roots, and we knew little of our own country. Hitchhiking became more than flight from a powerful family – our discoveries themselves became an esthetic and a disclosure. The people we met ... became the clue to our finding roots...[17]

Writing poetry was integral to living; to discovering 'American roots', and in the 1930s the Oppens shed class and privilege and involved themselves as political activists with the deprived and dispossessed people of their society. Through travels and work they came to feel 'at home in our country'. This ideal of 'American roots' has a tragic resonance when considered in relation to their subsequent experience of persecution and exile. For Oppen, his experience called in question everything he believed in, and led to a bitterly ironic idea of his poetic 'roots' – a word associated for him with 'route', and not dissimilar from Heidegger's *weg*. 'Of Being Numerous' begins from the position of the poet as a casualty, in the sense of 'Route' 8:

> Cars on the highway filled with speech,
> People talk, they talk to each other;
>
> Imagine a man in the ditch,
> The wheels of the overturned wreck
> Still spinning –

---

[17] Mary Oppen, *Meaning A Life* (Santa Barbara, CA: Black Sparrow Press, 1978), p. 68.

> I don't mean he despairs, I mean if he does not
> He sees in the manner of poetry.[18]

'Of Being Numerous' starts from the wreck, conceived in the figure of Crusoe: 'the shipwreck/Of the singular'. Seeing and speaking are at its centre: seeing with imagist intensity of vision, and the poet's desire to speak with others in a meaningful language. It is a poem tense to the point of breakdown. Its triumph springs from the fact that Oppen's mind does not break, but faces 'the place' he enters, the 'distances' within his society, with all 'intensity of vision'. It is necessary here to invoke the American Dream, an overused and abused term, but relevant to both Oppen and Reznikoff. The latter includes a section in 'Jerusalem the Golden' called 'The English in Virginia, April 1607', based on the words of Captain John Smith, who describes a newly discovered world rich in trees, flowers, birds, and 'running/everywhere/ fresh water' (74). The implicit contrast is with 'the glistening river/where the sewers empty/ their slow ripples' (21). This original vision of a pristine natural world (albeit inhabited by what the colonists perceive as 'savages') harmonizes with the concept of a promised heavenly city on which the poem is based. 'Of Being Numerous' is equally a poem that retains a sense of the meaningful life that should prevail in the modern city. The sense of what *should be* results in the near-despairing depiction of *what is*: the failure of an ethic. There is, for example, nothing in *The Waste Land* as bitter as Oppen's depiction of meaningless sexual encounters: 'The girls/Stare at the ceiling/Blindly as they are filled' (23). He feels, in particular, the plight of the young who need to construct new roots, but are used by their society for murderous or empty purposes:

> Who if they cannot find
> Their generation
> Wither in the infirmaries
>
> And the supply depots, supplying
> Irrelevant objects. (26)

'Of Being Numerous' is the work of a poet for whom 'It is not easy to speak'. This difficulty, and the courage with which Oppen confronts it, define its importance for the survival of poetry as a shared language.

---

[18] *New Collected Poems*, p. 198.

Section 17 is crucial in this respect:

> The roots of words
> Dim in the subways
>
> There is madness in the number
> Of the living
> 'A state of matter'
>
> There is nobody here but us chickens
>
> Anti-ontology –
>
> He wants to say
> His life is real
> No one can say why
>
> It is not easy to speak
>
> A ferocious mumbling, in public
> Of rootless speech (17)

The section is immediately followed by an indictment of the Vietnam War, with 'atrocity' stemming from the apex of government: 'An event as ordinary/As a President'. The executive power results in 'A plume of smoke, visible at a distance/In which people burn'. 'Distance' has entered into the very fabric of American society, which in consequence has become unreal. Words have been severed from their roots resulting in 'A ferocious mumbling, in public'. Graffiti ('There is nobody here but us chickens') characterizes the city's public spaces, so that 'subway' virtually becomes synonymous with 'subhuman'. 'Anti-ontology' replaces the realm of Being, in which people observing a common ethic speak with one another, and share a sense of what is not simply 'matter', but truly real.

In this situation in which what he sees brings Oppen close to despair, he falls back upon sustaining personal relationships, with his wife and daughter and friends, and other named individuals: men with whom he served in the Army, 'Muykut and a sergeant/Named Healy' (14). Oppen's feeling for women, for their value as human beings and their quality of perception, expressed supremely by his sense of Mary as a collaborator in his work, is a counterbalance to the sense of personal shipwreck in the poem. He lingers on names: Mary-Anne and Phyllis. Both are associated with the particular; Mary-Anne with 'a brick/In a brick wall', which was 'waiting/Here when you were born' (21). Instead of 'matter', we apprehend here the solidity of the built city, made for human habitation, as opposed to the glassy towers of late capitalism. The brick is one of the little words on which so much depends: a material object no less valuable than 'the little waves of the bay, the little leaves of the hedge', with which, in 'Jerusalem the Golden', Reznikoff says: 'I school myself to be content' (67).

Phyllis is invoked at a point in the poem where, for the poet, speech has become almost impossible:

>   Coming home from her first job
>   On the bus in the bare civic interior
>   Among those people, the small doors
>   Opening on the night at the curb
>   Her heart, she told me, suddenly tight with happiness –
>
>   So small a picture,
>   A spot of light on the curb, it cannot demean us (11)

We might think of this as a Reznikoff moment – in fact, it is a moment that Oppen shares with the spirit of his friend. It is the 'small' things that matter most: 'the small doors/Opening', the small picture, 'A spot of light on the curb'. Oppen proceeds to say: 'I too am in love down there with the streets/And the square slabs of pavement': a sentence whose syntax places him in the streets, not as one observing from a distance. Love of the city and of particular people confirms the survival of humanity, of shared values, in a time of madness and unreality.

'Of Being Numerous' and 'Jerusalem the Golden' are poems that give the lie to J. B. Harmer's statement, in *Victory in Limbo: A History of Imagism 1908–1917*, that: 'Imagist methods are unsuitable to a long poem'.[19] Both are poems that build capacious spaces, analogues to the size and diverse life of the modern city, and large and loose enough in structure to enable free play to the poet's mind. In these spaces the poet can move around, seeing, thinking, feeling, and making discoveries. The reader has to enter and inhabit them, learning more with each reading, while recognizing that they are too large and intricately complex to

---

[19] J.B. Harmer, *Victory in Limbo* (London: Secker & Warburg, 1975), p. 83.

allow summary. The poems, built from the imagist intensity of vision, and constructed on principles analogous to the mosaic or collage, have certain affinities. In their sense of awe, and of the Other, they show, to different degrees, the poets' Jewish inheritance. But in this and other ways they also differ radically. Each poem is a response to a different phase of American history in the twentieth century, and to New York as a changing city subject to different pressures. 'Jerusalem the Golden' has a distinctively Biblical perspective. Reznikoff may call himself 'barbarian', but he is intimate with the religious poetry and myth of Jerusalem and Athens. As he sees the life of the modern city with its squalor and human deprivation, so he sees it also in the light of the promise of the heavenly city. His 'angelic' vision in this poem is a vision of benevolence, of sad and wise understanding; its spirit of life is a spirit of hope. Oppen is a poet less certain of his Jewish identity, but troubled, nonetheless, by ontological questions, and questions involving the fate of a people, of humanity, that are ultimately religious. His intensity of vision in 'Of Being Numerous' is an intensity that tests his very limits as a man and poet. It is a poem concerning the relationship of the one to the many, and the poet's 'place' among his fellows that questions the very meaning of poetry itself in the modern world. In his questioning, in his response to the crisis the modern poet faces, Oppen is a poet who makes poetry possible.

Roy Fisher, Magician of the Commonplace

The development of Roy Fisher's poetry from *City* (Migrant Press, 1961), to his latest major collection, *Birmingham River,* published by Oxford University Press in 1994, owes a great deal to his defeat of what he has called, in a dialogue with Paul Lester, 'the demon of fixity and solidity'.[1] The 'demon' determines the kind of seeing that dominates *City*: an eidetic recall that freezes both the seen and the seer, petrifying him in front of a static urban world. *City* has, indeed, vivid visual qualities, but these are also symptomatic of the poet's alienation, his situation as virtually a thing among things, like a statue. As Fisher acknowledges in the poem, he is 'afraid of becoming/A cemetery of performance'.[2] There are also, however, qualities that work against stasis in *City*, and it is partly with the aid of these that Fisher has broken out of the prison of extreme self-consciousness.

There is, for example, his ability to read the shapes and signs of the urban world as a system by which authority determines social and psychological 'reality'. Another strength is his sense of cosmic energy, especially in the form of the sun, without which there would be no seeing and, indeed, no life. The *fluidity* of Fisher's finest poetry over the past thirty years has a lot to do with his increasing awareness of Nature not only as a force but also as a spring of imaginative energy, with which the human mind makes and dissolves its constructions. Thus water, for Fisher, is both life-giving source and a metaphor for the creative faculty. He has recorded his original awe in face of it in 'Rudiments', in which he remembers his father showing him *'The Canal'*: 'A black/rippled solid, made of something/unknown, and having the terrible property/ of seeming about to move, /far under our feet. I'd never/seen so much water before' (*Poems*, p. 165). This is Fisher's equivalent of the 'darkness' induced in Wordsworth's mind by the huge Cliff striding after him, 'the unknown modes of being'. Fisher's experience, though, is remembered by a man acutely aware of how images and works of art structure our sense of the world, so that for him the force of the common word, *water*, is felt

---

[1] *Paul Lester and Roy Fisher: A Birmingham Dialogue* (Birmingham: Protean Pubs, 1986), p. 28.
[2] Roy Fisher, *Poems 1955-1987* (Oxford: Oxford University Press, 1988), p. 24, hereafter referenced *Poems* in the text.

in the terrible and awe-inspiring presence it points to, that exists beyond all images and names.

What I wish to emphasise in talking about *Birmingham River* in particular is that Roy Fisher is a major modern poet in the Romantic tradition, from which he draws an idea of the imagination as the principal agent of liberation from repressive political and social and psychological systems. A statement from 'Metamorphoses', in *The Cut Pages,* is central: 'No system describes the world'.[3] If Roy Fisher is a difficult poet to classify, that is partly because he works to free the mind from classifications, to liberate particular identities from the tyranny of the general. The project is Blakean, and is based on Fisher's conviction, expressed in an interview with Robert Sheppard, that 'The human mind makes the world'.[4] My concern here is with Roy Fisher as a poet who renews a central energy that drives English Romantic poetry, but there is no contradiction between this and his affinities with American poets such as William Carlos Williams and Wallace Stevens, European painters such as Klee and Kokoschka, and a jazz musicians such as Coleman Hawkins. In each case, it is the work of the mind upon the world of things, the creative freedom of imagination, and the reality of human subjectivity that form the link.

Stranger connections appear as we look closely at Roy Fisher's work. More and more in his later poems, for example, he emerges as a lyrical poet within the tradition of English landscape vision, with links to poets as diverse as Clare and Tennyson, and with a subversiveness toward ideas and images of 'Englishness' that is also an element within the tradition. For a poet from a working-class family, we do not find Fisher in the company where conventional ideas would place him – with Richard Hoggart and the tradition of 'Arnold-through-Leavis-through Raymond Williams', which Fisher described to Sheppard as the line of 'bourgeois guardianship'.[5] The strangeness of Fisher's Birmingham is more real, truer to human experience, than established class moralities allow for. Fisher has written movingly about the poor of Birmingham, especially in 'Wonders of Obligation', a poem in which he fulfils his obligations not only by witnessing the terrible harshness of common experience, but also by assuming, without a hint of condescension, that common

---

[3] Roy Fisher, *The Cut Pages* (London: Fulcrum Press, 1971), p. 14. Also *Poems*, p. 84.
[4] Robert Sheppard, *Turning the Prism*: An Interview with Roy Fisher (London: Toads Damp Press, 1986), p. 13.
[5] Ibid., p. 12.

human-ness is also, and pre-eminently, the capacity to escape the prison of system by being and seeing differently. In fulfilling his desire to 'de-Anglicize England'[6] Roy Fisher dissolves class stereotypes of Englishness and visual clichés of urban and rural scenes, with the result that he renders life-experience in the English Midlands with memorable and moving veracity. His landscapes are true to the strangeness of reality, and have visionary qualities comparable to those of Geoffrey Hill and Basil Bunting. The following passage, from the end of 'Calling', the first part of *A Furnace,* provides a fine example:

> Gradbach Hill, long hog's back
> stretching down west among taller hills
> to the meeting of Dane river
> with the Black Brook skirting its steeper side,
> the waters joining
> by Castor's Bridge, where the bloomery
> used to smoke up into the woods
> under the green chapel;[7]

Thus begins a wonderful evocation of an area of North-West Staffordshire close to where three shires meet, an area of elemental beauty, rich in industrial remains, and with a powerful literary association to 'the composition of *Gawain and the Green Knight*'.[8]

Among other things, *Birmingham River* defines the human in terms of the creative imagination. The first poem in the book is about the poet's encounter with 'Sikelianos' – not the living poet but his name and his statue, the 'marble/ head and shoulders' of which are described as 'a little grander/than human'.[9] Statue and name are human constructs, but they define the human negatively, by the absence of the living mind with which Sikelianos used the given materials to construct his world. Fisher is too respectful of the materials to reverse Williams's famous formulation to read 'No things but in ideas', but things in this and other poems gain an extraordinary poignancy from being animated by the ideas of dead men and women. It is in the gap between image (in this case, statue and

---

[6] Ibid., p. 25.
[7] Roy Fisher, *A Furnace*, p. 7.
[8] Ibid, p. 10.
[9] Roy Fisher, 'The Collection of Things', *Birmingham River* (Oxford: Oxford University Press, 1994), p. 1, hereafter referenced *BR* in the text.

145

name) and the forces that create identity that Fisher makes his poems. His awareness of death is not morbid, but a means by which he defines life and the living.

He explores the gap between public sign and subjective reality differently in 'A Sign Illuminated' (p. *BR*, p. 6). Here, it is the perception of little boys that makes a familiar double-decker bus, altered and decked out 'in honour of something or other' – some public occasion – a luminous sign, an 'emblem'. The altered double-decker was 'less than a bus', but to the boys it was a thing of wonder. The most remarkable quality of the poem is that ordinary language carries a sense of the marvellous, which is not the poet's privileged possession but the imaginative capacity of the little boys. Revelation of the beauty and wonder of everyday language is one of Fisher's major achievements. His scepticism of signs and meanings handed down by authority helps to make him a magician of the ordinary, a poet who reveals our common right to the marvellous. By depicting what is 'grander than human', or 'less' than an object, he illuminates the magic of identity.

Roy Fisher the magician owes a debt to John Cowper Powys. As he acknowledges in the Preface to *A Furnace*, he is 'indebted to his writings for such understanding as I have of the idea that the making of all kinds of identities is a primary impulse which the cosmos itself has: and that those identities and that impulse can be acknowledged only by some form or other of poetic imagination'.[10] Like *A Furnace*, the central poem in *Birmingham River*, 'Six Texts For A Film', is about the making of 'identities' in Birmingham and the surrounding area – making and unmaking, in which the poet finds imaginative means 'to invoke and assist natural processes of change; to persuade obstinate substances to alter their condition and show relativities which would otherwise remain hidden by the concreteness'.[11] The making and unmaking are historical, from Anglo-Saxon settlements to late twentieth century dismantling of the industrial structure. The history is related to Nature, and especially to water, to the River Tame, 'the Dark River that "mothered the Black Country"' (BR, p. 17). The making is autobiographical too, in that it returns Fisher to his imaginative sources, the springs of what he has called, in a piece in Denise Riley's *Poets on Writing*, 'the fluid medium of my inner life'.[12]

---

[10] *A Furnace*, p. vii.
[11] Ibid., p. vii.
[12] 'Poet on Writing', *Poets on Writing: Britain, 1970-1991* ed. Denise Riley (Basingstoke: Macmillan, 1992), p. 273.

'Talking to Cameras', the first part of a six-part poem, begins: 'Birmingham's what I think with. //It's not made for that sort of job, /but it's what they gave me' (*BR*, p. 11). The plain language carries, as I have suggested in discussing other Fisher poems, a sophisticated point of view – I would call it a philosophical position, which it is, except that it is first evidently Fisher's way of apprehending the world. It is a view which both acknowledges the 'given' and affirms the activity of the individual mind in perceiving it and imagining it anew. Fisher has a wonderful perception of the intricacy and complexity of his urban structures, of the wrought materiality, the subterranean channels, and the sheer pressure of human uses on elemental substances. He recalls the things with eidetic vision, but renders them with a fluidity that arises both from his subjectivity and from their existence in other minds. There is, I think, no urban poetry like this in English, not even in Williams's New Jersey or Charles Reznikoff's New York. The closest to it, perhaps, is George Oppen's, a poet with a different sensibility from Fisher's, but an equivalent awareness of the work of the mind in making the world.

In keeping with his sense of material and subjective mutability, Fisher describes Birmingham in terms of provisional metaphors. The magician, as John Cowper Powys demonstrates, is the most sceptical of beings. As he is sceptical of all systems, so he suspects his own verbal and visual formulations, and shows his openness to life by dissolving their fixity and solidity. Thus, instead of speaking directly about the city's bedrock, Fisher says, 'If you get systematic, /and follow power around, you arrive/at a bedrock out of a book' (*BR*. p. 12). But since he also has a sense of cosmic power that makes identities, and of the imagination that in some sense participates in this *natural* process, he asks: 'But what is it/when you're first set loose in it, with only/your nostrils, fingertips, ears, eyes/to teach you appetite and danger?' And he answers with another question, which acknowledges water as the primary life-giving power, though human beings freeze it into their structures: 'Is it the primal ocean, condemned/ and petrified?' (*BR*, p.13) It is with the help of a myth, then, that Fisher has overcome 'the demon of fixity and solidity', the myth that Nature, the source of creation, is also the power behind the imagination. It is a myth whose great virtue is that we can *feel* with all our senses that it is true.

True to his Romantic heritage, the idea takes Fisher back to his childhood and the source of the magical view of life. He connects Delphi and Handsworth, saying that he has held in his hands the 'Omphalos-stone, the single centre, //not of the planet, but of the earth's shifting/ surface, the live map'.

> To touch
> the centre keeps everything round it
> fluid, just as it did
> when I still lived at ground level
> and centred the universe
> just beyond the mid-point of the garden path
> of Seventy-Four Kentish Road, Handsworth. (*BR*, p. 14)

It is authority of one kind or another that shapes the material and social world and gives it to us in the form of signs and systems. The original source of freedom is childhood, when, for Roy Fisher, it was a 'pair of big spilt pebbles set in the path' that 'governed'. With the pebbles in mind, Fisher says he's 'always been a two-moon man' (*BR*, p.14). The expression is a characteristically humorous way of saying that he rejects 'Single vision & Newton's sleep'. Fisher has a jokey way of saying things that are central to the Romantic tradition – the tradition which he renews, and uses to explore the very foundations of the city, and of the metaphysics on which our materialism is based, as no English poet has done since Blake. Indeed, Fisher is one of our funniest poets, a distinction he shares with Edwin Morgan. In *Birmingham River* 'Seven Figures From Anansi Company' and 'Every Man His Own Eyebright' show the range of his humour from the teasingly ironical to the zany and the hilarious. Humour is an expression of Fisher's wide anarchical streak.

It is also an aspect of his humility. It is absence of ego that helps to make Roy Fisher's best poems so marvellously unpredictable. This is not the same as absence of personality. On the contrary, the person is present in the way of seeing and imagining, present as a human being with all his needs. This presence, this fluidity of mind, is the freedom Fisher has won in his combat with the demon. Unfortunately, freedom to use the imagination as a way of envisioning the world is little understood in England, where readers seem to prefer poems which are performances of the self, coloured but also limited by the ego. In responding to the poet whom we feel to be 'one of us', however, we are in danger of admiring our mundane selves in the mirror, instead of responding to the liberation from fixed ideas and images that a poet such as Roy Fisher offers. What Fisher has to give are poems, ways in which the mind works in the world, not pictures of himself. On the whole, English taste for 'new' poetry tends to prefer cemeteries of performance, or statues, providing they look like ourselves.

It should be evident why Fisher quotes Blake in the first part of 'Six Texts For A Film'. 'What hand, what eye' echoes 'The Tyger', a poem whose vision Fisher has drawn on in his previous book, too, which he constructed in 'the furnace' of his brain. Like Blake, Fisher is preoccupied by the energy that empowers Nature and human making. He sees the city as 'an artefact', 'the work of one protracted/moment, an impulse to make'. It is

> a work of art that's at the same time
> the by-product of a spastic purpose,
> oozing as miraculous drops
> from a sort of spirit into a sort of matter,
> gathering in pools, trickling to fill
> wrinkles, indentations, then congealing as
> masonry: factories, floods of houses,
> shallowing as they spread, converted
> again to spirit in the understanding. (*BR*, 15)

Imagination reveals spirit congealed in matter, and the 'infinities of notions under one urban sky'. Like Blake with his 'furnace', Fisher derives metaphors for his mind from the processes of a mechanical civilisation – the 'Brummagem screwdriver' of 'Six Texts For A Film' is a case in point – and he uses them to subvert the mechanical world-view that reduces the many to the one, plural imaginative vision to collective cliché.

The Romantic tradition Fisher renews is a tough-minded one. Its visions are built upon particular impressions; it honours personal and historical experience, and is acutely suspicious of any authority and its generalisations and systems; its magic is not whimsical, but has the uncanniness of an earlier age of Romance, as Fisher's Midlands landscapes recall *Sir Gawain and the Green Knight*; it recognises Nature as creative and disruptive force. The latter relates directly to Fisher's sense of duality: the two moons that keep the mind from complicity with single vision, and the public and private faces of images and names. Thus, the aptly named River Tame has been thoroughly domesticated by human uses, but is also 'the Dark River', which recalls the 'something unknown' and 'the terrible property' of water in 'Rudiments' (*Poems*, p. 165) which symbolises an unpredictable power. The creative energy lives in and under the city's structures, as 'the Dark River' is hidden in 'Tame'. But there is no callow optimism in *Birmingham River*, no evasion of the meanness and viciousness that characterise human making and marketing in the modern world. In one poem he speaks directly of 'our own/proprietors' who 'have had the waters/poisoned for profit' ('Our Own', *BR*, p. 5) – a timely condemnation in view of the polluted summer just past, but with a related and more far-reaching significance for the waters of life poisoned by all the powers bent on selling us images and ideas that enslave our minds. Politically, Fisher is a poet who restores an idea of the 'common' by liberating the one, the individual imagination, from all repressive systems. He is, so to speak, a poet who is on the side of Nature, the life-giving force that judges and sometimes disrupts what we make of it, and the ultimate source of identity for the poorest he or she. On the face of it, the conclusion to 'Abstracted Water', the final part of 'Six Texts For a Film', is bleak. The canal is a place of

> Secrets
> half-guarded, absorbed; secrets forgotten,
>
> left to decay, bursting apart,
> letting the dead stuff spill out. Sunlight
>
> under bridges stays enclosed,
> lattices to and fro. There's a law
>
> dirt grows out of. (*BR*, pp. 22-3)

Here is a reminder of 'Brick-dust in sunlight' from *City* (*Poems*, p. 20), but also of the knowledge from 'Wonders of Obligation' that 'hereabouts/comes into being/the malted-milk brickwork/on its journey past the sun' (*Poems*, p. 155). Here, too, is 'Spirit/filtered through brickwork' from the first part of 'Six Text for A Film' (*BR*, p. 15). The enclosed sun is not trapped; it is still the force by which everything including the brick-maker 'comes into being'; and even in decay the water remains generative. Life grows out of dirt, but what Fisher actually says is, 'There's a law//dirt grows out of'. What this means, I think, is that all 'the dead stuff' goes back to the creative matrix. On the evidence of the filth we make, it is quite possible that we will destroy ourselves, but with the human mind and its capacity for making drawn from Nature, all things are possible. That, I think, is a 'message' we may draw from Fisher's work, but as he said in his 'The Poet's Message', in *The Thing About Joe Sullivan*, 'what sort of man/comes in a message?'[13]

---

[13] Roy Fisher, *The Thing About Joe Sullivan* (Manchester: Carcanet Press, 1978), p. 59.

Christopher Middleton:
The Poem as Act of Wonder

'We are in the midst of a great death of imagination.' Christopher Middleton's poetry, over more than forty years, has been an art of resistance to this death, which he described in introducing his collection of expository writings, *Bolshevism in Art*. Middleton described the 'suffocating situation' in an imagery of obstructions and airlessness: 'a world of impenetrable obstacles, a clotted and contrived world', in which 'authoritarian mystiques ... choke the life-currents'. In contrast to this, 'the poetic reality is ... a reality of first things, of the fresh roots of mind, the well-being of earth, the springtime of our suffering and passionate species'.[1] It is clear from Middleton's argument and the imagery with which he supports it that he is a poet for whom there is a profound connection between natural and imaginative creativity, nature and mind, and that he apprehends seeing and imagining differently as an act which has political implications, and opposes all forms of tyranny.

The first poem in Christopher Middleton's latest book, *Intimate Chronicles*, concludes:

> That fatal daybreak passes in a flash,
> Perfect, for its makings and unmakings
> While you wet a toothbrush in the old stone trough;
> So, tasting a brioche, you wonder still what's what.[2]

Situated in history and nature, both with their 'makings and unmakings', the human subject ('you') going about its daily tasks and pleasures, and intensely conscious of the temporal nature of beauty, remains prone to wonder. In fact, it is the poet who is the wondering man, and his poems are artefacts that open the reader to wonder. In terms of the colloquialism, the object of wonder is 'whatness'. It is a philosophical concept: quiddity, 'the real nature or essence of a thing; that which makes a thing what it is' (*SOD*). At the same time, it is the object or being the poet encounters,

---

[1] Christopher Middleton, *Bolshevism in Art and other expository writings* (Manchester: Carcanet Press, 1978), p. 17, hereafter referenced *BA* in the text.
[2] Christopher Middleton, 'Valdrôme Gallo-Roman', *Intimate Chronicles* (Manchester: Carcanet Press, 1996), p. 3, hereafter referenced *IC* in the text.

and to whose 'otherness' he responds. The imagination, as Middleton defines and exercises it, is rooted in wonder, and responds to the presence of 'things' by making texts which 'speak' their essential being. In terms which he defines in 'Reflections on a Viking Prow' he is an 'artificer poet' committed to 'figurative speech, as a time-tested access to truth in finite existence, and more, as speech which tells of the impact of the world upon the body'.[3]

In the Introduction to *Bolshevism in Art* Middleton links Dada with the Yoruba trickster god and with the anti-rationalist thinker Leon Chestov. He quotes Chestov's view that the aim of philosophy should be to find 'that frontier beyond which the might of general ideas ceases' (*BA*, p. 8). Dada, the mischievous god, and Chestov all free the mind from the tyranny of a world framed by system and rationalism, and open it to other spiritual or magical possibilities. Middleton himself is, in this sense, a metaphysical poet: his poetry crosses the frontier of general ideas and makes, differently in each poem, the spaces of a personal vision. He too creates, as he has written of Robert Walser, 'out of the most quotidian encounters with beings and in the text things, unique images of personal reality' (*BA*, pp. 109-10).

It is evident from his expository writings, as well as his poems, that Christopher Middleton has thought deeply about the nature and capacity of imagination and its workings in the world. In examining 'the sound-meaning nexus' of poems by Eduard Mörike, for example, he supposes that it 'marks a survival of a tradition of the sacred word, of the word which initiates being' (*BA*,. p. 13). 'Mandelstam to Gumilev 1920' invokes the same idea:

> The word you said, stars in terror of it
> Clung to the moon; eagles folded their wings;
> Men ringed it with number, dreading its radiance.
>
> Our sounds, woven of that radiance, were sacred,
> You said – but now what a stink of dead words:
> Dead bees, old hive deserted.[4]

---

[3] Christopher Middleton, *The Pursuit of the Kingfisher* (Manchester: Carcanet Press, 1983), p. 85, hereafter referenced *PK* in the text.
[4] Christopher Middleton, *The Lonely Suppers of W. V. Balloon* (Cheadle Hulme: Carcanet Press, 1975), p. 20.

While the Russian poets were to suffer, in the most literal way, 'the great death of imagination', they were committed in their work to keeping it alive. This meant being true to a different concept of 'reality' than that espoused by the State, a life-giving idea, in which (as the image of the hive emphasises) the poet served his people. The sacred word, the word which initiates being, acts on 'externals as a scenario waiting to be created, not fixed but transmutable' (*BA*, p. 130). Contrary to materialist philosophies, this belief values the singularity of the poet in a universe of singular entities, and poetic subjectivity as a force capable of transforming externals into 'a vision of being'. Imagination is thus known by its power to transform and reveal; the poet exercises freedom to transform external 'reality' into the world or cosmos of a poetic vision.

This belief has ancient antecedents. Middleton defends "that sense of the sacred, the authentic 'other' which happens to have fostered authentic creative work ...since Aurignacian times' (*BA*, p. 146). Poetic language is opposed to all kinds of clichés, 'the zombie shocktroops of power' (*BA*, p. 156). Middleton's engagement on this front lends some of his utterances a refreshing optimism: 'We can dismantle the grey cardboard world devised by the phrase-makers. We can offer, in the precision and zest of our writing, correctives to the language-rot which is killing the spoken and written word in most public areas, writing itself included' (*BA*, p. 156).

Poetry, in the tradition in which Christopher Middleton writes, unmakes the external world to show 'how life might be differently perceived'. Poetry 'can enable imaginations to see through general ideas (the terrible simplifications) to the naked living universe. By anatomizing idols, a good text overthrows them' (*PK*, p. 50). This is not, of course, a tradition confined to the English-speaking world; indeed, Middleton, more than any other modern English poet, draws strongly on literature and art from continental Europe and from world cultures, and scorns 'the somnolent, message-laden rationality, the moralistic sog, of cerebral or literary poetry a *l'anglaise*' (*PK*, p. 11). It is part of his achievement, however, that he enlivens our sense of an alternative tradition within British and American poetry: in Lawrence's poems about birds, beasts and flowers; in the Negative Capability of Keats, poet of 'the act of wonder', at 'the threshold across which [he] listened to the nightingale, and on which he constructed ... a Grecian urn' (*PK*, pp. 180-1); in Pound's idea of the poetic image affording 'a sense of sudden growth'; and in Hopkins seeing 'the inscape though freshly, as if my eye were still growing'.[5] Again, the

---

[5] Middleton quotes Pound and Hopkins in *The Pursuit of the Kingfisher*, p. 90.

organic image is more than a metaphor for Middleton; mind participates in the creation it perceives; awareness of inner depths and of the other grows with the overthrowing of idols that constrict and disfigure the sense of being.

'At Porthcothan', the first poem in Christopher Middleton's *Selected Writings*, introduces his characteristic stance towards experience. It is a poem of encounter, in this case between the poet and a sea-bird. The poem begins and ends with the unknown, and responds to the mystery of being with verbal precision. It is a true encounter, in which man and bird both lie open to question, and the bird's intelligence 'seemed to pierce the mind of the observer'. In rendering the bird's presence and otherness the poet reveals life as the force that makes and unmakes material forms:

> Such bodies best belong, far from bathers, among
> The elements that compose and decompose them,
> Unconscious, strange to freedom, but perceptible
> Through narrow slits that score the skin of things.[6]

In a later poem, 'Wild Horse', Middleton both distinguishes his poetic art, with mischievous good humour, from a native tradition of natural vitalism, with which he has, nevertheless, certain affinities, and exercises his greater imaginative freedom:

> As a more or less literate person
> Who writes down things that have
> Some connection with the English language
>
> What should I do with a wild horse
> Suddenly presenting itself to my thoughts
> In Berlin this winter morning [7]

The tone is deceptively casual; every word is significant. Christopher Middleton is, of course, highly literate (but too civilized to wear his learning immodestly), and his literacy enables him to draw deeply on his

---

[6] Christopher Middleton, *Selected Writings* (London: Paladin, 1990), p. 12. 'At Porthcothan' originally appeared in Middleton's first book of poems, *torse 3 Poems 1949-1961* (London: Longman, 1962), pp. 9–11.

[7] Christopher Middleton, *Carminalenia* (Manchester: Carcanet Press, 1980), p. 86.

'connection with the English language' in order to 'do' something with the living presence of images that act upon him. Again, the poem springs from an encounter which opens both poet and 'other' to question. Middleton is not, as he says, 'the savage Mr Ted Hughes'; he is conscious of his literacy in a positive way, and does not assume an elemental encounter with an actual wild horse – his relation is to an image that presents itself to his mind, not on a moorland, but in an urban centre of a culture which in recent times has let loose the murderous energy of its own myths of wildness and savagery. What Middleton does with the 'wild horse' is, so to speak, to allow it to take his imagination for a gallop, in which body-consciousness and the literate mind with its power of figuration work together, enabling freedom and control. The Nietzschean terms Dionysian and Apollonian are appropriate here, as in all of Middleton's best poems, which combine an exciting dynamic energy with cunningly wrought iconic forms. As he says in 'Reflections on a Viking Prow': 'Imagination, precisely because it is deceptive and demonic, needs artifice, needs the pressure of craft, the pleasure of artistry, for a dialectical counterpart' (*PK*, p. 85). In 'Wild Horse' the imaginative gallop leads finally to the source of imagination in 'this blaze the universe': a source fed by sexual energy and under the guiding influence of 'the magician'. 'Wild Horse' offers a paradigm of Middleton's modernism. The poem stems from an impulse received at a centre of European civilization; in awareness of the continuing catastrophic history, it forms a highly sophisticated ordering of 'wild' powers for the purposes of spiritual revelation and aesthetic delight.

Christopher Middleton is concerned with 'the inaugural making of meaning' (*BA*, p. 271). He is a poet not of 'given experience', but of experience that 'consists in the activity of creating, which the event or object only goes so far as to provoke' (*BA*, p. 220). While he protects himself with sceptical intelligence against religious ideas, as much as any general ideas, he shows faith in the spiritual and magical properties of imagination, which he sees as 'a relic, still radio-active, of the original cosmogonic process, embedded in man' (*PK*, p. 147). He writes under the magical guidance of images or figures of speech that connect the human mind and nature, transformative and liminal images such as the snake, the tree, the boat in the water.

One of the main aims of Christopher Middleton's poetry of encounter or relationship is to achieve vision, and by shattering conventional ways of seeing, reveal life in its very quick. He is aware of the impossibility of achieving the latter absolutely, and that it may be approached only in the makings and unmakings of figurative language:

> The great blaze of sense-impressions in which we live looks otherwise than it is or was, as soon as we attempt to freeze it. The most we can look for is some kind of approach to the moment, behaving as if we intended to take it by surprise. Even then, the intent itself may obstruct the unfolding of the true moment, if there ever was or is a moment one can call true, a moment with a coherence having greater magnitude and integrity than the constructions we place upon it.
>
> ('A Memorial to the Room-Collectors')[8]

Poetic vision as Middleton exercises it is thus an act that involves unknowing, making strange, and unselving – climbing 'forever/out of myself", as he says in 'Avocado Plant'. It is an act of wonder. One consequence of his ability to shed his ego and open himself to the mystery that lies within and outside is his capacity to express plenitude, gratitude for gifts given and received, and joy in life, which few contemporary poets can equal. This goes together with his sense of the elusiveness of the living moment, and (as he said in an interview with Ian Hamilton) his 'experiences of the strangeness of being alive, of the strangeness of living things outside oneself'.[9] Reading Middleton is a sometimes baffling but always surprising experience, as his acute sensitivity to the singular manifestations of being animates poem after poem, in figurative language that crystallizes, dissolves, and forms again in a new image.

The poems in his new book, published at the age of seventy, have a heightened awareness of time, memory, and the disappearance of human purposes. 'The Old Tour Guide – His Interpreter' reflects upon the difficulty of realizing a vision:

> Few have spelled out into the pleasure of a heartbeat,
> Into a knot of mind, once and for all,
> The loops of light they see spreading at sunrise,
> The braid that snakes down a girl's bare back.
> When we go to see what is there to be seen,
> The knots and braids easily slip;
> We learn to know how little we understand. (*IC*, p. 31)

---

[8] Christopher Middleton, *Pataxanadu* (Manchester: Carcanet Press, 1977), p. 98.
[9] Ian Hamilton, 'Four Conversations', *The London Magazine,* November 1964, Vol. 4 No. 8, p. 81.

Like Chekhov, in 'On a Photograph of Chekhov', Middleton has a correspondingly acute awareness that people 'cling … to their fatal fictions' (*IC*, p. 56). Middleton's aim, however (to use one of his favourite images, which recurs in the poem about Chekhov), is to make images like boats, which 'can float across a century, be put to use' (*IC*, p. 55). The artificer's poem has the reality of handmade things in a pre-industrial culture, which 'become real, because they were brought to life by currents of formalized energy, desire crystallising as it passed from imagination to skilled hands, through to treasured materials, and back again in a circuit never broken" (*PK*, p. 80). In this sense, the 'circuitry of response to the world' is Middleton's concern.

He is a poet who celebrates primal energy, but as a sea to navigate, not a savage or wild element to let loose imaginatively in deranged behaviour or murderous exercises of power. He is also a playful and witty poet, who has fun at the expense of academic prose style and logic, for example, as in 'From the Alexandria Library Gazette' in *Pataxanadu*, and enjoys 'absurd' writing which upsets habits of categorising and classifying or authoritarian ideas of order or literary decorum. Like Chekhov and the Dadaists and Native American tricksters, Middleton delights in subverting the powers of the world, and revealing possibilities not dreamt of in their philosophies. As in 'Moon Climbing', first published in *Serpentine*, 1985, he invokes the living powers of present images (moon, geese, wren) 'To blot from thought if only for a little time/ /… The symbols of power that make brutes of men'.[10] Middleton is capable of anger at brutalizing powers, but his is naturally a generous imagination which delights in 'the thousand things', all the manifestations of whatness and otherness. True to the Coleridgean ideal, he both expresses and orders strong feeling. In a poem of longing for the past, 'Catacomb', in his new collection, he writes 'Time just enough to imagine it was I who said://All your theologies, all, are fragments/From Aphrodite's shattered mirror' (*IC*, p. 29). It is a marvellous moment, in which the longing is at once expressed, and the self, conscious of its provisional imagined form, places itself among the subjects of desire.

In 'Wild Flowers' Christopher Middleton traces the evolution of flowers and humans:

> On roadsides they exist. Songs in our hands
> They go along with us. A passion

---

[10] *Selected Writings*, p. 143.

> Means us to pick them, so
> Responding to early light we stop; then drive on home
> To draw blankets back
> And make our love while sensing them,
> Their far fields, their darkness.[11]

In harmony with Middleton's faith in imagination as 'a relic, still radioactive, of the original cosmogonic process', 'Wild Flowers' explodes evolutionary determinism and materialistic notions that void matter of spirit. Together with flowers, songs and love are principles of creation. Constituent elements in the making of the human world (voice, song, love) belong with flowers as vital forces, and there is a profound reciprocity, embedded in language and the structure of the mind, between humans and plants and other creatures. In this and other poems, Middleton frames what in 'Discourse on Legend' he calls 'speech for an exchange/Of natures/Between things and people'.[12] Another way of expressing this would be to say that he puts mind in its place as a faculty that responds imaginatively to the creation it is part of.

Christopher Middleton shares with the English poets he is closest to, Keats and Hopkins and Lawrence, his wonderful empathy for other beings. His poetry of encounter is also, often, a poetry inward with processes of becoming or making. His many poems about artefacts celebrate the art of cultural phases in which the imagination responding to the nature of its materials produces objects of beauty that serve human needs. 'Small Carvings at Arycanda' presents 'a cluster of grapes' which 'hangs/Bursting from its marble slab, /Halfway liquid in your mouth'. Both Middleton and the old carver exercise 'the life/Of carnal imagination working as a hinge' (*IC*, p. 59). Their images are liminal and transformative, and expand our sense of being. Both sculpted and poetic images are thresholds between matter and spirit, and the living and the dead.

Middleton's description of the emergence of a cicada in 'Bivouac' shows him to be equally inward with natural processes:

> Finally, mute and dull, an oval pellet had shrugged the pupa off.
> The pellet put a leg out, soon another leg. Its back was turning
> emerald, then golden emerald, with wings that lay flush with the

---

[11] Christopher Middleton, *Two Horse Wagon Going By* (Manchester: Carcanet Press, 1986), p. 127.
[12] *Carminalenia*, p. 24.

pellet, exceedingly frail, then larger, unfurling into twin networks of golden emerald filigree tracery. And the head, with eyes, had woken up, was turning this way and that way; now the wings could move and lift. The cicada glowed as if dusted with pollen out of which, for the sake of argument, the breath of a beyond conjectured the world's first agile anatomies. Pristine forest contracted to the volume of a singing bird's egg. A fiery drop of universe at the other end of a tunnel through time.[13]

From 'At Porthcothan' to 'Bivouac' and his new poems, close observation and exact description are means by which Middleton opens ordinary things to show us the extraordinary magic making them what they are.

In twentieth-century poetry that retains a sense of the sacred, 'things' usually prove to be of central importance. No general idea will explain why this is so, or draw together under one heading poets as different from each other as Rilke, Ponge, W.C. Williams, George Oppen, David Jones, and Christopher Middleton. It would be of some relevance to Middleton to invoke the names of writers and thinkers with whom he has affinities, and some of whom have influenced him: Goethe, with his wonder at living entities and their conditions; Maritain, whose thinking on the relation between things and human consciousness influenced both Jones and Oppen; or Nietzsche and Heidegger; or Rilke. No idea, however, is adequate to account for poetry which casts off the bonds of generality and system, and honours singularity in poet and reader as well as subject.

Certainly, Middleton's poetry is integrally a response to existential and historical crisis, and is committed to making meaning in the face of conformity to meaningless or murderous authoritarian ideas. He reacts to the situation described by Walter Benjamin as 'loss of aura'.[14] 'Reflections on a Viking Prow' is *inter alia* a meditation on things and texts in this situation. Here, Middleton explores more fully the 'great death of imagination', which he perceives as 'a nightmare of designification' (*PK*, p. 87). More than in any other expository writing, he shows how 'image', 'sign', 'thing', and 'being' are vitally connected in his thinking.

A measure of the essay's richness is the confinement to a note of Middleton's connection of the Sanskrit *vastu*, meaning 'abiding essence', 'subject of concern', 'object', 'property', with *vástu,* 'becoming light',

---

[13] *Two Horse Wagon Going By,* p. 132.
[14] See Walter Benjamin, 'On Some Motifs in Baudelaire', *Illuminations* London: Collins/Fontana Books, 1973), pp. 189-90.

'dawning', 'morning'. He comments: 'The words might be related, within a preliterate, pre-selfconscious semantics of "disclosure", so that at a certain stage in the evolution of consciousness a thing could be experienced as an opening on being, a dawn of being" (*PK*, p. 198). The essay begins with his affirmation that: 'Some poems, at least, and some types of poetic language, constitute structures of a singularly radiant kind … We experience these structures … as apertures upon being (*PK*, p. 80). Of the 'artificer poets' of whom he writes in the essay, Middleton says: 'Almost they put us in perceptual contact with being; almost we perceive, in their organization, being as most subtle and integral form' (*PK*, p. 84). In his resistance to the 'great death of imagination', Christopher Middleton has achieved a poetry of this type. In his sense of the relation between poetic language and structure and the cosmogonic process, he has revived and revalued the idea of imagination, as a source of delight, and in opposition to the 'vacuum', which, 'having eroded the presences of original things, artifacts and handiworks, is eating away the awesome reality of individual human lives' *(PK*, pp. 86-7). He is a poet who feels 'the magic of presence', as he calls it in 'A Memorial to the Room-Collectors', the presence in which 'you were free to be everything the living universe had planted in your flesh and in your mind'. In the words of 'Holy Cow', his poems are acts of wonder that serve nature's 'radiant/free/ongoing creation'.

Taking Words for a Walk:
The Recent Poetry of Philip Gross

In this essay I draw upon four collections of poetry which Philip Gross has published since he settled in Penarth in 2007: *The Water Table* (2009), *Deep Field* (2011), *Later* (2013), and *Love Songs of Carbon* (2015).[1] Gross is a prolific author, who in this period has published other books, including two collaborations with artists. Here, I attempt to show that, while his poems respond to 'spirit of place' in his Welsh home, he achieves in his recent poetry a deepening of themes present in his work from the beginning. His original Cornish 'heartland', surrounded by the Atlantic Ocean, was a strong influence upon his earlier work. So also was the legacy of his Estonian father, a wartime refugee, displaced from the far north, beside the Baltic Sea. Living now beside the Severn Sea, Gross responds to his new environment, but with a mind for which water has always been vitally important. Water is the protean element. For Gross, it means the edge of the world. It means also seas and seaways as channels for migrating peoples with their history and myth. Especially in his most recent poetry, water, as a basic constituent of the material world, including the human body, excites his imagination. Indeed, it is the element that provides him with the principal metaphor for his poetry. As he writes in 'Betweenland' 1 in *The Water Table*:

> A body of water: water's body
>
> that seems to have a mind (and
> change it: isn't that what makes
>
> a *mind*, its changing?) (*WT*, p. 10)

'The Moveable Island', another poem in *The Water Table*, begins with changing water, and the changing mind:

> …shifts, like the hull of a boat
> left drifting, grounded on a different shoal

---

[1] I focus here on these books, all published by Bloodaxe; referenced in the text *WT*, *DF*, *L*, and *LSC*.

> each morning, in the midway, out
> where the Severn is letting, has let,
> itself go into sea, like a thought into sleep:
> now you're there, now you're not. (*WT*, p. 40)

'Shifts' is a keyword in Gross's vocabulary. Shifting is what water does; it is partly what makes it such an apt metaphor for the dreaming and thinking mind, and the writing mind that expresses itself through shifting and changing movements. The poem offers a view of an island, which it doesn't name – naming might distract from the fact that it is not primarily a 'poem of place'. The location is the poet's mind. 'The Moveable Island' is an act, a process, of thinking. As with many of Gross's poems, it begins *within* the act of thinking and perceiving. The ellipses, followed by the word 'shifts', are like a dot in Paul Klee's 'A line is a dot that went for a walk'. Paul Klee, a man in whom the child stayed alive in the painter's adult vision, is an artist dear to Gross, whose poetic practice may be likened to Klee's drawing. Whereas Klee takes a line for a walk, Gross takes a word. The writing that ensues is an exploratory, indeterminate process that involves instinct, wit and play, and calls upon the full resources of the poet's mind and art.

The major event influencing Philip Gross's poetry written in the period since he settled at Penarth was his father's gradual loss of language and sense of identity in his final years. This was a process that the son felt keenly, so that the poems that arose from witnessing his father's experience are full of love and pain. But the poems are also deeply concerned with philosophical and metaphysical issues, since aphasia calls into question the relation between language and world, and language and a sense of self. As Gross writes in 'Several Shades of Ellipsis' 6 in *Love Songs of Carbon*, what is lost with his father's aphasia is 'not/just the meaning but the one who meant it, stepping off//the marked path and into/abeyance'. (LSC, p. 69) Major sequences, notably 'Betweenland' (*The Water Table*) and 'Something Like the Sea' and 'Vocable' *(Deep Field)*, provide Gross with space not only to respond to witnessing loss of meaning and loss of self, but to explore the theme of the relations between language and world and self. He is writing in response to existential crisis. As his father loses language and memory so his own idea of self comes into question. At the same time, he draws upon his father's whole ambiguous legacy as refugee and man from Estonia.

His father's 'stepping off the marked path' initiates a journey for the poet. This is a journey within himself, and into the environment, and back into personal and ancestral memory. In all these respects the journey marks a deepening of Philip Gross's imaginative world. In 'Something Like the Sea' 3 (*Deep Field*), the son's witness of his father's failing language takes his mind back, beyond his father's displacement from Estonia as a refugee, to something far older. In the syllables of broken Estonian words he hears 'bird-hordes//ululating on the Northern edge/of things'. (*DF*, p. 55) Birds are present in many of Gross's poems, and the idea of 'edge' is a key concept. Through his father, his Estonian heritage is not only one of displacement; it is also a world of ancient myth, in which birds are associated with voices of the dead, and with mystery. At this edge between the living and the dead the figure of the shaman enters the poem:

> what the birds were saying,
>
> the old timers knew. Half outcast on the scrubland
> in his turf shack,
>
> the rag-skirted shaman, the tribe's
> cracked interlocutor, crooned under his breath,
>
> unmanned, his voice stolen by birds – his soul
> flown north
>
> with the wildfowl, for news –
> the price, when he returned, his human speech. (*DF*, p. 55)

At this point it is well to pause and remind us that Philip Gross is a witty poet with a vocabulary that draws widely upon the contemporary world, including popular culture. He does so with humour, and without diminution of metaphysical and philosophical seriousness. Thus, in 'Barry Island with Dante and Ducks' (*Later*), yellow plastic ducks serve to question the distinction between soul and appetite, and the nature of human 'wanting'. This is lightly done. 'Thinks Bubble' (*The Water Table*) plays as lightly with references to Doctor Johnson and Bishop Berkeley, Buddha and the Beano, in seriously exploring the nature of thought. Nowhere in the modern world escapes Gross's intellectual curiosity. 'Fantasia on a Theme from IKEA', in *The Water Table*, is subtitled "*seven descants on 'ground'"*. With a reference to *The Tempest*, the second section of the poem uses shopping to pose questions about our fundamental nature that later poems in *Love Songs of Carbon* will pursue further:

> … dreams. We are such stuff:
> flesh, matter. No wonder they can't look away,
> all those ideals and angels. Where else to found
> their celestial cities but on grit and clay,
> hormones and DNA? Where else to ground
> their being? (*WT*, p. 19)

It is characteristic of Gross that a shopping expedition should raise basic questions of ontology. Another example of his playful sense of humour occurs in 'Storm Surge', in *Love Songs of Carbon*, where he likens the surge coming up channel to thud on Penarth pier to a rugby scrum. The remarkable thing about this kind of wit in Gross's hands is that it cohabits with a sense of awe.

As it has developed, the play of mind in Philip Gross's poetry has been strongly influenced by his knowledge of new sciences. This is more than a matter of references to phenomena such as fractal geometry, string theory, Brownian Motion, or dark matter. It is the recognition of what he calls in 'Epithalamium, with Squirrels', a playful poem in *Love Songs of Carbon,* 'the play of material things' (LSC, p. 56) in the quantum universe. This affects the perspectives of the poems, which move between the subatomic world and the far reaches of the cosmos. In 'Mould Music' (*Love Songs of Carbon*), for example, the perspective shifts between mould spores on plum skin and human life seen from space:

> from a farther remove
> what's the shimmery bloom
> on the rind, the lichen
>
> on the rock in orbit,
> but us: cave-
>
> moss bristling
> its tiny luminescence
> in the black of space? (LSC, p. 14)

The image of human life as 'cave-moss' recalls 'Vocable' 11, in which the prehistoric cave is the original human home animated by the voice.

Gross's perspective upon the universe, from particle to outer space, incorporates the indeterminacy fundamental to the Uncertainty Principle. He takes to heart the lesson of modern physics 'that the clear space between thing/and thing is all trouble … either that/or delight, *jouissance*, a fine/discontent at molecular level' ('Brownian Motion', *Love Songs of Carbon*). The idea of 'the play of material things' takes us back to Paul Klee and the dot or line taken for a walk. The word 'walking' returns us to the creativity of language:

> *Hom. sap.* – the vocambulant species
>
> walking the talking the walk
> to the ends of the earth and
>
> into our inheritance of tongues
> as into our vestments of features
> and skin, our coat of many colours. (*DF*, p. 39)

It seems likely that 'vocambulant' is a Gross coinage. It is a word combining voice with the activity of walking that aptly describes the evolution of the human voice in the movement of migratory peoples. Language is the humanizing process, as integral to us as our skin. The implicit politics of the poetry is manifest in 'our inheritance of tongues', and 'our coat of many colours'. Gross honours cultural differences within a humane universalism.

This openness to human diversity is consonant with the value that, as a Quaker, he places on listening. He combines this attentiveness with his long-held interest in Buddhism. In an interview he has spoken of the Buddhist Void, 'the place of endless and emergent possibility', and said that: 'At best, Quaker worship looks towards that fertile space'.[2] This is a religious position, but it is not immaterial. The poems in *Love Songs of Carbon*, with their rich factual and metaphorical use of the carbon and water that constitute the basis of the material world, including the human body, bring to a focus Gross's concern with 'us who are matter'. He is a spiritual materialist who looks unblinkingly at the fact of death.

---

[2] See Interview with Philip Gross by Bryan R. Monte, 'Philip Gross – Oh, So That's Where We Were Going', *Amsterdam Quarterly*, 2014.

It is a fact, however, that does not negate mystery. A central credo occurs in 'Brownian Motion' (*Love Songs of Carbon*): 'Take this from the heart/ of things: that nothing will be fixed'.

'Legacy', in *Later*, returns to the metaphor of migrating birds to express his deep sense of human connection in and across time:

> Somewhere too far
> or near to see, feel the rippling lift into flight: birds
> on their centuries'
>
> migration, out of the distance in us (we're
> a resting place, a night stop), out of our far-north
> ancestors, and gone
>
> into the dark of our descendants, through
> that space called *me* at one time,
> at another, *you* or *you*. (*L*, p. 49)

The self (*me* or *you*) is not lost but defined by its life within the temporal process, and in connection with ancestors and descendants. The human being in this vision is essentially migratory. Even a settled people carry within it the story of human origins.

Philip Gross writes spacious poems – poems that are spacious on the page, and poems that describe a generous space for cultural diversity and for life on earth. This openness owes a significant debt to his original homes in the South West peninsula and his father's displacement. An earlier poem, 'The Duke of Nowhere', in *The Son of the Duke of Nowhere*, 1991, begins:

> I was the son of the Duke of Nowhere.
> Nowhere was home.[3]

What we may expect following this beginning is a poem about loss, caused by his father's life as a refugee. This poem about 'our exile' refers to the Gross family's move from Delabole in north Cornwall to Plymouth. From here, the boy perceived the sea as 'the edge of the world'. 'Edge', as

---

[3] This poem appears also in Philip Gross, *Changes of Address: Poems 1980-98* (Newcastle: Bloodaxe Books, 2001), p. 99.

we know, was a word that was to acquire a special resonance for Philip Gross as the edge of language, which brought him to deeper questioning of the relation between self and language, and language and world. The Cornish location carries his mind out from 'the edge of the world':

> On a clear day I could watch grey frigates
> climb it and slip over. I woke one night
>
> to singing in the streets that suddenly
> grew small as all the hooters of the fleet
>
> brawled up together, blurting
> *Home* ... as if any such place
>
> existed, over the horizon, anywhere.

We may detect a hint of melancholy in this if we think of homelessness. What we may see in the poem, however, is openness to the world beyond Cornwall, and the attraction of elsewhere. This looks forward to the fuller appreciation of the father's legacy in later poems. That legacy raises crucial questions about world and self. It is also the legacy of a migratory people, a people moving on, evolving, never 'fixed', but carrying with them an ancient mythology of life and death, and a sense of mystery. This is a genetic inheritance, the inheritance of the species (*'Hom. sap.'*) that learned to stand upright and to walk: the beings that acquired a voice to speak with one another, and to relate to the world in which they lived. Situated in Penarth beside the 'betweenland' Severn Sea, it is in this human spirit that Philip Gross takes his words for a walk, opening generous spaces for readers to enter.

Poets, Language and Land:
Reflections on English-Language Welsh Poetry since the Second World War

This essay is not intended to be a survey or thorough exploration of English-language Welsh poetry published since the Second World War. Instead, drawing where possible upon poems which have appeared in anthologies during the period, my discussion will concentrate upon ways in which poets from three generations write about the relationship between language and the land in Wales. This is a recurring concern of English-language Welsh poets, but one treated differently by different poets, and with variations governed in part by the exigencies of particular historical 'moments. Accordingly, my aim is also to make some comparisons and contrasts between poems published at different times during the period. In reflecting upon the present situation of the Welsh poet writing in English, I shall conclude with some personal observations.

Keidrych Rhys's anthology *Modern Welsh Poetry* (1944) includes both Dylan Thomas's 'Poem in October' and R.S. Thomas's 'A Peasant'. 'Poem in October'[1] constructs a powerful version of the theme of the connection between language and the land. The poem begins with the speaker exposed to the elements: 'Especially when the October wind / With frosty fingers punishes my hair'. By the end of the first stanza, however, he has subdued nature to language, which is imaged as being integral to the human organism:

> My busy heart who shudders as she talks
> Sheds the syllabic blood and drains her words.

The speaker, who is evidently the poet, asserts the role of the poet as maker:

> Some let me make you of the vowelled beeches,
> Some of the oaken voices…

---

[1] Keidrych Rhys, ed., *Modern Welsh Poetry* (London: Faber and Faber, 1944), p. 124.

The poet has the function of magician, too: 'Some let me spell you of the raven's sins'. In this context, what the speaker calls 'the loud hill of Wales' suggests a Wales constructed by poetic voices. This both invokes and reverses a trope central to Romantic poetry – that of nature's voice or voices, in which the poet finds meaning, as, for example, both William Wordsworth and Edward Thomas do.[2] The landscape of 'Poem in October' suggests nature's voices, but does not attempt to speak through them; it is, rather, a landscape inseparable from its maker's language, which is English.

This is a celebratory poem, but also a guilty one, in which both the poet and the land are being 'punished'. One reason for this may be that the poet is conscious of having stolen the breath of inspiration – traditionally attributed to God or nature – in making himself, with language, its master. He is 'Shut, too, in a tower of words'. The function of a tower is to stand firm, whether as sacred enclosure or military bastion. In historical fact and as a metaphor, the tower shuts in and shuts out, providing security for those inside, but with the capacity of becoming a prison, and isolating its inmates. In terms of a metaphor to which we shall return, the poet in his tower of words might find himself an astronaut in a spacesuit, 'free' of Earth.

'Poem in October' is at once a boast and the expression of a predicament. For English-language Welsh poets who followed Dylan Thomas, the tower of words tended to represent a predicament: English words, imposed on the Welsh landscape, subjugating the native language. R.S. Thomas appeared to offer an escape from the tower. Seen in this light, the key words in his poem 'A Peasant'[3] were 'ordinary man', 'bald Welsh hills', and 'the vacancy of his mind'. 'Bald Welsh hills' evoke a treeless landscape that had a particular appeal for Thomas, and although it is described in English words, 'Welsh' points unequivocally to the land to which the hills belong. 'The vacancy' of the mind of Prytherch, an 'ordinary man', is a vacancy the poet can choose to fill. Thus, with 'A Peasant', R.S. Thomas clears the ground for the poems he will construct upon it. Or for what he will find – his approach appears to be more modest than Dylan Thomas's, more that of a priest, one who listens, serving a mystery, than of a magician, who exercises power over words and things.

---

[2] There are many instances in Wordsworth. To my mind the most evocative occurs in 'There was a boy' in *Lyrical Ballads*. There are many in Edward Thomas too. See 'The Unknown Bird', for example.
[3] *Modern Welsh Poetry*, p. 130.

One thing R.S. Thomas rediscovers is the Romantic trope. In 'A Priest to His People':

> I have taxed your ignorance of rhyme and sonnet,
> Your want of deference to the painter's skill,
> But I know, as I listen, that your speech has in it
> The source of all poetry, clear as a rill
> Bubbling from your lips…[4]

It is the speech of his people that is 'the source of all poetry', and the water imagery forms an organic connection between people, landscape, and the land of Wales. With its renunciation of mastery over language, the metaphor places the poet in a humble, receptive relation to his subject. It was however to prove problematic for R.S. Thomas, since the organic connection of the Welsh-speaking Welsh to their land implied the inorganic disconnection of the English-speakers claiming to be Welsh. Thus, 'An Anglo-Welsh writer is neither one thing nor the other. He subsists in no-man's-land between two cultures'.[5]

What R.S. Thomas built on the ground he cleared with 'A Peasant' was, in Raymond Williams's useful term, a structure of feeling and, such was its power, other poets were quick to occupy it, and build their own poems in the shadow of R.S. Thomas's: John Tripp, for example, in 'Soliloquy for compatriots', which was included in the anthology *The lilting house* (1969).[6] Here, the English reader is immediately confronted:

> We even have our own word for God
> in a language nourished on hymn and psalm
> as we clinched to our customs and habitats.

Thus, the poem begins as a boast. It continues however as an elegy:

> But now the strangers come to bang more nails
> in the battered coffin of Wales.

---

[4] R. S. Thomas, *The Stones of the Field* (Carmarthen: The Druid Press, 1946), p. 29.
[5] R. S. Thomas, *Autobiographies*, trans. Jason Walford Davies (London: Dent, 1997), p. 22.
[6] John Stuart Williams and Meic Stephens, eds., *The lilting house: An anthology of Anglo-Welsh poetry 1917-1967* (London and Llanddybie: Dent and Christopher Davies, 1969), pp. 170-71.

At the end it returns to being a boast:

> How could they know
> for one moment of the steely wonder
> of pride in legend in a sunken past,
> the stiff stubborn strap to our backbone
> that makes others still seek us out?

In his Introduction to the anthology in which 'Soliloquy for compatriots' was included, Raymond Garlick notes that the poems 'are Welsh in that they are ultimately statements about what it is like to be a Welsh human being'.[7] Judging by this and other poems, this certainly meant being conscious of a history and defining identity in relation to land and language; in fact, languages, one of them apparently a tower which no longer keeps strangers out.

    R. S. Thomas developed a variant of the organic metaphor connecting language and land which Dylan Thomas had deployed differently, as a function of the poet as maker and magician. In R. S. Thomas's use of the metaphor the effect is, as suggested above, humbling: more to do with response than mastery. Gillian Clarke's 'The Water-Diviner'[8] immediately establishes a religious perspective: 'His fingers tell water like prayer'. The poem restores the 'voice' the diviner hears to nature; it is the water's voice, to which he listens. This is water that is 'responsive' to human beings, as the owls are to the boy in Wordsworth's 'There was a boy'. But the water's answer does not come from nature alone; it rises from the depths of a culture, shouting

> a word we could not say, or spell, or remember,
> something like 'dŵr ... dŵr'.

'The Water-Diviner', then, figures the Welsh language as a deep cultural resource, integral to the land under which it flows. Like many of Gillian Clarke's poems, it is about being at home in Wales, which means being in touch with the Welsh language perceived as a nourishing and shaping force in the land itself. Like R. S. Thomas, Gillian Clarke sees the poet as servant of a culture rather than master of an art. Unlike R. S. Thomas,

---

[7] Ibid., xxi.
[8] Gillian Clarke, *Collected Poems* (Manchester: Carcanet Press, 1997), p. 71.

she is able to feel at home in Wales, in the English language.[9] This is affirmed in her early poem 'Blaen Cwrt' (anthologized in *Green Horse*, 1978),[10] in which her home in Ceredigion is described as having 'all the first/Necessities for a high standard/of civilised living'. As with the poems by the two Thomases, it is worth quoting the familiar lines again in the present context, for what they reveal of the relationship between poet, language, and land. The necessities are:

> silence inside
> A circle of sound, water and fire,
> Light on uncountable miles of mountain
> From a big, unpredictable sky,
> Two rooms, waking and sleeping,
> Two languages, two centuries of past
> To ponder on, and the basic need
> To work hard in order to survive.

Silence connects the cottage to sound and its elemental surroundings; the position of 'two languages' in the lines links them to the rooms and the centuries, to the present living space and to historical continuity. The cottage is thus at once a cosmic, a cultural, and a personal 'centre'. The implied coexistence of the two languages, Welsh and English, may be historically inaccurate in this part of Ceredigion, where Welsh alone would have been spoken until quite recent times. But it is an aspiration, which relates to the present linguistic situation in Wales. For Gillian Clarke Blaen Cwrt with its two languages is home, and home is Wales.

Since his early 'A Welsh Wordscape' Peter Finch has periodically played witty variations on the dual land / language inheritance from Dylan Thomas and R. S. Thomas. 'Hills' (included in the anthology *The Bright Field*)[11] reveals a poet who 'thinks of Wales as important to him as Dada'.[12] A glance at the poem on the page shows that it is a concrete

---

[9] I discuss Gillian Clarke's and R.S. Thomas's use of organic metaphors in Chapter 2 of my *Imagining Wales: A View of Modern Welsh Writing in English* (Cardiff: University of Wales Press, 2001).

[10] Meic Stephens and Peter Finch, eds., *Green Horse: An anthology by young poets of Wales* (Swansea: Christopher Davies, 1978), p. 34.

[11] Meic Stephens, ed., *The Bright Field: An Anthology of Contemporary Poetry from Wales* (Manchester: Carcanet Press, 1991), pp. 105-6.

[12] I take this from the back cover of Peter Finch's *Antibodies* (Exeter: Stride, 1997). The source of the information is unknown to me, though it strikes me

poem, which constructs a tower of words. Ostensibly it deconstructs the second and third lines of 'A Peasant':

> Just an ordinary man of the bald Welsh hills,
> docking sheep, penning a gap of cloud.
> Just a bald man of the ordinary hills,
> Welsh sheep gaps, docking pens, cloud shrouds.
> Just a man, ordinary, Welsh doctor, pen weaver,
> cloud gap, sheep sailor, hills.
> Just a sharp shard, hill weaver, bald sheep,
> Pilot pen rider, gap doctor, cloud…

This is witty play, which brings the spirit of Dada into an unlikely context. It is also an analysis and reconstruction of a cultural artefact – R. S. Thomas's 'making' of an 'ordinary man of the bald Welsh hills'. The poet Thomas himself is taken apart and put back together. 'Penning a gap of cloud', Thomas both 'writes Wales', as a contemporary critic might say, and encloses Wales in his vision. Thomas rather than Prytherch is the 'man'. And Thomas is 'Welsh doctor, pen weaver, /…. sheep sailor…' A man who offers himself as a healer, a writer, a maker of enclosures, a man at sea, a man whose father was a sailor. Above all, perhaps, Thomas was 'gap doctor'. Certainly, the word 'gap' and its variants are the main 'bricks' from which Finch constructs his tower of words

> Just grass gap, bald gap, garp grap,
> gap shot, sheep slate, gap grap.
>   garp gap
>   gop gap…
>   gwint gap grog gap
>   growd gap gost gap
>   gap gap gwin gap
>   gag gop gwell gap…

'Hills' exhibits the exhilaration and wit of its making: a tower made of English words, with an admixture of Welsh words or parts of Welsh words. It is thus a concrete figuration of the 'Anglo-Welsh' situation, and, we might think, a visual representation of 'the wind-bitten towers' in R.S. Thomas's 'Welsh Landscape'. The main word is 'gap', in several

---

as being quintessential Peter Finch.

senses: breach, break in continuity, divergence, chasm. This defines the Anglo-Welsh situation, as R. S. Thomas saw it: the gap between two languages, two ways of life; the 'cultural wound', in Bobi Jones's famous description,[13] which R. S. Thomas offered to doctor – by radical surgery, we might think. But I am now constructing a meta-poem around Finch's poem, as he makes it hard not to do.

Finch's tower is in danger of falling down. It is top-heavy, most eroded where made of 'gap' words. And the whole structure balances precariously on a negation:

> The problem gaps, ordinary television,
> nationalist garbage, insulting ignorance,
> shot sheep, uninvited bald interference,
> don't need real sheep where we are,
> sheepless, sheepless, Welsh as you are, still,
> no gasps, gogs or gaps for us,
> no,
> point our aerials at the Mendip Hills.

'No' is the single brick on which the tower of words stands, and where its foundation should be there is none, as Welsh people turn their backs on Wales, pointing their television 'aerials at the Mendip Hills'. The poem, therefore, both embodies and deconstructs R.S. Thomas's foundational poetic tradition, which it shows resting now on an indifference among Welsh and English people that will bring it tumbling down. All these solid words make an airy construction, from which the people have turned away, towards Anglo-American televisual culture. Yet there the poem stands, as do the 'Welsh hills'.

The contrasting metaphors, which, as we have seen, have played a dominant part in the poetry of English-language Welsh poets born between 1913 (R. S. Thomas) and 1947 (Peter Finch), continue – with important differences – to feature significantly in the work of younger poets. Here I turn first to the Seren anthology *Oxygen*, in which new poets from Wales appear to reveal a major difference between contemporary English-language and Welsh-language poetry. The English editor, Amy Wack, says: 'The English language poets here seem less concerned than previous generations with questions of identity'. The Welsh editor, Grahame Davies, says that many

---

[13] See Bobi Jones, 'Anglo-Welsh: More Definition', *Planet* 16 (Feb/March 1973), pp. 11-23.

of the poems in Welsh 'address questions of politics, identity and culture which are crucial to the condition of belonging to a minority linguistic community'.[14] It would appear from these editorial comments that Roland Mathias was right when in his introduction to the anthology *Green Horse*, he doubted whether the 'future will long contain what could meaningfully be called 'Anglo-Welsh' poetry'.[15]

The contents of the anthology bear out the difference of emphasis between the Welsh and English-language Welsh poets. Interestingly, this is true even when a younger poet plays a variation on the traditional nature/culture metaphor, as Owen Sheers does in 'Learning the Language'. The poem begins:

> Beneath the old oak in Llanddewi,
> in tiny brains of mistletoe
> showing in silhouette against the white sky;
>
> this was where to find them.
> Hard knots of hair and mucus
> the paper twistings of a nervous hand,
>
> packaged and pulled in the guts of an owl,
> dropped with an upward swallow,
> a single feathered heartbeat in the throat.[16]

Sheers wittily recycles the metaphor of Welsh as a natural language and R. S. Thomas's image of Wales as the corpse of a nation. The owl pellets 'translate in the warm water', 'disclosing broken histories of bone'. From the resulting patterns the poet arranges 'death sentences'. This is an ambiguous image: it might refer to the Welsh language, or to what the language means to the poet. Welsh might therefore be either a dying language, or a language that kills. 'The old oak in Llanddewi' provides a resonant setting, bringing together the Druid tree and Dewi Sant; 'tiny brains of mistletoe' reinforce the suggestion of the Druid inheritance. But what does it imply? Does it mean that if Sheers were to adopt the mantle of bard in a traditional sense he would be passing a death sentence

---

[14] Amy Wack and Grahame Davies, eds., *Oxygen: beirdd Newydd o Gymru: new poets from Wales* (Bridgend: Seren, 2000), p. 11.
[15] *Green Horse*, p. 22
[16] *Oxygen*, p. 14.

upon his ambition as a poet writing in English? Or could it mean that he, like Dylan Thomas, might become an established poet in English through covert use of Welsh 'magical' powers? The questions probably are not the point of the poem, but I think they are not entirely beside the point. Certainly, the final focus of the poem is not upon the language, but upon the poet himself:

> Laying out their patterns beneath the bright lamp,
> I try to piece it together on the damp black paper –
> arranging death sentences.

One may reflect that with the cultural marginalization of poetry, poets tend to withdraw from issues affecting the larger community, in which they may feel themselves to be an alien presence, into a preoccupation with poetic processes and functions

The title poem of *Oxygen* is by Kate Bingham. It begins thus:

> Before you make a start there may be something else
> you want to say, perhaps in a professional capacity
>
> or just because it came up recently in a dream,
> advertisement, or conversation and seems important.
>
> This is the diminishing return you have to fight all afternoon
> because a poem is like a rocket and the difficult bit
>
> falls back to earth with a terrific crash which no one notices
> for their ears are beating with drums and blood.[17]

As I suggested earlier, a rocket may be described as having affinities with a tower of words. Unlike actual views of Earth from space, the view from Kate Bingham's rocket is not highly exhilarating: 'Stones, tracks, / flowering cactus trees shrink into a khaki ocean'. The excitement is generated by the poetic 'flight' itself – the act of writing. And the poet describes the world to which she returns, in Larkinesque terms, as circumscribed by distant communication and mortality: 'the clock, the telephone, / the song of ambulances'.

---

[17] *Oxygen*, p. 14.

'Oxygen' appears to be a poem about the experience of poetic creation – an experience which distances the poet from the everyday world. The final line is: 'Say what it's like to be so far from home'. It would probably be a strained interpretation to claim that 'Oxygen' is a poem of exile, which plays a variation on a dominant theme of earlier English-language Welsh poetry. However, it does remind me of Joseph Brodsky's argument in his essay 'The Condition we call exile'.[18] There, Brodsky speaks metaphorically of the writer gravitating outwards from Earth in the space-capsule of his language. It is a positive image for Brodsky, an image befitting the idea of the poet as an autonomous individual, on which, as a man who had experienced totalitarian tyranny, he placed a high value. If this is relevant to Kate Bingham's poem, the reference is to the woman poet celebrating the liberating power of her imagination.

The question for any of us, of course, is what we are free *for*. Gwyneth Lewis, who is represented in *Oxygen* by poems in English and poems in Welsh, has written a poem in memory of Joseph Brodsky, and he is in fact quoted on the cover of Lewis's *Zero Gravity* (1998) as saying: 'Felicitous, urbane, heartbreaking, the poems of Gwyneth Lewis form a universe whose planets use language for oxygen and thus are habitable'. There, again, is the Russian émigré's idea of the autonomous imagination, of poetry forming a universe in which the poet and his or her readers can live. Even in her 'space' poem, 'Zero Gravity', however, Gwyneth Lewis is more down to earth, and true to her Welsh tradition which locates the universal in the particularities of Wales. As a poem that is both an elegy and a celebration, 'Zero Gravity' is in a major tradition of both literatures in Wales, and its corresponding concerns are: love, death, time, identity. The fourth section turns upon a castle:

> Bored early morning down on Cocoa Beach,
> the kids build castles. I know my history,
> so after they've heaped up their Norman keep
> (with flags of seaweed) I draw Caerphilly's
> concentric fortress. Five-year-old Mary,
> who's bringing us shells as they come to hand,
> announces, surprised: 'I am the boss of me'.
> She has a centre. In our busy sand
> we throw up ramparts, a ring of walls
> which Sarah crenellates. Being self-contained

---

[18] Joseph Brodsky, *New York Review of Books*, January 1988.

> can be very stylish – we plan boiling oil!
> But soon we're in trouble with what we've designed.
> So much for our plans to be fortified.
> Our citadel falls to a routine tide.[19]

As the poet says: 'I know my history'. Welsh poets usually do. And history, in the context of Wales, raises questions about relationships: between Wales and the outside world (especially Norman and English invaders), and between compatriots. Here, the little girl announces: 'I am the boss of me'. The Americanism expresses, in a childish way, the ideology of capitalist individualism. Her 'centre' harmonizes with the self-contained sandcastle, which perhaps refers ironically to the castle image or symbol that recurs in poems from Wales. This has a stylishness which summons up offensive actions – expressed light-heartedly, but the point is serious: 'we plan boiling oil!'. The sandcastle falls to natural processes, as real castles do. The latter fall as a result of human agency too: in the Welsh context, fortifications do not keep others out, or keep compatriots apart from each other, in stylish or aggressive isolation. John Donne said something similar: no man is an island. It is especially poignant to think that in Wales no woman, or man, is a castle either, whether made of sand or stone or words.[20]

Gwyneth Lewis's castle image and her sequence call to mind Gwyn Williams's eloquent description of the Welsh poetic tradition, which he perceived behind the poetic compositions of David Jones and Dylan Thomas. This is worth quoting at length:

> The absence of a centred design, of an architectural quality, is not a weakness in old Welsh poetry, but results quite reasonably from a specific view of composition. English and most Western European creative activity has been conditioned by the inheritance from Greece and Rome of the notion of a central point of interest in a poem, a picture or a play, a nodal region to which everything leads and upon which everything depends. The

---

[19] Gwyneth Lewis, *Zero Gravity* (Newcastle upon Tyne: Bloodaxe Books, 1998), p. 16. In the same book, 'The Pier' is 'in Memory of Joseph Brodsky'.
[20] The most sustained and complex exploration of castles as metaphor, symbol, and historical fact is Tony Conran's *Castles* (Llandysul: Gomer Press, 1993). It would be beyond the scope of this essay to deal with Conran's long poem adequately, though there are some points at which essay and poem touch.

dispersed nature of the thematic splintering of Welsh poetry is not due to a failure to follow this classical convention. Aneirin, Gwalchmai, Cynddelw and Hywel ab Owain were not trying to write poems that would read like Greek temples or even Gothic cathedrals but, rather, like stone circles or the contour-following rings of the forts from which they fought, with hidden ways slipping from one ring to another. More obviously, their writing was like the inter-woven inventions preserved in early Celtic manuscripts and on stone crosses, where what happens in a corner is as important as what happens at the centre, because there often is no centre.[21]

Gwyn Williams's idea of decentred poetic composition strikes me as being, after more than forty years, still relevant to the special opportunities open to poets drawing on Welsh poetic traditions. In the main, however, the opportunities are being neglected, so that one has an additional reason for wondering whether Roland Mathias was right in doubting the future of "what could meaningfully be called 'Anglo-Welsh' poetry".

Oxygen contains highly-accomplished work, quite a lot of which, in English, could have been produced anywhere, in the space capsule of the poet's language. Much of it centres, in one way or another, upon the self. We shall certainly see more work of this kind. I would like now however to say what I hope to see, as well. Some of the most notable English-language poetry from Wales during the past half-century has been in the form of sequences. One thinks of work by David Jones, Tony Conran, Chris Torrance, and of the prevalence of the poetic sequence among work by women poets: Lynette Roberts, Gillian Clarke, Christine Evans, Sheenagh Pugh, Catherine Fisher, Hilary Llewellyn-Williams, and Anne Cluysenaar. It might be suggested that one of the main reasons for the importance of the sequence to these and other poets is that Welsh poetry, in both languages, is primarily a poetry of relationship: between persons, between the individual and the group, between the poet and God, between people, language, and the land. The sequence offers, as it were, a stage that is large enough for the poet to explore relationships in depth and approach them from a variety of directions. Unlike the first-person lyrical poem, or even the dramatic monologue, the sequence affords opportunities for the adoption of multiple points of view.

Clearly there are special reasons why, since the 1970s, women, even more than men, have been forced to rethink questions of relationship;

---

[21] *The Burning Tree,* p. 15.

above all there is the issue of patriarchy and all that it implies. But while English-language Welsh women poets, such as Hilary Llewellyn-Williams, and Gillian Clarke in 'Letter from a Far Country', have tackled assumptions of male authority critically the women poets have approached the subject of relationships in other ways too. Gillian Clarke also introduced into 'Anglo-Welsh' poetry of relationships the experience of the poet as mother. Ruth Bidgood extended the tradition of writing about the connections between the generations, in a landscape which the living share with the dead. At this point in discussing such a subject one needs to be especially careful to avoid defining poets narrowly in terms of gender. Male poets, too, write about relationships, and Wordsworth, in his 1802 Preface to *Lyrical Ballads*, famously defined the Poet as 'carrying every where with him relationship and love'. It is clear, nevertheless, that women poets, since the 1960s, have gained the confidence to deal questioningly with every aspect of traditional relationships, in ways that would have been inconceivable to Wordsworth, for whom the Poet was 'a man'.

In Gwyn Williams's terms, the sequence is a form especially suited to showing that 'what happens in a corner is as important as what happens at the centre'. By means of this form, I believe, male and female poets will continue to explore, from many different angles, where, and what, and who they are. In Wales, moreover, they will continue to reveal the 'corner' as the 'centre' that it is.

A poetry of relationship can scarcely be divorced from a concern with identity. In the 1960s and 1970s in English-language Welsh poetry this had a strong nationalist emphasis. This has diminished generally in the past twenty years but not vanished. The question of Welshness and all that it implies in cultural and political terms is hard for a poet to escape from in Wales, even if he or she wants to. It is also difficult for the poet in Wales to take to the space capsule of language – the triune reality of history, land and language itself militates against it. Movements that have occurred elsewhere in the West since the 1970s have taken place in Wales also, with special emphases – for example, the rise of women's poetry, and the growth of poetry with an ecological concern. Poetic competence is widespread – a happy development due in part no doubt to the emergence of creative writing courses. By the same token, real originality is rare; but it always is. There is a craft tradition in Wales, which gives priority to the 'well-made' poem. This can be an advantage, and the expert handling of traditional forms can result in a highly original poetry, as we see in the work of poets as different from each other as Roland Mathias and Tony

Conran. There can however be disadvantages to established conventions whether of free verse or formal verse, too. At a time of changing relations between human beings and the world, as in new ecological thinking, any conventional making can be a liability: craft conventions, no less than 'free' self-expression, can work against new ways of seeing and thinking, which require formal and linguistic innovation. In my view younger Irish poets are currently showing more imaginative daring than their counterparts in Wales.[22]

But there are always poets who, because of their originality, we do not hear about – as, for example, most of his contemporaries did not know about William Blake, and, among Victorians, only a very few of his friends had any knowledge of Gerard Manley Hopkins's poetry. This is a time of variety in English-language Welsh poetry; only consider three recent books, lloyd robson's *cardiff cut*, Mike Jenkins's *Coulda Bin Summin*, and Samantha Wynne Rhydderch's *Rockclimbing in Silk*. These would suggest that at least three markedly different kinds of poetry are alive in Wales: the agile personal or dramatic lyric, the dialectal voicing of personae, and the demotic epic monologue, drawing on Welsh urban lifestyles as the American Beats drew on their lives and times.

In each case the writing has some bearing on the subject of the poet, language and the land. Consider for instance Samantha Wynne Rhydderch's 'The Lighthouse Keeper's Daughter', from *Rockclimbing in Silk*:

> was the first to see the dead musician's
> eyes at dawn, blue and immense
>
> as Llangorse Lake where his voice
> would echo from water to rock to
>
> water. That was before the migraines
> bleached her tongue, combing her skull
>
> each night until mute with pain she
> polished cobalt vowels in the wind.
>
> The whiteness throbbed round
> and round, firm and eternal as

---

[22] For a study of the Irish poets Randolph Healy, Billy Mills and Maurice Scully see David Anwn, *Arcs Through* (Dublin: Coelacanth Press, 2002).

> this glass tower, a prism
> practising madness: light, limb, dark,
>
> blade, light, clover, dark, lake, light,
> dark, wound, dark, dark.

With its startling images and intense, elliptical lyricism, this communicates an essentially personal experience of pain, loss, mental distress; not private, but experience such as another person may feel, without necessarily being able to articulate it in other terms. One may think it a poem in which the poet has expressed something barely expressible, but formative of her sense of language, her imagination. What is especially interesting, then, is the role of the public images in the poem, the specifically Welsh references: to Llangorse Lake and the Merlinesque 'glass tower'. As with the poem by Owen Sheers, it is not clear whether these are intended to invoke the meanings they carry in Welsh mythology, or whether they are being 'translated' into the language of the poet's inner world.

Mike Jenkins's use of language in *Coulda Bin Summin* is very different from Samantha Wynne Rhydderch's. The Merthyr voice in 'Gwyn Alf' celebrates the late socialist historian:

> ee spoke like one of us...
> Ee brung it up t'date,
> constructin a buildin
> o' sights an smells
> is stammer a-drillin
> ands framin windows,
> is fag the chimlee.
> An oo owns 'is ouse?
> ee seemed t'say...
> ee laid a track
> f'tram or train, is spinnin brain
> 'maginin a future town
> where we'd get off, t'larf
> an eat an sing under-a roof
> of-a place we'd made.

As the historian may have given a voice to his people, yet drawn his gifts from their human worth, so Jenkins the poet aspires to speak 'like one of us'. The poetic risks in this are enormous, but one feels that Mike Jenkins, like Wilfred Owen, cares more in case one of the people whose experiences he is voicing should say 'No Compris!',[23] than that a literary critic should find fault with his poetic art. He does, nevertheless, employ traditional means. Here, for example, the image of the building is as central to the poem as the tower is to Dylan Thomas's 'Poem in October' or the cottage to Gillian Clarke's 'Blaen Cwrt'. And it holds its place in the poem for the same reason that the other images do in theirs: the building is an embodiment of the relationship between poet, language and land. Thus, the building in 'Gwyn Alf' is effectively an extension of Gwyn Alf Williams ('is fag the chimlee'); it is made out of the historian and his words, however, only in the sense that he showed the people the places they themselves had made, and of which they could take possession. Not a castle or a cottage or a lighthouse or a space capsule in this case, but a Merthyr (and by extension a socialist, working-class Wales) the people could call their own.

The best way to give a fair impression of lloyd robson's *cardiff cut* in a brief discussion of it is probably to quote the opening, since this suggests the kind of writing it is, though without doing justice to its variety. This, then, is how the writing begins:

> sunnyday but cold & slightwindy, gallopt inta town on the back of a cupa/bacon sarnie, turnd me ankle on corner of newport & fitzalan, leaping out the way of a taxi. nasty stitch in the bargain.
>
> jumpt train wi no ticket as standard. rode the silverbrown doublescore to newport, graveltrack run of quadruple scars watchin steelbars curve soar curl across cities & moorland, via splottbridge hundred yards from me own front door, but no platform.
>
> dock cranes & powerstat, transporter bridge & landfill site, westbound train goes passt window, inches from me glasssquasht nose in the corner of doorwell & toilet the corridor someone askt if i've change but i'm distant.

---

[23] The reference is to Wilfred Owen's comment on his poem 'Spring Offensive' to Siegfried Sassoon.

This is egalitarian writing – witness the absence of capitals, which includes the poet's name among the entire 'materials', and the social attitudes that are immediately apparent in this passage. lloyd robson's use of demotic language, however, is quite different from Mike Jenkins's. *cardiff cut* is a consciously literary work, which does not present itself, as *Coulda Bin Summin* does, as if it were speech. It suggests literary influences as diverse as e.e. cummings, James Joyce, Gerard Manley Hopkins, Jack Kerouac, but these are less important than its foregrounding of the fact that it is *writing*. Hence the compound words with their compact imagism; hence the sense impressions and dynamic, kinetic verbal expression. What is most impressive about this is that the persona and his way of life (which includes his way of seeing and feeling) are *in* the language and the rhythms. And he is *in* the place, so that what he renders in words is a Wales that has never been seen before, as Roy Fisher revealed Birmingham in *City*. A Wales not seen only, but, in a particular way, lived in. *cardiff cut* shows us 'cities and moorland' – the subject of other English-language Welsh writing – but it also shows us places, and ways of being and seeing and speaking in those places, that have not been revealed so intimately before. As a castle can embody the relationship between poet, language, and land in other poems, it is life in the city streets that performs a similar function here.

As these works by Samantha Wynne Rhydderch, Mike Jenkins and lloyd robson show, there is a good deal of diversity in English-language Welsh poetry today. If variety is good for poetry, then this is a healthy time for poetry in Wales. What I wonder, though, is who the readers are. That is to say, are Rhydderch, Jenkins, robson and other poets specialists reaching different groups of readers, or is there a readership genuinely open to different kinds of poetry? My fear is that the former may be the case. If it is, then poets who see differently – outside any of the prevailing orthodoxies or established alternative currents – will have a lean time of it. But, it may be said, they always do. What poetry needs is more readers with disinterested critical passion, more openness to the unexpected. The protean Taliesin is the symbolic genius of Welsh poetry in both languages. Our need is to be able to follow that genius as it manifests itself in new and surprising incarnations.

'Adventurers in Living Fact': The Poetry of Dick Davis, Robert Wells, and Clive Wilmer

Shade Mariners, published in Cambridge in 1970, brought together poems by three young English poets, Dick Davis, Clive Wilmer, and Robert Wells. They had been students at King's College, Cambridge, and the selection of their poetry had an introduction by their former supervisor, Tony Tanner. It is a deservedly serious introductory treatment, in which Tanner describes how the poets differ from one another, while discerning 'in the book a certain homogeneity or inter-relatedness of interests'.[1] Now, nearly forty years on from that early selection, when each poet has achieved a considerable body of work, affinities are still discernible, although the differences between the three poets are strongly marked.

A common characteristic of Davis, Wilmer, and Wells from the outset was the need they felt for formal control, and the pleasure they took in it. Tanner mentions Thom Gunn as an influence on their work. More surprisingly for the period, he says 'they have been influenced by such different writers as Emily Dickinson, Tennyson, and William Collins respectively'.[2] Each still bears the marks of these early influences. Davis's shorter poems show what he has learned from Emily Dickinson, Wilmer has benefited from his studies of Victorian poetry and prose, and Wells from his reading of 18th century poetry. But their use of tradition goes far deeper than the naming of influences suggests. Each has developed a contemporary voice from an intelligent use of diverse traditional resources, and their originality lies partly in the creative relations they have established with the past.

Formal control in the poems in *Shade Mariners* coexists with inner turbulence and experiment. None of the poets is concerned only with the expression of his subjectivity, although each is embarked upon a search for identity, conducted in an uncertain time, and under the shadow of what appear to be past securities. Each has a strong sense of the world over against the self, and may be described, in the words of a poem by Yvor Winters, as an 'adventurer in living fact'.[3] Dick Davis would later

---

[1] Tony Tanner, 'Introduction', *Shade Mariners* (Emmanuel College, Cambridge: Gregory Spiro, 1970), p. 1.
[2] Ibid., p. 7.
[3] 'Quod Tegit Omnis', *The Collected Poems of Yvor Winters* (Manchester:

write a fine book on Yvor Winters, *Wisdom and Wilderness*, and the tension between these terms, between the mind or grounded self and the forces with which it has to contend, define from the outset the area in which the three poets venture.

A mere glance at the shapes of Dick Davis's poems on the pages of his new book, *A Trick of Sunlight*, reveals his passion for formal control. The resulting impression is both true and potentially misleading. As well as a poet, Davis is a leading Persian scholar and translator, a man of culture with a wide range of cosmopolitan interests. He has a gift for epigram and a wit both funny and mordant, but there is nothing of the 'academic' poet about him. Reading Davis, in fact, reminds us that the truly cultured poet is the one who knows wildness, and the need to create order. The first poem in his new book discloses the inwardness that is perhaps the principal source of Davis's verse:

> 'The heart has its abandoned mines…'
> Old workings masked by scrub and scree.
> Sometimes, far, far beneath the surface
> An empty chamber will collapse;
> But to the passerby the change
> Is almost imperceptible:
> A leaf's slight tremor, or a stone
> Dislodged into the vacant shaft. [4]

Here, the most intimate experience is given classic expression, and hidden subjectivity gives shape to objective form. Another poem, 'Chagrin', begins: 'In middle age, to my chagrin I find / That death and sex preoccupy my mind' (*TS*, 27). This is neatly expressed, but not merely clever. The title poem of an earlier Davis collection, *Touchwood*, likened 'identity' to 'this twisted tree / The lightning struck'.[5] Another poem speaks of 'that sense / Of self-inflicted psychic violence, / A mayhem of the spirit that destroyed / My youth and left a suicidal void'. In the new book 'Getting Away' (*TS*, 3-4) recalls childhood experiences which indicate that the choice before the young Davis was between self-maiming or being scared to death. He is not a confessional poet: he does not involve the reader

---

Carcanet Press, 1978), p. 102.
[4] Dick Davis, *A Trick of Sunlight* (Athens, OH: Swallow Press/Ohio University Press, 2006), p. 1, hereafter referenced *TS* in the text.
[5] Dick Davis, *Touchwood* (London: Anvil Press, 1996), p. 23.

in details of his personal suffering; he does however show the pressures involved in shaping both a life and a poem.

Davis, then, is a classical poet who opposes a sense of order to inner and outer forces threatening human identity. Like Yvor Winters, he has a sense of underlying darkness, and the need to resist it with wit and clarity, as well as humour. The result in his best poems is a rare poise, like a graceful dancer on the edge of an abyss. His art is in a profound sense defensive. As in the following poem, where the snow represents chaos, he is aware of the attractions as well as the dangers of the forces he needs to resist.

> Do you remember those few hours we spent
> Enchanted by the pictures at the Frick?
>
> Whole rooms – thank God! – abandoned to mere charm,
> To versions of *douceur* and dignity
>
> (As if the two of them encompassed all
> That might be said of life without a shudder);
>
> And in the atrium the fountain plashing,
> The almost silence, and the little frog.
>
> Then, as we stepped outside, the swirling snow. (*TS*, 19)

Davis's gift for epigrammatic brevity is one aspect of his considerable range as a poet, which includes a magical lyricism, as in 'Water' (*TS*, 5), and acid or exuberantly humorous satire. The poet who writes a four-line poem beginning, 'I lay down in the darkness of my soul' (*TS*, 35), is the same man who produces 'William Macgonagall Welcomes the Initiative for a Greater Role for Faith-based Education' (*TS*, 43).

Tony Tanner does not mention Yvor Winters in his introduction to *Shade Mariners*, but the spirit of Winters may be assumed as a guide for Robert Wells and Clive Wilmer as well as Dick Davis. Clarity, control, and order mattered equally to the three young poets. In each instance, one is aware that, as for Winters, their need to find and maintain a secure identity required the exercise of these virtues. For Davis and Wilmer their sense of the historical or mythical past has helped to shape their quest. Wells is no less of a literary traditionalist, as his fine translations of Virgil and Theocritus show, but he is also, first and last, a nature poet. From the start, physical work in the countryside has been one of his principal subjects. He is a superb descriptive poet, as this passage about catching crayfish from his new book, *The Day and Other Poems*, shows:

> Ducking beneath its roof of leaves we entered
> The riverbed, I following - and waded
> Upstream, bent over to scrutinize the pools.
> There crayfish hung by ones and twos unmoving
> In still grey water out of the main current,
> Or stalked invisibly, grey as the water,
> Or scooted backward with a flap of the tail
> Through a sudden clouding of stirred mud, our hands
> Darting to take hold of them as you showed me,
> Between finger and thumb, clear of the pincers
> Behind the whiskered head, and lift them away,
> Tail aflap and pincers impotently stretched
> (You held one out, smiling at its vain flourish).[6]

Wells's mature poetry, as here, has a wonderful lucidity. But there is more to it than the word 'description' accounts for. He has shown sensitive attention to physical details since his early work, as in the 'The Winter's Task'. But that poem also showed something else, a shadowing of the spoken by the unspoken. This may be described also as an absence or a lack, which the later poems help to explain.

Wells is a poet of desire, and a poet of companionship. He is a poet who seeks, above all, bodily contact with the other, and with the world. This means he has, too, a sense of separateness, of incompletion as well as completion. In 'The Forester: Five for S.A.' he writes of a companion with whom he worked on Exmoor:

> A quickening knowledge
> Joined you to what surrounded you, vast views
> Of near and far, spacious and intricate;
> A field of adventure in which you moved
> Secret and cautious, or running like a boy;
> Calculating as far as you could, then reckless,
> Agilely daring... (*DOP*, 10)

---

[6] Robert Wells, 'Adamo'. *The Day and Other Poems* (Manchester: Carcanet Press, 2006), p. 29, hereafter referenced *DOP* in the text.

'Quickening knowledge' describes well the knowledge Wells seeks, which results in a pastoral poetry touched with eroticism. The theme is beautifully encapsulated in the first poem used as an epigraph to his new book:

> *He knelt, placing his hands*
> *On the stones beside the stream*
> *And bent his face to the water*
>
> *For the lips*
> *That would not shape themselves to his.* (*DOP*, 8)

Wells writes poems of explicit desire, notably in the third section of his new book concerning his Indian lover, but the sexual and spiritual elements in his poetry also express an attitude towards reality, a desire for participation, for being fully present in the world. As both love poet and nature poet, his subject is also in a sense metaphysical, since it concerns both the relation of body and spirit, and the quest for wholeness. The poles of experience defining the 'field of adventure' in Wells's poetry are immersion and separateness, belonging and isolation. Looking back now at the passage about catching crayfish one can appreciate how subtly the description of entering the riverbed realises a shared experience of participation in reality. The Exmoor and Italian landscapes of his new book are more richly peopled than is usually the case in his earlier work, but, whether implicitly or explicitly, Wells's poetry has consistently sought identity through relationship between self and other, and man and the natural world.

Davis, Wells, and Wilmer can all be described as metaphysical poets, who are concerned with fundamental questions of human identity and relationship, and with the realities of sex and death. Like Winters's idea of the poet they are 'adventurers in living fact'. But whereas the first two show a classical stoicism in their attitude towards experience, Wilmer has emerged as a Christian poet. 'Inwardness', 'ghostliness' and 'nothing' are among the words haunting his new collection, *The Mystery of Things*, whose central long poem is 'Stigmata', and George Herbert, Henry Vaughan, and Dante are among the poets he quotes or alludes to. The epigraph to 'Stigmata VII', 'Spiritual Biography', quotes Johannes Tauler on Christ as 'the Door': 'We must enter by this door, by breaking through nature, and by the exercise of virtue and humility'.[7] Love is the shaping

---

[7] Clive Wilmer, *The Mystery of Things* (Manchester: Carcanet Press, 2006), p. 52, hereafter referenced *MT* in the text.

experience of the book: a painful and ecstatic experience of sexual love, which involves the wound of desire: 'The body vulnerable to its desire // Seeks out another who is vulnerable' (*MT*, 53). Violence ('breaking through nature') is integral to love as thus experienced and understood:

> There is no faith or hope that does not know
> The odour of carnality, nor love
>
> The neighbourhood of animals: lost sheep,
> The ox and ass, the reek of stable straw,
> The child at the swollen breast nodding asleep,
>
> Who born in pain will end in pain, his bonds
> Unbroken breaking him, his inwardness
> Leaking into the world through his five wounds. (*MT*, 53)

In the past Clive Wilmer's poetry has drawn sustenance from his interest in Victorian literature (Tennyson, Ruskin, the Rossettis, Morris) and culture. With the emphasis of his new poetry, Shakespeare and the metaphysical poets of the 17th century are his models. From the beginning, his interest in monoliths and architecture has corresponded to a sense that he 'builds' his poems with care. This is still the case, but the model now is Donne rather than any Victorian writer:

> Monuments of the time of the Black Death
> Might house two effigies: beauty above
> In all its earthly splendour – like a meadow
> Embroidered with the thousand flowers of May;
> The other effigy, laid out beneath,
> Foretells the flayed cadaver. You, my love,
> Who walk with death, lie down beside his shadow,
> The focused knowledge of your own decay. (*MT*, 51)

In 'Stigmata' and other poems in his new book Wilmer renews the language of incarnational poetry. Wounded in body and spirit, he writes at the bidding of an impulse composed of pain and passionate desire that evidently breaks through his own defences. Breaking through nature in this sense results in an access of poetic power. He explores his themes in terms shared with mystics and metaphysical poets, but also, like Donald

Davie and Thom Gunn, he keeps open connections between Ezra Pound's modernism and Winters's classicism. 'The Falls', for example, is a modernist composition, which, while echoing Dante and Henry Vaughan's 'The Waterfall', Ruskin and St Paul, is formally akin to Davie's modernist 'poems about the sacred', in *To Scorch or Freeze* (1988):

> the sun and the other stars
> > the beating heart
> > > the snow-melt
>
> driven, crying
> of this steep place afraid
> > > the common pass
> ...
> immutable change
> > made and remade
> laws finer than any known of men
>
> from things made
> > being seen and understood
> > > the invisible things
>
> each frill and fibre
> > > eternal power (*MT*, 41)

With delicacy of touch as well as with 'strong lines' Wilmer takes on the challenge of writing a modern religious poetry. His book is dedicated 'To the Memory of Masters and Friends'. These include Donald Davie, Tony Tanner, and Thom Gunn. Tony Tanner, of course, identified some of the preoccupations of Clive Wilmer and of Dick Davis and Robert Wells in his intelligent and generous introduction to their work in 1970. He was convinced that their poetry 'deserves to be discussed in an entirely serious way'.[8] Sadly, it has rarely received sustained discussion despite the fact that over the past thirty-five years it has more than justified Tanner's expectations. One may reflect that this is due in part to the originality each poet has shown in developing his work in relation to traditional poetic methods. One result of this is that they have kept open connections with the past, showing the life to be found in established

---

[8] *Shade Mariners*, p. 1.

formal and linguistic resources, but also drawing upon wisdom contained in classical and religious traditions. 'Adventurers in living fact', they have boldly ignored fashions from which, every decade or so, 'new' verse is made. In honouring their art, they have achieved a rare seriousness.

A Story of a Poem and a Sculpture

The story begins with a visit to the site of the Garden Festival at Ebbw Vale one Saturday morning early in February, 1992. Lee Grandjean, the sculptor, and I had been working together for several years on an exhibition and a book, *Their Silence a Language*, involving sculpture and drawing, poetry and prose. Now, late in the day, we had been invited to collaborate on a project on the Festival site. Neither of us was a complete stranger to this part of Wales, but we were both outsiders, and we approached the place attentively, alert to the possibility of a work that would respond to the nature and history of the valley, instead of imposing an alien vision.

At first, the experience of being shown over the site by the Visual Arts and Crafts Co-ordinator was rather depressing. Pavilions and other brightly coloured buildings had been put up in the middle of the valley, where the great British Steel Corporation works had formerly stood, and they looked, even from a short distance, like an outpost of Disneyland set down frivolously in the midst of a ruined industrial landscape. In fact, work on the Festival buildings, and on clearing the site, was still going on, and men wearing hard hats were drilling and driving dumper trucks and bulldozers and lorries in and around the area, in which numerous sculptural and artistic projects were already *in situ*. Our purpose was to find a place for our project. In grassy areas beside the rough tracks winding steeply up the hillside, I noted a shallow covering of soft earth over iron-hard slag.

Once out of sight of the Festival encampment, I came alive to the place and Lee began to see possible sites for a sculpture. Just over a ridge that hid the pavilions below, but still within the Festival area, a small pond of blue-grey water was rippling and brimming its banks, filling the hollow of what had once been an opencast mine. On the other side of the fence alongside the pond three ponies were grazing in a green field and on the far side of the field was a farm, which had been there before industry came to the valley. Standing by the pond looking back across the valley to the other side, we could see several rows of terraces, which seemed to end arbitrarily, on moorish hillsides that swept on, up and up, high above them to a mountainous ridge. Above us, slopes with outcrops of rock, sheep that appeared to be the same greeny-grey colour as the thin grass, and rock quarry faces, rose as steeply to a facing ridge.

From here we could see something of where we were – below us, the dead industrial valley (but with the noise of men at work on the Festival site), a vast area of heaped-up and partially cleared and levelled slag, and farther up, under the town of Ebbw Vale (which couldn't be seen from where we were standing), the valley of living industry, with long roofs of the tinplate works and tall, smoking chimneys.

We looked at the trees on the hillside above us – oaks and beeches, standing apart, black against the grey-green slopes. There was also a blueness round about – in the water, in shale, in the slate-roofed terraces, in mist in the valley.

The trees were not big, but they were gnarled and looked very tough. 'They've fought their way into existence,' Lee said; 'you can see it by their shape.' Near the pond was an old birch, a tree that forked from its trunk and had a great shock of twisting branches; it too, like the oaks and beeches, showed the struggle to grow. An old oak post was stuck in the ground in front of the birch: a fence post with strands of rusted wire bitten into it.

What could we make in this place? I had been thinking of Waldo Williams's cloud of witnesses; of some kind of witness that the trees and the fence post seemed to bear, and of the pond as an eye. It was a place for looking; and I was all the time uneasily aware that we could only look, not knowing the life of the valley as it had been, or the life as it was, but looking with the respect and imagination that is the least we owe to people who have borne the passage of a great history in their bodies and minds, and is perhaps the most we can pay. Later, I was tempted by a romantic gesture. Remembering the clouds over Mynydd Bach and feeling the fascination of mountain ridges and views from on high, I thought of Idris Davies standing in the ruins of Dowlais seeing 'the ghosts of the slaves of the Successful Century/Marching on the ridges of the sunset' and hearing them curse him because 'they could not forget their humiliation'.[1]

And what, now, of the language of socialism, which had been spoken in the Valleys of south Wales with rare force and meaning, and is still spoken there, but with little power? A political vision was forged in this place, a vision which achieved, practically, welfare for all, or at least an approximation to that ideal; and is now widely scorned or met with indifference, and can seem as derelict as the industries whose peoples once sustained it. This was not Waldo Williams's *bro*; but in the Valleys,

---

[1] Idris Davies, *Gwalia Deserta* (London: Dent, 1938), p. 16.

for all the demoralization of unemployment, perhaps one might still feel that a sense of brotherhood isn't only to be mocked as an outmoded sentiment.

In making anything here there would be a problem of language, in case one's words were only alien, or too loud, or sentimental. A sculpture, it seemed to me, might be the shape of witness; and a passage between past and present, standing at an edge between earth and sky, the natural and man-made worlds, and the living and the dead. And it might be so more effectively for its silence; or perhaps it might incorporate a few essential words, forged in the fire of the necessity to be simple, which belongs to the place.

At the site we had chosen there would be sounds: sounds of the wind 'that pulls the architecture about, that pushes through' (Lee); sound of the stream running by mossed rock outcrops down the hillside; sound of the train that will bring visitors to this part of the Festival site, (and once the rails that transformed Britain and joined the world in iron circuits were manufactured here). Thinking of this, Lee remarked that the valley would once have been full of sound – hammering, scream and shout of the rolling mill as it shoved steel through.

Steel and coal had carried the valley out of itself. People escaped from their work to the tops. Men brought their women up from the valley, and women brought their men. Poets found solitude in which to write poetry (as Idris Davies did in his valley). People could come here to get a whole sense of the valley, to see it as a container, as a story. A buzzard circled high in the sky, hung still, floated, glided, giving us another imaginative perspective. 'A place for a place,' Lee said.

* * *

What I have written above is more or less what I noted at the time, and set down more continuously soon afterwards: my impressions, my ideas and Lee's ideas and ideas we arrived at together. Then, in just over a fortnight after our visit to Ebbw Vale, I received from Lee a packet containing a sheaf of drawings, some with words alongside them, and a couple of pages of notes. Although we have worked closely together, in different places, it is important to understand that he in no way conceives sculpture in literary terms, or in any terms other than its own. Nor do I think of poetry as word made sculpture, in any literal sense. Our collaborations have been made possible by close imaginative affinities, expressed through different arts, with a sense of what we may learn from each other, provided the essential differences are recognized.

With regard to words, whether mine or his own, what Lee sees and isolates is their suggestion of sculptural potential, as image, shape and form. From his drawings and words, it was evident that the images he had drawn from Ebbw Vale, primarily from his own perceptions, but also from my notes and our exchange of ideas and impressions, were of forging and crucibles, 'fingers of flame', anvil and pulpit, and 'rooted witness'. By now the words were very much secondary to him, and he was working towards a group of vertical oak-carved sculptures, which combined shapes of flame and pulpit and crucible and vestigial human form, and integrated them impressively – that much was evident from the dynamic drawings, which already delineated forms that the sculptures would body forth. At this stage, the words he was considering incorporating in one or more of the sculptures were FLAME, HEART, WIND. His thinking about what he was making could also be inferred from his notes, which sometimes have the poetic quality of mind intent on stripping its vision to the bare essentials. For example:

Consider a high pulpit. Where the hands rest, a word is inscribed. There is the high seat from which to bear witness.

The strong and simply built, rooted, essential. When all else has been blown away. Fingers of flame rise from a great crucible held between rooted witnesses; still as posts. That which remains is a stronger tempered heart.

The imagery of flame is common to our way of seeing, as is the sense of a dynamic contained force. It isn't for me to say exactly how much I owe to Lee Grandjean's work, or he to mine; nor could I. All I want to do now is to place in context the poem I wrote as a contribution to our project, and after looking at Lee's drawings.

* * *

THE WITNESSES: EBBW VALE

1
Tongues of fire
that transfigured the earth,

joined it in iron circuits –
what have they left?

Three ponies graze
in a green field
above the valley.

These, and an old post
with strands of rusted wire,
keep out despair.

2
If there are spirits
they are like the trees
on the mountainsides
whose shape is the struggle to grow.

Iron did not master them.
Still they burn, over the seared
and dross-hard ground:

shocks of black, windblown flame.

3
What word will you carve
to speak for the dead
and not dishonour them
who forged a new world in the heart?

If there are sounds
they are valley voices,
twined with the turns of the wind
and the falling stream.

When silence fell
on the last hammer-blow,
what remained in the air
but a strand of their song?

4
If there are witnesses
the wind blows through their mouths,
rain pricks their eyes
as it dints the mountain pond
which was once a mine.

And around them weathers circle,
as the high buzzard turns,
drifts and falls,
and the far ridge crumbles away.

5
What do they see but defeat?

Eyes that have watched so long
see violence woven with hope.

When all has been blown away
what lasts is a twisted flame. (*CL*, pp. 284-86.)[2]

* * *

What I had attempted was at once an honouring and a questioning: an honouring of the place, the history, the life of the valley; a questioning both of our ability to render honour and of what remained, outlasting the dereliction. These are among the functions of poetry in which I still believe, in a time of tedious if sometimes brilliant 'self-expression', which marks the essential sameness of enclosed ego-experience, shut off from the struggle to uncover and articulate deep common human needs, in relation to our 'place' in nature and our spiritual being, which I believe is the concern of all serious art today. I owe my sense of these poetic functions partly to my years in Wales and to my awareness of writers such as Waldo Williams and Gwenallt, Emyr Humphreys and Idris Davies and David Jones. And as I believe in attempting to recognise what is common, in the depths, so I loathe populism in all its forms. The

---

[2] Subsequently 'Ebbw Vale', incorporated as part 2 of 'Variations on a theme by Waldo Williams' in my book *Our Lady of Europe* (London: Enitharmon Press, 1997), pp. 124-25.

common one discovers in one's own fundamental needs or not at all; populism is based on an external, condescending idea of 'the people' and what they need, and exploits and betrays them.

In the event, there was, literally, no place for our project at the Garden Festival, since the Committee turned down Lee's proposal for a group of sculptures incorporating words by the small pond. We can't say, therefore, exactly how that project would have developed. Lee went on, nevertheless, to make a sculpture in response to the place, and since I had written a poem, and we had enjoyed and benefited from our time together at the site, there is only one thing about the whole episode that I regret.

Lee Grandjean's sculpture *Witness* is in my view a great work of art. It is a sculpture with massive 'presence'. It combines images – crucible, steps, flame, column, abstract human form – and it belongs recognisably to his exploratory sculptural 'language'. But it can't be read like a poem, (or as a poem should not be read), separating image from image, disintegrating what the imagination apprehends as a whole into constituent parts. The sculpture is a sign that points within itself, a symbol that is the real thing; rather than being about a witness, it is an act of witnessing. In this work, too, as well as carving the wood, Lee has worked with fire, burning the hollow base of the column – the crucible image – black. And he has stained the oak with iron sulphide, blackening it, as the tree on the mountainside at Ebbw Vale had been blackened. It is a work that would have done honour to the place for which it was conceived. Initially, to people not familiar with the 'language' of Lee's sculpture, it would probably have seemed strange. But initial strangeness is almost a guarantee of authenticity in modern art, arising from and bodying forth a deep conception, erupting with rude force into the world of received ideas and conventional perceptions that most of us live in most of the time. But it is in such works that we can recognise what we are, and what is the shape of need that human life bears. When I saw Lee's *Witness*, it was standing against the wide East Anglian sky and the broad, undulating land, and in relation to the massive church towers that stand up out of the landscape. Since it was at Lee's home, with other works by him in his garden, and not far from his barn studio with its multitude of formed and partly formed sculptural images, I couldn't say that it was out of place. Yet this is my deep regret: that it will not bear witness to the place that inspired it and to which it is a powerful and moving tribute.

Mametz Wood:
The photographs of Aled Rhys Hughes

In Aled Rhys Hughes's photographs taken outside Mametz Wood rich sunlit corn fields end abruptly at a dark wall of trees. The juxtaposition of light and dark is an instance of the duality that characterises Hughes's photographic technique. Dark and light in this place are at once actual and metaphorical. Mametz Wood has a terrible history. Seen in relation to the open land the line starkly dividing light and dark calls up ideas of good and evil, past and present, life and death. In the shadowy interior of the wood dark and light are ambiguous, an entangled border more than a sharp division. In this liminal place, the evil of war was inextricably mixed with the heroism and endurance of men.

In the period 7-11 July 1916 Mametz Wood was the site of the 38th (Welsh) Division's first major engagement. Robin Barlow, in *Wales and World War One*, describes the wood that the Welsh troops were ordered to capture from the Germans:

> Mametz Wood occupied an area of approximately 220 acres, covered in thick undergrowth of hawthorn and briar intermingled with fallen trees and branches from previous bombardments, all of which would impede any progress on foot. Also on the floor of the Wood, there was a considerable amount of wire, which had been laid by the enemy during the respite from fighting after 1 July. There were still considerable numbers of standing trees of oak, beech and ash, averaging thirty to forty feet in height. The Wood measured about one mile from north to south and three-quarters of a mile from east to west at its widest point. Mametz Wood was divided by two straight rides and longitudinally by a third.[1]

The thick wood occupied by elite German troops formed a formidable objective. This was made more lethal by the line of attack, which was down a slope and then uphill in open country. Thomas Dilworth, in

---

[1] Robin Barlow, *Wales and World War One* (Llandysul: Gomer, 2014), p. 65.

David Jones and the Great War, draws on *In Parenthesis* and other first-hand accounts to describe the attack of 7 July:

> No man's land was 500 yards of wild, uncropped grass, thistles, wild flowers, and self-grown mustard and wheat. Like a mechanism perversely preset to move slowly, they walked across 60 yards of plateau, scurried down a steep 30 to 50 foot incline, and slowly walked up the bare, gradually rising slope towards high ground where the enemy waited, firing at them. The walk took four minutes, a passage through a maelstrom of rifle and machine-gun bullets, shrapnel and shell-casing fragments flying at every angle – a thousand potential deaths and maimings with no protecting cover. The noise was beyond hearing, the quaking earth erupting, the air thick with smoke, chalky dirt, steel, bits of flesh.[2]

This was an episode, on a smaller scale, of the major Somme offensive, in which, on 1 July, the total number of British, French and German casualties was immense. Robin Barlow gives the figure of 911 NCOs and other ranks and thirty-seven officers belonging to the Welsh Division killed between 7-11 July in the battle of Mametz. 'In addition,' he says, 'many hundreds more men would have been posted missing, their bodies never recovered'.[3] As Captain Llewelyn Wyn Griffith remarked, the bodies of the dead represented 'those who had to fall to prove to our command that machine guns can defend a bare slope'.[4]

The next major advance on the wood on 10 July was more successful, and after ferocious fighting and in scenes of terrible confusion, the wood was partially taken. Under a German artillery bombardment, the Welsh Division began to withdraw on 11 July. The withdrawal was completed the following day, when the 21st Division, which cleared the remainder of the wood, relieved them. Some weeks later German troops recaptured Mametz Wood, which they held to the end of the war.

Was the battle of Mametz, in which so many young men on both sides were killed or wounded, a success for the Welsh? Assessments of

---

[2] Thomas Dilworth, *David Jones in the Great War* (London: Enitharmon Press, 2012), p. 111.
[3] Barlow, p. 81.
[4] Ll Wyn Griffith, *Up to Mametz*, 1931 (Norwich: Gliddon Books, 1988), p. 228. All subsequent quotations from this book from this edition, referenced *UM* in the text.

both witnesses and historians differ. Siegfried Sassoon described the battle as 'a disastrous muddle with troops stampeding under machine-gun fire'. The historian, Colin Hughes, concluded that 'the Welsh Division, inexperienced and inadequately trained, pushed the cream of Germany's professional army back about one mile in most difficult conditions, an achievement that should rank with that of any division on the Somme'.[5]

But how is success or failure to be assessed in such circumstances?

Robin Barlow is right, surely, when he says: 'The name of Mametz Wood, perhaps like those of Aberfan or Senghenydd, is embedded deep in the Welsh psyche, immediately conjuring up images of needless loss of life, bravery, chaos and self-sacrifice'.[6] But how can a photographer today, or any of us, know anything about the reality of the battle? As Llewelyn Wyn Griffith said: 'there were two kinds of men in the world – those who had been in the trenches, and the rest'. (*UM*, p. 43.)

This is a truth of which a sensitive visitor, such as Aled Rhys Hughes, is acutely aware. He will avoid voyeurism by acknowledging its risk. According to Robert Adams, the American photographer: 'What we hope for from the artist is help in discovering the significance of a place'.[7] Hughes comes close to revealing the significance of Mametz Wood by acknowledging his distance from the events that made it famous. Moreover, he knows it as a place embedded in his psyche, as a Welshman. And he knows what the witnesses have told us, so that when he walks in Mametz Wood with his camera he will be mindful of a passage such as this from Llewelyn Wyn Griffith's *Up to Mametz*:

> Years of neglect had turned the Wood into a formidable barrier, a mile deep. Heavy shelling of the Southern end had beaten down some of the young growth, but it had also thrown trees and large branches into a barricade. Equipment, ammunition, rolls of barbed wire, tins of food, gas-helmets and rifles were lying about everywhere. There were more corpses than men, but there were worse sights than corpses. Limbs and mutilated trunks, here and there a detached head, forming splashes of red against the green leaves, and, as in advertisement of the horror of our way of life and death, and of our crucifixion of youth, one tree held in its

---

[5] Hughes and Sassoon are quoted by Barlow, pp. 82-3.
[6] Ibid., p. 59.
[7] Robert Adams, Beauty *in Photography* (New York: aperture foundation, 1987), p. 16.

branches a leg, with its torn flesh hanging down over a spray of leaf. (*UM*, pp. 231-2)

Part 7 of David Jones's *In Parenthesis* covers the same ground as *Up to Mametz*. Jones was a Private in B Company, Griffith a Captain in C Company. They came through the battle, survived the war, and, some ten years after the war, wrote their remarkable accounts of the battle of Mametz Wood. *In Parenthesis*, one of the greatest of all war books, was what first drew Aled Rhys Hughes to Mametz Wood, which he has visited on several occasions, making photographic studies, and entering deeper into its mystery. The writings, and especially David Jones's epic poem, have influenced his sense of the place, whose meaning he explores in his photographs.

There is a significant connection between poetry and photography in relation to war. Since the advent of photography in the nineteenth century photographs have worked together with poetry in evoking war landscapes and revealing the reality of war. Photographs and poems have memorialised war and fixed its images in our minds. Thus, Roger Fenton's *Valley of the Shadow of Death* brings to the Crimean War battlefield associations with Tennyson's 'The Charge of the Light Brigade' and Psalm 23. We see the American Civil War battlefields through the photographs of Matthew Brady and his associates and through Walt Whitman's poems. If the former emphasize desolation, the latter express personal emotion – though this is not to say photographs lack emotion. Wilfred Owen collected photographs of the dead and maimed to show to ignorant civilians, and Owen's poems, together with photographs of the Western Front, have contributed to our understanding of the First World War.

Some modern thinkers, notably Susan Sontag and Roland Barthes, associate photographs with death. This is not only because they show dead people, as in gruesome pictures revealing the horror of war, but because they show what is past. Photography bears the mark of mortality, and is the art most confined by the past: it reminds us that once living subjects are dead; it isolates person or object or event, separating them from the stream of life. Actual photographs of the First World War picture landscapes of death, with dead or wounded men, ruined buildings, shattered trees, and torn earth. Some subliminal sense of these is likely to emerge into our consciousness from time to time as we look at Hughes's photographs, which contain signs of the carnage and devastation that once made a waste land of Mametz Wood. His subject, however, is by no means exclusively death or horror, any more than these are exclusively the subject of *In Parenthesis*.

In Hughes's photographs the landscape in which Mametz Wood is situated appears today much as it would have done to the men of the 38th (Welsh) Division in July 1916. Except, of course, that we see it in the shadow of the slaughter that, for them, was to come. But the sun shines in these pictures of hilly chalk country interspersed with groups of trees, beyond the dark edge of Mametz Wood. To the troops arriving on 5 July 1916 with orders to take the wood, the landscape would have been reminiscent of parts of southern England, with which it shares geology and a history of cultivation. To them, it must have appeared at once homely and sinister. The names they gave to this French landscape, such as White Trench, Bunny Trench, Acid Drop Copse, and Caterpillar Wood, both designated military locations and laid claim to an uneasy intimacy. With hindsight, we know that the area that the men called Happy Valley, in which Jones's battalion went into reserve for brief respite on 8 July, became Death Valley. The sun still shines on it in Hughes's photograph of the area, but we see the innocent landscape with bitter knowledge.

Woods have been powerful presences in human history, and to this day they have kept something of their ancient aura. Woods are traditionally homely and alien, beautiful and sinister, 'dark' places in which the hero loses himself, and perhaps his life, or completes his quest. They are sacred in the dual sense of being both blessed and cursed, and they nourish a rich, ambivalent poetry. *In Parenthesis* includes an especially powerful evocation of the significance of woods. The scene occurs around Christmas 1915, some 7 months before the attack on Mametz Wood, when John Ball, 'posted as 1st Day Sentry, sat on the fire-step; and looking upward, sees in a cunning glass the image of: his morning parapets, his breakfast-fire smoke, the twisted wood beyond':

> Across the very quiet of no-man's land came still some twittering. He found the wood, visually so near, yet for the feet forbidden by a great fixed gulf, a sight somehow to powerfully hold his mind. To the woods of all the world is this potency – to move the bowels of us.
>
> To groves always men come both to their joys and their undoing. Come lightfoot in heart's ease and school-free; walk on a leafy holiday with kindred and kind; come perplexedly with first loves – to tread the tangle frustrated, striking – bruising the green.[8]

---

[8] David Jones, *In Parenthesis,* 1937 (London: Faber and Faber, 1978), p. 66. Subsequently referenced *IP* in the text.

The evocation of Biez Copse as 'the woods of all the world' comprehends the whole range of human experience, with a wealth of allusions to Malory and Arthurian Romance, *Y Gododdin* and *The Golden Bough*, Celtic history and myth, and folksong. To woods men

> Come with Merlin in his madness, for the pity of it; for the young men reaped like green barley,
> for the folly of it. (*IP*, p. 66)

The passage reinforces the intimacy between men and nature that characterizes *In Parenthesis*, and enhances the poignant imagery of men and trees entangled in a common destruction in Mametz Wood: 'stamen-twined and bruised pistilline/steel-shorn of style and ovary/leaf and blossoming/with flora-spangled khaki pelvises'. (IP, p. 170) In Mametz Wood, the poetry of 'the woods of all the world', as perceived in Biez Copse, continues in a different key, and David Jones's depiction of the war shows graphically 'the pity of it', and 'the folly of it'.

The emotions of the scene recall Wilfred Owen and other poets, unsparing in their rendering of the pity and folly of the war. But with David Jones there is a difference. Begun 10 years after the end of the war, *In Parenthesis* has the advantage of perspective. It combines the immediacy of terrible experience with a vision of ultimate meaning in the form of religious myth. Through images such as that of 'the young men reaped like green barley' David Jones intimates a metaphysical order, which is sacrificial and redemptive. It is a Christian vision that assimilates ancient pagan myth.

Aled Rhys Hughes's view of Mametz Wood has certain affinities with this vision of a restorative metaphysical order. He is not, however, a trespasser on the ground of the men who fought there, men like David Jones and Llewelyn Wyn Griffith, who won the right of a larger understanding. Questioning marks the spirit in which Hughes approaches Mametz Wood. Robert Adams, in *Beauty in Photography*, a book with special significance for Hughes, describes Beauty as 'a synonym for the coherence and structure underlying life'.[9] Art affirms Form: 'a framework that is larger than we are, encompassing totality invulnerable to our worst behaviour and most corrosive anxieties'.[10] These words can be applied, with caution, to what Hughes shows in his pictures of Mametz Wood.

---

[9] Adams, p. 24.
[10] Ibid., p. 25.

Seen in the light of 'a framework that is larger than we are', the beauty of Hughes's photographs shows in Mametz Wood and the surrounding land a restored nature and agriculture – a life continuous with the life that preceded the war. But things do not go on the same, blotting out memory. The landscape shows stark contrasts of light and dark, and the interior of the wood is green, with natural shadows that also evoke the darkening of hindsight. Light against dark suggests conflicting opposites: life and death, good and evil, peace and war. Shadows represent memories, but also foreground indefiniteness, the difficulty of seeing clearly, of knowing exactly what we are looking at. The uncertainty is first in the mind of the photographer. He shares his questions with us. What does it mean, this landscape of memory – other men's memory – this landscape of the dead, with shell craters and trench systems that look like ancient earthworks, and physical mementoes of the war lying among leaves and fallen timber?

A picture of branches fallen crosswise may suggest Llewelyn Wyn Griffith's 'crucifixion of youth'. But, as Hughes knows, it is not for a visitor long after the battle to impose a meaning on the place. Meanings may, however, be suggested. The fact of the many young lives lost or ruined, together with the witness of writers who participated in the battle, haunt the photographer, and help to determine what he sees. However much he observes the delicate beauty of new growth, the pressure of appalling memory makes his seeing ambivalent. Duality is written into the landscape and the photographer emphasises it through use of scale and compositional rhythms – in sunlit, open cornland and dark wall of the wood, in chalky, flinty fields pitted by craters and harrowed by trenches, in shadow and light among the trees. Some analogies with painting suggest themselves. In Paul Nash's post-war paintings of southern England, for example, the landscapes remember his war paintings. The 'new world' men have made, the world of dead men and shattered trees in cratered landscapes, has become assimilated to the ancient burial sites, and to the very configuration of the rolling chalkland hills.

The risk of voyeurism is a challenge to the photographer, as to any visitor or viewer. The Mametz War Memorial, sculpted by David Petersen and erected in 1987, makes a bold statement. The Welsh Red Dragon tearing at the barbed wire in which it is entangled says what it means. Hughes's photograph of young soldiers of today paying formal respect at the memorial makes a poignant image, reminding us how young many of the dead were, and warning us of the fate that may await these young men. But what are the motives of tourists with cameras? Do they remember the bitter humour with which the fighting men ironically foresaw 'a Cook's tourist to the Devastated Areas'? (IP, p. 186) Hughes certainly remembers; he knows that by 1919 Michelin's illustrated guidebook to the Somme had appeared, and Mametz village was being talked about as a picturesque ruin. He takes his pictures in full knowledge of the irony. His emotions are complex, and guilt is part of them. This, though, is not disabling. It is, rather, a moral quality, and a creative unease, which determines him to meet what Rowan Williams calls the photographer's challenge to 'stereotypical images and stock or sentimental responses'.[11]

As in his photographs of the Welsh landscape and coast, Aled Rhys Hughes is an artist drawn to liminal and numinous places, places where a patient artist attentive to mysterious presences may discern a sense of metaphysical order. Open to meanings not of his own making, he has a keen sense of what may be intuited but cannot be easily seen or shown. For the soldiers themselves, the battlegrounds, where they lived with death, were haunted places. The Western Front generated in the men a sense of the uncanny, as memoirs and art of the war show. *In Parenthesis*, more than any other book, captures this atmosphere of mystery, in a place charged with the presence of death. In this respect, its distinguishing feature is David Jones's use of pagan Celtic myth and Arthurian wasteland imagery. As a Welshman, Hughes is especially sensitive to the way in which this illuminates the life and death struggle enacted in Mametz Wood.

Woods are both naturally and symbolically mysterious places. Even today, any wood contains an echo of the primeval wildwood, and of forests that for centuries were dangerous places, the abode of robbers and outlaws, the lair of wild animals. For Britons, and especially for the Welsh, their aura recalls holy groves, places of worship and sacrifice for their Celtic ancestors. Any wood is both inviting and daunting, making us pause at the threshold with a sense of fearful excitement. What will we find if we walk or push our way in? Will we become lost? What is true of any wood is immeasurably truer of Mametz Wood. As Hughes's photographs show, it is naturally alive with green, leafy trees and undergrowth; but it is also a dark place, a place of evil memory, where the photographer walks with uncertainty. One of his most evocative photographs shows the shadow of the Welsh Dragon Memorial. The shadow lying on land outside the wood points along the line of advance to the dark wall of trees. What remains of all that heroic sacrifice but shadows?

---

[11] Rowan Williams, *The Edge of Words* (London: Bloomsbury, 2014), p. 195.

As well as shadow, Mametz Wood is full of mementoes. Sometimes, like the branches fallen crosswise, these form natural symbols. More often, they are enigmatic – signs that raise questions. Some we can only see in the photographs by looking closely – as the photographer has looked, requiring of the viewer an equivalent attentiveness. A faded photograph pinned to a tree suggests a story we can only guess at. Does it show a soldier killed or wounded in battle, and placed in the wood by a descendant as an act of homage? The wood is full of fragments telling unknown stories. We know what poppies mean. But what is the meaning of the numerous small Welsh flags attached to trees? Do they lay claim to the place for Wales? And what would that tell us about Welsh nationality and its debt to historical memory? The name Mametz may resonate in the mind with Aberfan and Senghenydd. As a grievous event, it may be embedded in the Welsh psyche alongside Gruffudd ab yr Ynad Coch's poem on the death of Llyweln ap Gruffudd, when 'the oaks beat together'.[12]

Entering Mametz Wood through Hughes's photographs we are entering this psyche. This is a place of old wounds, mental wounds, as real as the remains of trench systems, and of pride at heroic sacrifice. We may think of the sculpture of 'The Dying Gaul', the noble figure in which David Jones saw the Celtic 'defeat tradition'. The tradition is profoundly ambivalent, for upon the memory of defeat the Welsh have founded their survival as a nation. This is what can be seen in the spirit of Mametz Wood as Hughes reveals it: in half-light and darkness, in signs of the past in the present, in images of life and death. It can be seen too in contrasts between sharp definition and blurred focus, which emphasise uncertainty.

Mametz Wood was where men and nature underwent a mutually destructive action. Here, natural growth was subjected to mechanical destruction, and men and their machines were entangled in undergrowth and killed by falling trees. Human and natural powers were locked in deadly embrace, as were the Welsh and German soldiers. *In Parenthesis* is founded upon this polarity, as we see at the conclusion to the passage evoking 'the woods of all the world':

> Keep date with the genius of the place – come with a weapon or effectual branch – and here this winter copse might well be special to Diana's Jack, for none might attempt it, but by perilous bough-plucking.

---

[12] Gwyn Williams includes the original Welsh poem, 'Marwnad Llywelyn ap Gruffudd', and his English translation side by side in *The Burning Tree*, pp. 80-85.

> Draughtsman at Army made note on a blue-print of the significance of that grove as one of his strong-points; this wooded rise as the gate of their enemies, a door at whose splintered posts, Janus-wise emplacements shield an automatic fire. (*IP*, p. 66)

In his later work, David Jones would develop the two kinds of 'significance' shown here – poetic, mythological, religious in opposition to the mechanically functional – into his philosophy of conflict between sacred sign and utility. Aled Rhys Hughes, too, is an artist who evokes 'the genius of the place'; and in his photographs of Mametz Wood he shows how the war brought men and nature together to share an intimacy that destroyed both.

The war created a literal closeness to the earth. Men dug into it, seeking shelter; they were drowned in waterlogged trenches and craters; they were entangled in branches and crushed by falling trees. It created, too, a sense of kinship between men and nature, a common suffering, seen in a kind of equivalence between broken men and shattered trees. This intimate relationship between suffering men and ravaged nature appears in writings and paintings and contemporary photographs. What can be said of it positively is that it has influenced the modern ecological imagination.

It is with this imagination, in knowledge of the close relationship between men and nature, that Hughes approaches Mametz Wood. He shows a tree severed from its roots, hanging, without ground to grow in – an actual tree, but also a tree that bears the larger, symbolic significance. The image both reminds us of what the war did to men and trees, and prevents easy thoughts about nature's regenerative power. But that power is not denied: Mametz Wood today is once more a living wood. Another photograph shows a live shell among corn, which the farmer has ploughed round, as the agricultural year continues in spite of the war, and the earth absorbs its mementoes. Artillery shells rest by the base of a tree, unnatural but harmless occupants of the wood. Wood has grown round a shell, in what looks like a protective embrace. Other photographs show gnarls on trees caused by shells or bullets, but not unlike natural growths. Some look like totems. Overgrown trench systems might be ancient tumuli. A shell that looks like a strange creature has taken up residence on the woodland floor. Mametz Wood, originally used for hunting, has its own wild life, which includes deer and wild boar. Since the war, shell cases and other military fragments have become native to the place.

The photographs show how the fallen are remembered throughout the wood. Crosses and wreaths of poppies make small, but definite, statements of human value against the magnitude of the trees. They are not leaves, but they look as if they belong here. Welsh flags maintain a strong Welsh presence. They are commemorative, but we may wonder what claim they are also making, since flags are used to lay claim to places. This wood in France is a Welsh wood, a wood of Welsh memory, an outpost of the Welsh nation. But do the flags also claim victory? Here, we return to our question on first entering the wood: what is victory in such circumstances? It is what the photographs show that makes us especially cautious about offering opinions or making judgements.

Hughes is careful not to interfere with mementoes he comes upon in the wood. He has, however, photographed examples of trench art, such as a candleholder made from a shell case, and a paper knife made from a bullet. Each object speaks of a story we do not know. Objects represent the German dead too: a lamp, the sole of a boot, a belt buckle. Most evocatively, the photograph of a photograph: a funeral card that prays for 20-year-old Leonhard Schachtner, Soldat, 'Tod furs Vaterland'. One name, one brief history, but it stands for the tragedy of all the young lives lost in the battle of Mametz Wood.

Symbols occur as if naturally through the photographer's art. Cornland and ploughed, chalky fields, rolling hills, the dark wall of the wood, all reveal the presence of the past they have absorbed, a tragic modern history assimilated to the ancient dead. In the photographs we are seeing a landscape almost a century after a battle. At the same time, we are seeing it much as the men of the 38th (Welsh) Division saw it on 5 July 1916, with the homely yet alien hills at their backs, and the formidable wood, concealing the enemy, below and in front of them. Taken outside the wood, a photograph shows docks, like blood, moving towards the dark wall.

The men knew Mametz Wood as the Queen of the Woods on the Somme battlefield. David Jones gave the name a special significance in *In Parenthesis*:

> The Queen of the Woods has cut bright bows of various flowering.
> These knew her influential eyes. Her awarding hands can pluck for each their fragile prize.
> She speaks to them according to precedence. She knows what's due to this elect society. She can choose twelve gentle-

men. She knows who is most lord between the high trees and on the open down. (*IP*, p. 185)

Colin Hughes concludes his study of 'In Parenthesis as straight reporting' by recalling Jones's reaction to being shown photographs of Mametz Wood 50 years after the battle:

'It is clear from the photographs' wrote David Jones in 1969, remembering the wood only as a shell-torn waste-land, 'that the Queen of the Woods has revivified her groves. It reminds me,' he added, 'of the line from the folk song John Barleycorn,

    And Barleycorn stood up again and that surprised them all.'[13]

The folk song speaks of regeneration, death that gives rise to new life. It was poetry, in the form of religious myth, which for Jones ultimately held the significance of the battle of Mametz Wood. This was grounded in love, love of dead comrades, but also the sacrificial love that he perceived as the meaning of the universe. Llewelyn Wyn Griffith also saw the war in terms of his Christian inheritance. But his judgement of the battle was more sombre than Jones's:

Added to the burden of fatigue and grief, we were governed by a dark feeling of personal failure. Mametz Wood was taken, but not by us, it seemed; we were the rejected of Destiny, men whose services were not required. The dead were the chosen, and Fate had forgotten us in its eager clutching at the men who fell; they were the richer prize. They captured Mametz Wood, and in it they lie. (*UM*, pp. 259-60)

Jorge Luis Borges, in his lecture 'The Divine Comedy', quotes Homer, 'the gods weave misfortunes for men, so that the generations to come will have something to sing about', and Mallarmé, '"tout aboutit en un livre', everything ends up in a book". Borges concludes: 'something remains, and that something is history or poetry, which are not essentially different'. This chimes with Griffith's discovery:

---

[13] Colin Hughes, *David Jones The man who was on the field* (David Jones Society, 1979), p. 23.

> Common clay as we were, and far enough removed as we thought ourselves from the spun glass of the poet's imagining, we found ourselves betrayed into the very emotions they had sung. That the prose of war should prove the truth of poetry's tale of man's feeling – that it should now be easy to believe that some of those magic lines were indeed a reflection of the real thoughts of real men and women – that was an astonishing discovery. (*UM*, pp. 129-30)

It is true that what we know of the battle of Mametz Wood is poetry. This may be interpreted, in the broad sense of the word, as vision: the vision of *In Parenthesis*, and of *Up to Mametz*. Aled Rhys Hughes sees with his own eyes as an artist, but he also draws upon what these books have shown him. The result is a sequence of photographs that have their own visionary quality. In achieving this, Hughes's art helps us to discover the significance of the place.

The Experience of Landscape, Painting and Poetry

There is, I think, an art of seeing that applies equally to pictures and nature. It is a way of entering each attentively, and exploring what is there, and it enlarges the world, and induces a feeling of awe, which emphasises the bounds of one's knowledge and descriptive powers. It is an art which relates the person to the *other*, instead of reducing the *other* to the confines of the self. Thus, looking with delight at landscape art, as my mind and eye enter more fully into each composition, and at the same time recognise formal and thematic relationships among various works, I have an increasing sense of the limits of what can be said. As the Scottish poet Hugh MacDiarmid stood on a raised beach and felt, 'I look at these stones and know little about them',[1] so I stand in front of David Bomberg's *Trendrine Cornwall* and know the poverty of my vocabulary of colour, or in front of Mary Potter's *Sun on the Beach* and know that words like symbol and impression simply miss the painting's effect. The same is true of my experience of nature, which the pictures influence. I grew up in a home that was full of landscape paintings, mainly of water, light and trees, in constant movement and change. These were as 'natural' to me as the places outside the home that had inspired them. In course of time, I saw more in the places because of the paintings, and more in the paintings by the light of nature. But to see more is both to value what is revealed, and to feel acutely the difficulty of doing justice to it with words.

'Landscape' is a concept that points in two directions, to the picture in the frame and to part of the world outside the frame, and therefore raises unavoidable questions about the relation between art and reality. This is not the place to analyse that relation in depth, and in any case I would rather celebrate transactions between the two meanings of 'landscape'. To simplify, as I must in a limited space, it seems to me reasonable to suppose that each of the artists represented in the exhibition,[2] however proud or modest by temperament, first stood

---

[1] *The Complete Poems of Hugh MacDiarmid* Vol. 1 (Harmondsworth: Penguin Books, 1985), p. 423.
[2] *The Experience of Landscape*, paintings, drawings and photographs from the Arts Council Collection, South Bank Centre 1987-89. All the works of visual art discussed in this essay are reproduced in the catalogue. Except where noted otherwise, all the poems quoted or referred to are printed in the catalogue,

in front of a landscape and felt, like MacDiarmid, awed by something vastly greater than his or her knowledge. This supposition doesn't ignore the manifest differences between descriptive and visionary landscapes, as we see them in the window views of Charles Ginner and Winifred Nicholson, for example, or between different forms of abstraction, as in Brian Wynter's geometrical forms and Bomberg's painting, which calls to mind Van Gogh's prediction of an art 'closer to music, where colour would reign supreme'. Rather, it is based on the evidence of the pictures themselves, which shows that the artists have first experienced landscape, and that their work is an effort to attain further knowledge, whether through truth to impressions of the world or through non-descriptive elements. The Impressionist Alfred Sisley said, 'Every picture exhibits a place the artist has fallen in love with'. That has the vulnerability of all such general statements, but, as a description of landscape art, I like it very much, especially since love can take many different forms, and often includes or interacts with other, darker emotions.

Now, we are more inclined to look *at* pictures rather than *through* them, as if they were windows on their subjects. But although every real work of art is an object which makes creative use of its medium, I don't believe that a single one, from Palaeolithic cave paintings to the present day, exists *only* for its own sake. Art is a vision of the world, even if one describes it, less resonantly, as Emile Zola did, as 'a corner of nature seen through a temperament'. As far as the landscapes of Britain are concerned, artists such as Bomberg, Winifred Nicholson, Joan Eardley, and Michael Fussell do in their terms what Molly Holden does in her poem 'In this unremarkable island', which begins: 'We are always surprised by our weathers' (*EL*, p. 45). The artists too surprise us with remarkable, beautiful and mysterious effects of weather and light. Molly Holden was writing in a great tradition of English poetry, which includes contemporary poets as well as Wordsworth and Clare and Hardy. It is a tradition that shares the spirit of Constable's gratitude to the banks of his native Stour for making him a painter, and, like him, finds its art 'under every hedge and in every lane'. Coleridge describes Wordsworth's object in his poems in *Lyrical Ballads* as, 'to give the charm of novelty to things of every day, and to excite a feeling analogous to the supernatural, by awakening the mind's attention from the lethargy of custom, and directing it to the loveliness and the wonders of the world before us'. He is speaking, like Constable, about an art of seeing, without which 'we

---

hereafter referenced *EL* in the text.

have eyes, yet see not'. The experience of landscape art is, often, a seeing of common places and 'things of every day' for the first time.

Of course, it is not only a gentle beauty or mystery that artists disclose in unseen familiar places. Who would have thought Primrose Hill a place on fire with solar energy, where waves of red heat seem to break out of the ground? In Frank Auerbach's *Primrose Hill, Summer Sunshine* the paint looks trowelled on, gouged, handled with intense, even violent, yet sensitive feeling. It bears the marks of a struggle to convey a vision, which is what I value most in any art, and find, in different forms, in many works in this exhibition. And where better to show nature's solar and volcanic forces than in a place in which the eye dulled by 'the lethargy of custom' is least likely to see them? Auerbach, like Bomberg and Victor Pasmore and Roger Hilton, paints an '*active* universe', but with a more dangerous energy than Wordsworth perceived. Every artist of worth sees things differently, with a personal vision. But what all see is truer than a literal photographic description to the nature we live in and are part of, whether their truth is to atmosphere, or to underlying structures, or to elemental forces. A Turner, a Palmer, a Pasmore abstraction, all reveal to us *our* world: the world in which we really find ourselves, rather than the world we may think we possess. Long ago, I learnt from Paul Nash to see truths about downland that I would not have seen otherwise. Of course, without his work, I would have missed his vision. But Nash's art of seeing reveals correspondences between different objects and scales and forces that are actually there, in the life of the subject. Landscape art is a personal, partial revelation of nature. It enlarges and subtilizes our sense of a world in which, in the words of R. S. Thomas's 'The View from the Window', 'colours/Are renewed daily with variations/Of light and distance' (*EL*, p. 68), there is constant movement and change, and creation is at work on a painting that is never the same but always finished.

What does Winifred Nicholson reveal in her *Cumberland Hills*? Purple orchids in a vase at a window that opens on a view of azure uplands. Her medium is paint, but I have to revert to the language of music or poetry to suggest what she shows. Green leaves echo a green, globular vase, which in colour and shape echoes fields below the hills. Curtains and distant uplands are like forms made of the same light and air. It is a wonderfully fresh, delicate painting, which unites the near and the far, the inner and outer worlds, and discloses a harmony of plant, earth and sky. *Cumberland Hills* shows in manmade and natural objects the one sensitive life. Looking at it, I could see why the poet Francis Horovitz loved Winifred Nicholson's paintings.

In her poem 'Walking in Autumn', Frances Horovitz images treading on fallen crab apples, 'feet crunching into mud/the hard slippery yellow moons' (*EL*, p. 40). The image identifying apple and moon, heavenly body and earthly fruit, calls to mind the sun and moon images, and other images connecting different elements, that haunt a number of the pictures. Paul Nash has been called 'Master of the image',[3] and in *Nest of Wild Stones*, with its pebbles shaped like eggs or astronomical spheres, and flints which might also be Avebury sarsens, and are like skylarks, one can see why. He animates the inanimate, relates different scales in nature, and earth and sky, and his images are presences, charged with numinous power. This is a consciously symbolic art, which rearranges things in order to intimate the reality behind appearances, and it may usefully be called poetic. But although I'm tempted to use literary terms in describing some other works, they seem merely clumsy when applied to Winifred Nicholson's paintings, or to the thistledown sun in Joan Eardley's beautiful *A Field of Oats*, or to Mary Potter's *Sun on the Beach*. Nevertheless, it is not only what Charles Tomlinson in 'The Marl Pits' calls 'a language of water, light and air' (*EL*, p. 73) that landscape artists, like poets, seek, but also presences, or images that make the *other* present.

Sun on the Beach is a haunting painting of light and of contrasting, interacting objects and elements. The yellow sun is as much on the beach as a ball might be, and the boat, a pale curved shape linking beach and sea, is like a moon. The correspondence of sun and moon-boat is elusive, unselfconscious; I tried applying to it the word symbol but the picture rejected it. But this is not *only* a painting of things in sunlight. The winter shrub in the sea-garden has a spikiness (with just a hint of a Sutherland-like crown of thorns) and the objects on the beach a raggedness, which contrast with the smooth lines of beach and wall. A balance of opposing forces, light and dark, sun and moon, earth and sea, the enclosed world of room and garden and the unenclosed outer world, is implicit in the vision. Like sun and shrub and moon-boat, the strange, pale faces of cabbages in the sea garden are presences.

In other pictures, trees have an equivalent life. Robert Colquhoun's *Church Lench* is a wartime landscape. The shapes and dark green of tree crowns and trunks hold a tension between peaceful stillness and menace. There is a 'dark' feeling, which the one white tree intensifies, and reveals its cause as the threat of death. Something of the many different languages

---

[3] See Margot Eates, *Paul Nash The Master of the Image 1889-1946* (London: John Murray, 1973).

that trees are capable of providing may be seen, also, in the photographs by Paul Nash, the drawings by David Nash, and Elizabeth Vellacott's *Winter Trees*. Looking at David Jones's *Tree Trunks and Shed*, one might know nothing of his religious and mythological concerns, and still, in the stature and centrality of the foreground tree, in its reaching up and out, and above all in its sensitive organic being, see an image of the Tree of Life.

'I should paint my own places best – Painting is but another word for feeling.' Yes. But Constable's self-prescription is patently not applicable to many artists, who find places to fall in love with away from home, whether in Cornwall or Provence or Andalusia or Skye, and make them their own. It is a paradox familiar to me from poems of place that the art of seeing often involves, in some sense, distance from the place seen. On the one hand, I think of Richard Jefferies's statement in 'Meadow Thoughts' that in order to know a place, 'It is necessary to stay in it like the oaks'. And on the other, of the figure in W. H. Auden's 'The Wanderer', 'a stranger to strangers over undried sea', who dreams of home, and wakes to see nameless birds, and people making 'another love'. It is not only that at least some distance is necessary before one can see anything at all, but that a degree of estrangement renews the world, and may transfigure it. The artist is inward with the otherness of landscape, but often experiences it as a wanderer, bringing to it needs and feelings born of the distance between the human and the natural world. A dream of home pervades many British landscapes, in paintings and poems, and may express desire for one or several things: Paradise, Eden, a return to personal or cultural origins, union with the beloved or with nature, death. Coleridge links the aim of giving 'the charm of novelty to things of every day' and the aim of exciting 'a feeling analogous to the supernatural'. Indeed, there are few good landscapes in which one can separate the aims completely, or make a rigid distinction between an atmosphere arising from intimacy with the place, and an atmosphere expressing the vision of a wanderer or dreamer. Thus Michael Fussell, in *Heavy Rain over a Marsh (Winter Rain)*, uses curving strokes of charcoal with deceptive simplicity, expressing both the essence of weather and place, and a visionary mood. Ivon Hitchens, in another work rich in atmosphere, paints a leafy, watery otherworld in his *Garden Cove*. He succeeds in depicting England as an enchanted realm, because his vision is not based on cerebral fantasy, but rooted in physical, sensuous experience. His otherworld is, also, Sussex. In Sargy Mann's *River Box*, too, the place has been lived in, known from the inside, its conditions weathered; but it is not only natural knowledge arising from being in a place like an oak that shines in the glint of water and the tiny candleflame of sunlight, which lead deep into the formidable, dark mass of vegetation.

Responding to personal and cultural need, a number of the best modern British poets evoke presences in the landscape and landscapes charged with power, and, like the artists, they frequently use imagery of light and dark. They summon up the historical past and the life of nature, or they project a lost religion or integration onto landscape. David Jones in 'The Sleeping Lord' identifies potent elements of Welsh history and myth with 'the configuration of the land' itself (*EL*, p. 30). Landscape paintings may have an equivalent charge, in images and symbols, and perhaps above all in rhythmic movements of lines, colours and shapes. The artists don't exactly show 'history' as poets, let alone historians, treat it, but rather long-inhabited places, in which the relationship between man and the land is strongly defined. Sir William MacTaggart's *Winter Sunset, the Red Soil* (a title that is an imagist poem) is a painting whose dynamic rhythmic movements charge it with energy and meaning. Red sun and red-brown earth, irregular curved shapes of sun and trees and fields, all move in relation to one another, and man's place in nature, his home among solar and earthly powers, is implicit in the house with its red-brown roof. By contrast, Sheila Fell's *Woman in the Snow* conceives the human on a more heroic scale. Here, corresponding sombre colours and massy forms relate the woman's capacity for strength and endurance to the buildings'. Unlike the enigmatic and disquieting human presence in Carel Weight's work, the woman has a dependable solidity, and is more like a Tolstoyan peasant than one of Hardy's figures, 'slighted and enduring' in relation to Egdon Heath. Absence, too, can be a kind of presence, in pictures in which the external world is depicted with loving attentiveness, as if the artist, like C.H. Sisson in his poem 'Burrington Combe' (*EL*, p. 34), has revealed place as it is without him, or as in the loneliness that haunts L. S. Lowry's flat, blue-grey, empty *Seascape*.

Descriptive paintings, like Charles Ginner's *The Window* and Leonard Applebee's *Barns in a Field*, may remind us that landscape, which is itself an artefact, can seem to create its own abstractions by juxtaposing different objects with similar shapes. Indeed, different landscapes have different rhythms. I mean by this something more than the Classical concept of *genius loci*, or spirit of place, although this is part of it. The rhythms express a total environment: geological structure, soil type, native vegetation and wild life, effects of human occupation and labour, and also cultural significance, its symbolic shape in the imagination of a people. I don't mean that anyone sees all this, but that an artist, without deriving his art naively from them, may be most indebted to wild or cultivated landscape for a sense of its rhythms. For example, in Roger Hilton's *January 1964, Red*, in which the abstraction arises from a Cornish landscape of cliffs and mines, and from forms such as shells and the female body, and in Brian Wynter's *Landscape, Zennor*, we may see the relationship between perceived rhythms and abstract form. Victor Pasmore's *The Snowstorm: Spiral Motif in Black and White* reveals a similar, but more immaterial transaction between the imagination and the elements. The transaction is as old as the art of the caves, and it reveals not only a delight in creating formal patterns but the forces that create, destroy, and continue life.

The art of seeing petrifies, if it is not continually renewed. At first, I looked over rather than at Robert Law's *The White Horse of Uffington*, because it did not match the image of the original fixed in my mind. But how could it? The white horse, an image that is part of the land itself, and moves with its rhythms, is the most dynamic manmade work in these islands. But of course, Robert Law isn't competing with his subject. Looking again at his drawing, I saw that the words at the top are an integral part of the image: 'CROSS THE WAVING CORN PAST THE LOOKOUT POST TO THE WHITE HORSE OF UFFINGTON CASTLE'. Artist and viewer both *look across* the waving corn, but both also, in a sense, *approach* the figure, crossing the space bodily, over a distance evoked by drawing and words. The distance is physical, but the childlike waving corn and skeletal horse, like slivers of picked bone, also mark a temporal distance, between the primitive and the modern, and between child and adult artist. Or perhaps they mark the distance only to annul it, and unite past and present, child and man, rather as certain modern poets, such as David Jones and Seamus Heaney, return to personal and cultural origins. Another 'primitive' work, W.G. Gillies's *Eildon* – its dark green the colour both of our sombre northern wilderness and of the primordial vegetative world – also establishes a relationship between child's eye and artist's eye. In the horses that crop the grass, yet look like hill-cut figures, and in the bold, simplifying, suggestive lines in which hill shapes, horsebacks and beehive ricks echo one another, a connection is made, as in the Law, between the age of the hills and the individual human lifespan, and between the innocent eye and adult experience.

The words at the bottom of Hamish Fulton's *Seven days Alberta* are as much part of the image as Law's words are part of his drawing. In Fulton's work, they underline the experience of finding the sticks in the Rocky

Mountains and thus reinforce the authority of the artist, who has also arranged and photographed them. This is a sophisticated, selfconscious, actively imaginative form of 'found' art. Together with several other works, David Nash's *Larch framed with Larch* and *Ash framed with Ash*, Mark Boyle's *Bonfire Study*, John Latham's *Carberry Bing* and Terry Setch's *Penarth 111*, it reminded me of William Carlos Williams's famous poetic prescription: 'no ideas but in things'. Fortunately, the words are capable of several interpretations at least as various as these works. Thus, in the Terry Setch, the use of hot wax and oil paint creates an effect of the artist handling the actual substances of place – the clay, sand and pink stone of Penarth cliffs and beach. I have had an analogous sense, in writing poems about place, of working not only with words, but with the materials that the words name – chalk and flint, or shingle, mud, tar and salt water. John Latham's 'documentation', a photomontage which incorporates a jar of slagheap material, is a different treatment of the thing itself, although, as a celebration of the beauty that may be found in industrial waste, it also has something in common with William Scott's *Slagheap Landscape*, and, as an arrangement of multiple images, with John Virtue's atmospheric *Green Haworth*.

If Peter Lanyon's *Soaring Flight*, a beautiful, rhythmic painting of the sky seen from the sky, provides the least earthbound experience of landscape, it is difficult to imagine anything literally grittier or more down to earth than Mark Boyle's *Bonfire Study*. Here, it seems, is the very stuff of an actual place, just as it was in situ: 'coal, burnt wood, stones, ash and scorched earth' (and was the hayseed I saw clinging to it meant to be there?). But of course, this is not the debris of a bonfire but a bonfire *study*, in which the artist has used a fibreglass base, a secret method of composition, and substances already shaped or affected by human agency, and found a new way to play imaginatively with the relation between realism and abstraction, and art and nature. In that respect, as in some others, *Bonfire Study* is not different in kind from other works in the exhibition. For landscape art is by definition a transaction with reality, and experience of it opens our eyes both to the world of the picture and the world outside it. Some of the artists are drawn to wild places, remote from what Edward Thomas in *The South Country* called 'the parochialism of humanity', and others to the measured and manmade. But all bring us down to earth: to mystery, or the novelty of 'things of every day', or fiery energies burning in common places. They reveal or transform their experience in acts of personal vision, and disclose an art of seeing landscapes both in and out of the frame.

Natural Magic

An Eskimo has been said to have many words to describe snow, but no more, I would think, than there are shades of white and blue and brown and yellow in Winifred Nicholson's snow scene, *View from Studio Window*. Ivon Hitchens and Frances Hodgkins, the other painters represented with Nicholson in the exhibition,[1] *Influence and Originality*, at Djanogly Art Gallery, University of Nottingham, were also notable colourists. Writing in the exhibition catalogue, Liz Reintjes places experiments with colour among their shared interests. Such experiments were one of the elements of European Modernism which, from the 1920s, they absorbed into the British landscape tradition (though it should be remembered that the more 'exotic' Hodgkins was born in New Zealand, and drew upon Maori art). Other shared interests which they assimilated from Modernism were – in Reintjes's words – 'the manipulation of space, emulating a naive and primitive style of painting', and 'a fascination with the relationship between art and music'.[2]

Winifred Nicholson spoke of 'a Music of Colour', and Ivon Hitchens of 'visual music' and the 'musical appearance of things'.[3] The inclination to talk about painting in terms of other arts, and especially music, acquires a new significance with the advent of abstract art in the twentieth century. There is, I think, a connection between these artists' use of music as an analogy or metaphor for painting and Frances Hodgkins's frustration, at East Bergholt, one of the sacred places of the British landscape tradition: 'My brain reels trying to reduce this exuberant Nature to pictorial form – it is so gross green & lush… Here I feel lost in a deadening sea of growth'. It is not Constable's Nature she sees, nor are his means or terms of help to her as a modern painter. Set beside this cry of desperation Winifred Nicholson's matter of fact 'there are no words for colours, only a few flower names, a few jewel names, that is all, and quite inadequate to convey the myriad shades that our eyes perceive each moment'. The tone is different, but the words convey a similar sense of being overwhelmed

---

[1] 9 January to 10 March 1996.
[2] *Influence and Originality* (Nottingham: Djanogly Art Gallery in association with Lund Humphries, 1996), p. 12.
[3] Quotations from the painters, and from Liz Reintjes, are taken from the exhibition catalogue.

by a Nature that cannot be reduced to traditional terms, either verbal or visual.

There is, it seems to me, a parallel to be drawn between an artist's frustration at her inability 'to reduce this exuberant Nature to pictorial form' and the poverty of our language of colour to describe 'the myriad shades that our eyes perceive each moment'. 'Visual music' consequently offers a way of talking about something, in paintings and in nature, which words cannot adequately describe. It denotes the kind of harmony obtainable through use of colour and rhythmic movements and shapes in painting which has been freed by modern experiments from the dominance of the object in traditional art.

The positive side of Frances Hodgkins's sense of defeat in face of 'this exuberant Nature' is that 'sheer thrill' which, Liz Reintjes says, each of the three painters 'experienced before nature which they saw as a powerful and dynamic force which, at the same time, could be lyrical, romantic and mysterious'. Here, indeed, is a source of the British landscape tradition as it descends through Constable and Palmer and Turner to these modern painters, and which *requires* independence of vision in those who draw upon it. The source is nature apprehended as a force which awes the painter, even as he or she attempts to reduce it to pictorial form. The work of Hitchens, Hodgkins and Nicholson is, therefore, never purely abstract, for each, even as he or she translates the new language of abstraction into original vision, remains a maker of images and shapes which correspond to aspects of nature as a living force.

Each of the three painters evolved a sophisticated British modernism, in the sense that 'British' stands for a preoccupation with landscape and place; indeed, a modernism that was all the more sophisticated in that they asserted their independence, from European models and from each other, at the same time as they assimilated what they learnt about colour and form from Picasso, Matisse, Mondrian and others. This exercise of the spirit of independence upon 'provincial' materials, in effect, this different seeing which reveals Cumbria or Sussex as a universal 'centre', is in my view the main reason why the achievements of British modernism are not more visible to the eyes of critics who, for one reason or another, regard 'British' or 'English' and 'Modernism' as mutually antagonistic or exclusive terms. It is a view that is as damaging to our painting as it is to our poetry.

However abstract their designs, it is evident that each of these three painters stood in front of a landscape and looked at it. Ivon Hitchens may be regarded as the exception, but only in that, after his removal from

Hampstead to West Sussex in 1940, he stood within, rather than in front of, his woodland place: as much a participant in the natural world as an observer.

While Hitchens paints as though contained within the natural matrix, Winifred Nicholson frequently conveys a sense of cosmic space. Looking at her *The Red Flowerpot*, for example, one might be moved to parody William Carlos Williams's poem about a red wheelbarrow and ask what depends upon this pot of flowers. The answer is, *everything*. As Liz Reintjes has noted, the bowls of flowers standing in a window in Nicholson's paintings have an iconic quality. To Nicholson, flowers were 'the secret of the cosmos'. The secret is the reconciliation of opposites – nearness and distance, darkness and light, matter and spirit. It is with colours and shapes, then, that Nicholson unites the darkness under the soil with the brightness of the sun, the hidden with the visible, the near with the far, stillness with movement; and thus, instead of representing the flower face in an illustrational style, creates visual correspondences to the whole life of nature. In *Violas in a Window*, for example, shape echoes shape, the flowerpot, the round lake and the curve of hills and sky, and contrasting colours bring out the tones of each, uniting earth and water and sky. What the flower faces are, and what they 'see', here, is the secret of the cosmos. Another way of putting this would be to say that Nicholson paints her apprehension of what it means to be at home in the world. Her art is, at the same time, a way of controlling the forces she perceives, and of reaching beyond herself, the woman who stands by implication in the room behind the flowers in the window that opens on the cosmos.

Frances Hodgkins's vision strikes me as being, by contrast, essentially playful, even comic. Standing in front of her paintings, *Solva* and *Broken Tractor* for example, I find myself wanting to laugh aloud, and with delight as much as amusement. *Solva*, with its shapes of houses, river, stones, hills, clouds, animals, contains a whole world, but as a child's painting does – everything is in the process of coming into being, wonderfully sentient, at once individual object or creature and the fluid life that has not yet hardened into form. It is a world alive with colour, indeed a world in which the identity of things springs from colour. What could be more marvellously alive than the white sheep and red cow on the dark blue, oblong field which is only just big enough to contain them! Nor is it only natural things that are alive in Hodgkins's paintings. In *Broken Tractor* the machine squints at us – a cubist object with a sense of humour. It seems that everything to her is animate, a personage, but drunk with the mystery of its being, not sombrely mysterious, as images are in the world of Paul Nash. Look for example at the parrot in Hodgkins's *Wings over Water* (1930) and call to mind the hawk in Nash's *Landscape from a Dream* (1936-38). It is hard to say which painting is the stranger. But one thing a Paul Nash will never do is make one laugh. The title of another Hodgkins painting, *Enchanted Garden*, sums up her vision, which is of a humanised but magical nature. Magic, in the sense of imaginative play, is the presiding genius in her places, and magic, by which the external world is soluble in the mind, characterises the work of all three painters.

If, to use a gender-loaded term, there is *mastery* in Hodgkins's reduction of nature's exuberance to pictorial form, and in Nicholson's making of cosmic icons, Hitchens's mature techniques suggest an approach that is conventionally described as female. He appears to take the way of surrender to nature, of participation in its fluid rhythms. *Forest Edge no 2*, for example, suggests the waters of an aquarium, in which lighter coloured brushstrokes 'float' among the dark greens and reds, and the whole evokes an underwater world. Frances Hodgkins stood aghast before 'exuberant Nature'; Winifred Nicholson said, 'Art is the desire to resolve opposites – to find a path in the jungle of phenomena'; and Ivon Hitchens, in his woodland and woodland pool paintings, uses abstract means to draw the density and richness of an Amazonian rainforest from a corner of West Sussex.

Or so one might think if one has not looked closely, as Hitchens did, at a few square miles of English woodland. For his colours and the rhythmic play of horizontal and vertical lines in his elongated canvases, and his suggestions of image (in one painting, leaf shapes like hand marks on a cave wall), correspond to something seen and felt even in our domesticated landscape: movements of light and shadow, delicate sprays and downpours of leaves, water mirroring vegetation, coverts and brief openings, and everywhere the green force of nature.

There is abstract method – method *and* vision – in Hitchens's revelation of natural truths. But he is also, I think, a painter of psychological depth. The intense drama of his painting serves him in both capacities. *Winter Stage* creates drama with colour, and with movements that draw the eye up, across and, as in most of his paintings, deeply *in*. This is a theatre of inner event. After experiencing the sheer pleasure of Hitchens's 'visual music', the temptation is to try and read the painter's mind, though it is probable that one will only succeed in reading one's own. At any rate, it seems to me that his inner drama is one in which, through balance of male and female elements, he sought peace. In his dark wood, with its suggestion of cavernous and watery depth, and of structure and fluidity, Hitchens found solace. It is tempting to speculate about the painter's need for peace and integration, as one thinks of him being bombed out of his Hampstead studio, and going in wartime to live in Sussex woods. There is something in his paintings that suggests to me Wolf Solent's 'mythology', in John Cowper Powys's novel: a subaqueous inner world in which he 'resolves' the conflict of opposites, while in effect escaping from reality. The charge of escapism, especially in the twentieth century and above all in the context of war, is often brought against paintings and writings in the British landscape tradition. In our insular situation, and in the context of a national culture that positively discourages serious thinking, it is not a charge to be taken lightly. In Hitchens's case, however, it can only be brought at the cost of ignoring the tension and drama in his painting, which in *Woodland Landscape* (1940) rises to a tragic intensity. (But consider also the stroke of yellow in *Forest*, which is as dramatic as a meteor striking across a dark night-sky.) Now, though, with our new awareness of nature, informed by the ecological crisis and the new physical sciences with their emphasis upon complexity, interconnectedness, and the human situation within the web of nature, there is less excuse for us to think of a painterly obsession with nature or place as escapist. Moreover, if it is peace that Hitchens draws us into in his tangled woods and pools, rather than the darkness that Dante stumbled into, it is that peculiarly modern kind of peace, in which an ancient spirit of reverence has descended from empty heavens to invest itself in life on Earth.

By her organisation of the exhibition, and in the catalogue, Liz Reintjes allows the painters to speak for themselves. And one of the things they say is that 'originality', rather than being the opposite of 'influence', contains a sense of returning to, or drawing upon, origins. Origins, in the context of this exhibition, means the British landscape tradition, to which no one belongs except by virtue of a unique vision or, to modify Thomas Hardy's comment on late Turner paintings, a landscape plus a man's or woman's soul. But it also means nature as a dynamic force, the origin of all things, which renews the painters' art, because they learn to see it anew.

Gathering All In

Having spent several hours absorbed in the David Jones centenary exhibition, 'A Map of the Artist's Mind', at the Glynn Vivian Art Gallery in Swansea, my first thought on leaving was to doubt that Jones's work will be seen whole in my lifetime. A subsequent reading of two new books, Merlin James's book written to accompany the exhibition[1] and Jonathan Miles and Derek Shiel's *David Jones: The Maker Unmade*,[2] confirmed the doubt. For useful as both books are, especially in relating David Jones's painting to movements in both mediaeval and modern European art, James's book gives little sense of Jones's complementary achievement as a poet, which places him among the great modernist writers, and Miles and Shiel's criticism of what they see as the constrictions of Jones's Catholicism, and their treatment of his mental distress in Freudian and Reichian terms, raise more questions than they answer. Another new book, David Jones: *A Fusilier at the Front*,[3] consists in large part of his pencil drawings made during the First World War, drawings which were discovered by his nephew and niece after his death. Other discoveries which are being made among his papers are likely to alter our perception of the hugely ambitious poetic work which he laboured over during the last 30 years of his life, and of which *The Anathemata* and *The Sleeping Lord* are 'fragments'. Any comparison of David Jones and William Blake would need to take into account the great differences between them and their times, as well as certain affinities, but I will hazard the prophecy that it will take as long for a complete awareness of Jones's achievement as a poet and artist to form in the minds of those who come after him, as it did in the case of Blake. And, anyway, how many of us now know Blake in his entirety? Jones's work excites me partly because, 25 years after I first became aware of it, I still feel a beginner in exploring his whole imaginative world and the connections between his practice of the visual arts and his modernist poetry.

---

[1] Merlin James, *David Jones 1895-1974: A Map of the Artist's Mind* (London: Lund Humphries in association with National Museum & Galleries of Wales, 1995).
[2] Jonathan Miles & Derek Shiel, *David Jones The Maker Unmade* (Bridgend: Seren, 1995).
[3] David Jones, *A Fusilier at the Front*: His record of the Great War in word and image, selected by Anthony Hyne (Bridgend: Seren, 1995).

By 'whole' I mean not only his entire body of work, which, obviously, no one can know until it is all available, but also the integrity of his vision, the unity of its many diverse manifestations. A further meaning of the word refers to his religious perception of reality, which he struggled to embody in his work. He quoted with approval Stanley Spencer's reference to the making of a picture: 'All must be safely gathered in'.[4] He aspired to paint pictures that are 'contained yet limitless', or, as he said, 'to do Cézanne's apples again, after the nature of Julian of Norwich's little nut, which "endureth and ever shall for God loveth it"'.[5] Miles and Shiel see his attempt to reconcile 'a sensuous artistic disposition with the strictures of a religion not only based on suffering but that also advocated the denial of any sensuous urge not sanctioned by socially constraining codes' as the main cause of the 'great strain' he experienced.[6] What also needs to be said is that he found in Catholicism the meaning of life. He saw this as a meaning necessitating that 'all things worthy of our worship' are 'wounded'.[7] But for him it also meant the kindness of creation: the kinship of all creatures and the universality of the Creator's love. It may be argued that his kindness was instinctive: his childhood drawings capture the life of animals, his trench drawings are equally sensitive to the being of men and rats, and he never lost the ability to render the quickness of trees and flowers. But if an acute sensitivity to the life of beings and things distinguishes all his work, it was his Catholicism that formed his sense of the whole. In the words of 'The Tutelar of the Place':

> Gathering all things in, twining each bruised stem to the swaying trellis of the dance, the dance about the sawn lode-stake on the hill where the hidden stillness is at the core of struggle.[8]

Despite what I have said above, it may be that to know a few paintings well is better than to have encyclopaedic knowledge of an artist's entire work. Indeed, if the vision is whole it may be manifested in the microcosm of a single work. I would not however claim that this is the case with David Jones, since his works are also a record of struggle. Their

---

[4] *Epoch and Artist*, p. 243.
[5] *The Dying Gaul*, p. 142.
[6] *The Maker Unmade*, p. 142.
[7] Quoted in Rene Hague, *A Commentary on The Anathemata of David Jones* (Wellingborough: Christopher Skelton, 1977), p. 38.
[8] *The Sleeping Lord and Other Fragments*, p. 61.

very diversity – drawings, engravings, sculptures, watercolour paintings, inscriptions, poems, essays – is a manifestation not only of creativity, but of a search among different strategies to produce the significant image, the image that will signify the whole of sacred reality. He felt acutely that he lived in a time whose predominantly secular values had evacuated that significance. Yet there is, I think, a sense in which the metaphor of the dance, the dance of creation about the Tree of the Cross, may be used to describe Jones's formal experiments.

In *Roman Land* (1928) the religious sense of duality is implicit in the rhythmic play of different shapes and forms. This is a cultural landscape, in which a male will interacts with the natural forces on which it has been partly imposed. One may look at the painting without knowing anything about Jones's thinking about 'the Queen of Heaven and cult hero – son and spouse',[9] or about his ideas of culture and nature, or of unity and diversity. What one then responds to is a patterned visual image in which his thought and feeling about these things are grounded. Alternatively, it is possible to know about Jones's thinking in terms of complementary male and female principles and to reject his ideology. Whichever view one takes, it is evident that the play or dance of energies in his paintings owes a great deal to his religious ideas and feelings, and it is energy – a bruising energy, but also the energy that is eternal delight – which relates his landscapes to the strongest tradition of British landscape painting.

The centenary exhibition usefully simplifies Jones's themes, with sections on 'Art in Relation to War', 'The Tutelar of the Place', 'History and Romance', 'Of Metamorphosis and Mutability', and so on. It also makes evocative gatherings of his 'things', such as childhood drawings, books from his library, an annotated map of South Wales showing the prehistoric sites, and his annotated regimental history. The first exhibit, centrally placed, is *Human Being* (1931), the self portrait that reveals not the individual, but, in terms of Jacques Maritain's philosophy, the person, the man who is a maker, created in the image of God.

Paradoxically, the personal, in this sense, can serve a philosophy of artistic impersonality, by which the artist is concerned to depict not only the self but the reality of being, or as Eric Gill said of Jones, 'the universal thing showing through the particular thing'.[10] An autobiography of suffering can be read out of Jones's paintings – war trauma, sexual

---

[9] *Dai Greatcoat*, p. 227.
[10] Quoted in Thomas Dilworth, *The Shape of Meaning in the Poetry of David Jones* (Toronto, ON: University of Toronto Press, 1988), p. 23.

frustration, mental breakdown, agony at cultural decay – and his impressionist markings are often surprisingly violent for a medium – watercolour – which is usually thought of as gentle. What I am aware of in all Jones's work, nevertheless, is his art of containment. This manifests itself as an attempt to contain feeling and potentially disruptive personal experience within the form and image, and to understand the personal in terms of the human. An obvious example would be the Frontispiece to *In Parenthesis* (1937), in which the young soldier with his uniform half ripped off and tangled in the wire is the male as both victim and violator, implicated in unmaking nature and his kind, yet a spiritual being. There is a fundamental difference between self-expression and the artist's act of making a shape from the very things of which he is himself made to which Jones refers in the Preface to *The Anathemata*. This is, however, reconcilable with the 'agitation that borders on Expressionism' which Miles and Shiel perceive in the 'wild energy' of *Briar Cup* (1932).[11]

In *Manawydan's Glass Door* (1931), what might have appeared primarily as the shock of Jones's own loss as he remembered his companions killed in the war has been transmuted into a vision of extreme fragility in face of an awful power, with the ship racing before the same wind that blows the curtains into tangles and the stormy flux of sea and sea-facing room depicted as virtually a single element, which the protective features of door and lock and windows scarcely divide, so that the outdoors surges indoors. Force contained in form, force that sometimes distorts or shatters or dissolves form, seems to me to characterise the best tradition of British landscape painting, in Constable as well as Turner, and in modern painters such as David Bomberg with his paintings of Trendrine, and Joan Eardley in her paintings of Catterline. If the play or dance of energies relates David Jones to these painters, the difference is that he, true to the tradition of mediaeval illumination, paints the power of the spirit that is not of this world, though it is everywhere present in it. Thus, one reason why his window-view pictures differ markedly from those of the man he called 'my paragon' Bonnard is that for Bonnard the beauty of the world saturated in colour was its own justification. It would make more sense in terms of religious vision to compare Jones to Winifred Nicholson, the modern English painter to whom he is closest. In Nicholson, however, the sense of wholeness is incarnate in colour, whereas for Jones it is transparency and transmutation that express the divine spirit. Kandinsky's saying 'colour

---

[11] *The Make Unmade*, p. 135.

is a power which directly influences the soul'[12] is applicable to Winifred Nicholson, who was heir to the liberation of colour from form effected by Gauguin, van Gogh, Cézanne, Matisse and others. Jones, by contrast, is an artist of nervous – sometimes frenetic – lines and marks, of rhythmic pattern and the dance of forms.

His wood-engravings, superbly represented in this exhibition by the series illustrating The Golden Cockerel Press edition of *The Chester Play of the Deluge* (1927), show the sharply detailed and intensely dramatic rhythmic shaping that was to have an equivalent in *In Parenthesis*, the 'shape in words' Jones wrote substantially during the period from 1928 –1932 when he produced his finest landscapes and seascapes. In the mid-1920s he found a direction for his art in Welsh hill country, under 'the impact of the strong hill-rhythms and bright counter-rhythms' of the brooks.[13] In *Tir y Blaenau*, for example, the delicate and subtle colouring accentuates the rhythmic lines of hills and streams and horses' backs, of vertical tree trunks and horizontal branches. The vital abstract design corresponds to a rhythm perceivable in the landscape. Each tree and each horse in the painting is wonderfully sentient.

Capel-y-ffin, where David Jones stayed in the mid-1920s with Eric Gill and his family, is in the border country between England and Wales. But all Jones's paintings represent a kind of border. 'Man is a "borderer"', he wrote in his essay 'Art and Democracy'; 'he is the sole inhabitant of a tract of country where matter marches with spirit'.[14] (The pun on 'marches', meaning both 'moves together with' and the Welsh Marches, is characteristic, as is the military metaphor.) Jones's paintings are accordingly attempts to create images uniting matter and spirit, nature and the supernatural, time and eternity. What this meant in painterly terms was that he developed a peculiarly transparent and metamorphic style, combined with a detailed, loving perception of the particular. It is a style which aims, by analogy with the action of the Mass, to preserve the identity of being and thing in the act of transubstantiation. He found in Welsh folk-tales a quality obliquely connected with what he wanted in painting: a quality having 'to do with a certain affection for the intimate creatureliness of things – a care for, and appreciation of, the particular genius of places, men, trees, animals, and yet withal a pervading sense of

---

[12] Wassily Kandinsky, *Concerning the Spiritual in Art* (New York, NY: Dover, 1977), p. 25.
[13] *Epoch and Artist*, p. 30.
[14] Ibid., p. 86.

metamorphosis and mutability'.[15] He spoke of the Celtic folk-tradition which 'introduces a feeling of transparency and interpenetration of one element with another, of transposition and metamorphosis. The hedges of mist vanish or come again under the application of magic'.[16]

The paintings of his first great creative period, 1928-1932, have an equivalent quality. At the same time, in writing *In Parenthesis*, he was exploring a border between the past and the present, and history and myth, and life and death. In one sense or another, the border became a potent metaphor for many artists and writers affected by the First World War. It manifested itself in various forms of duality, in the need to resolve opposites or mend disconnections, or reunite inner and outer, consciousness and the depths of the mind. With the rise of cultural nationalism during the '30s, and the Second World War and its aftermath, the land itself increasingly became a border where the dualism found expression. In Paul Nash's late mythological landscapes, for example, life and death are embodied in the interaction between powers of earth and sky. For David Jones, the border was where he struggled, in different forms, to make images of man-the-artist 'whose man-hands god-handled the Willendorf stone'.[17] He sought, in opposition to the spirit of the age, to relate the human and divine in images of the whole creation.

There are continuities as well as differences between the earlier and late paintings. In *Y Cyfarchiad I Fair* (The Greeting to Mary, 1963), for example, the rhythmic shaping is similar to that of the wood-engravings and early Welsh landscapes. The painting attempts to gather all in, to contain the boundless, and is itself an enclosure, which, like other late Jones paintings, combines a use of illustrational detail with the fluidity of line he so valued – combines, or works against? Paintings such as *Vexilla Regis* (1947), *Trystan ac Essyllt* (1962) and *Y Cyfarchiad I Fair* need a strong central image to counter the tendency of crowded symbolic details to disperse the attention and fragment the coherence of design. There are grounds for arguing that Jones's methods in his late paintings are essentially literary, and are therefore realised more effectively in his poetry. I suggest this with hesitation, however, since, despite the excellence of some critical writing on Jones's poetry and painting, what we are not likely to have for some time is a full account of his complete imaginative effort as poet and painter, which reveals in detail the internal relations

---

[15] Quoted in Paul Hills, *David Jones* (London: The Tate Gallery, 1981), p. 48.
[16] *Epoch and Artist*, pp. 238-39.
[17] *The Anathemata*, p. 59.

between his techniques. In the absence of an awareness of the whole, I would rather point to similarities than make comparisons. Thus, in *Y Cyfarchiad I Fair*, Mary's long wavy hair, flowing like a mountain stream, joins the circling hills to the semi-circle of the wattle fence, and she is part of the land, its tutelary spirit, as Arthur is identified with the land in *The Sleeping Lord*.

Towards the end of his life it may have been easier for Jones to find words in which 'many confluent ideas are involved in a single image'[18] than it was for him to paint them. His most original use of tradition in his paintings was a late flowering, however. His painted inscriptions recall his debt to Eric Gill and look back to the world of classical antiquity; they are also distinctively modern works, which claim a high place among the products of abstraction. Not that they are wholly abstract, of course – on the contrary, they are laden with cultural significance and are the culmination of Jones's fascination with the incarnate word, and the word that is artefact and palimpsest. As Jones would have been quick to point out, all art is necessarily abstract, a cave painting as much as a Mondrian. It is true though, that with his literary and historical and mythological interests – all of them integrated in his perception of religious reality – he could not be purely abstract. It was the desire to embody meaning, in the terms proper to each of the arts he practised, that led to Jones's different experiments. The outcome was a psychic wounding, as he strained his nerves to achieve the impossible. It was a wounding that may be related to his personal problems, as well as to the cultural situation that he himself blamed for his difficulties. But I think it should also be understood by analogy with the action of the wounded healer who makes whole, which to Jones was the meaning of life. Irrespective of whether or not one shares Jones's faith, it seems to me that no modern vision of the whole could carry conviction that does not have at its heart, as his does, an experience of maiming and brokenness.

---

[18] *Dai Greatcoat*, p. 151.

Truth of Experience:
The Paintings of David Tress

David Tress's recent painting *A Hot Day, February (Tretio)* is a fine example of his work. It is a painting of a place experienced under particular conditions of light and weather at a certain time, but well known to the artist from many visits over the years. The landscape has a sensuous immediacy, but, rather than being a fleeting impression, it is immensely earthy: a place forged by natural forces, and charged with a sense of geological and historical time.

Looking at the painting, one sees a blaze of yellow – an image which conveys not just the appearance of gorse, but an impression of its flaming energy. This blends with the quieter movement of white clouds. The gorse flares in a swirl of colour out of the subdued ochre and yellow and brown of the rocky, uneven ground. All in the foreground is intensely alive, a fluid, dynamic movement, but belonging to an earth marked by ancient human presence. As one's gaze settles so it comes to rest on distance – a line of silvery-blue hills blending with blue sky. Now the whole image combines energy with depth. This Pembrokeshire landscape, experienced at this moment of time, is a palimpsest, an intensely living place layered with the past.

The wonderful freshness and vigour, combined with a sense of the ancient and enduring, is characteristic of David Tress's personal vision. He would echo, I think, John Constable's 'painting with me is but another word for feeling', where feeling is for both artistic medium and subject. 'Art,' as Peter Abbs says, 'involves a sensuous embodiment. … It is an intensely physical activity – an erotic activity – working towards the spirit, towards meaning, towards value.'[1] The implication, as we see with Tress, is that his whole person is involved in the act of painting. The viewer is consequently awakened to the life in things, and experiences landscapes infused with spirit.

David Tress is an artist of independent mind, who has chosen his way of working in full knowledge of the art scene he is rejecting, which values concepts over physical making. He was born in London in 1955,

---

[1] Peter Abbs, 'Harold Mockford: Acts of Discovery', *Images of Earth & Spirit*: A Resurgence art anthology, eds. John Lane and Satish Kumar (Totnes: Green Books, 2003), p. 161.

and has lived in West Wales since 1976. He studied Fine Art at Trent Polytechnic, and learnt from aspects of Abstract Expressionism, especially its use of dynamic gestures, and the sense of the painting as an action. He learnt also from the detailed precision of Pre-Raphaelite painting. Having absorbed the lessons, he moved on, arriving at his mature vision by a process of experimentation. This involved both development of his techniques as an artist using watercolour and other media, and participation in a landscape, immersion in it, in all weathers and seasons: intimate knowledge of his subjects, gained over a period of time.

Tress's originality springs from his relationship to the tradition of British landscape painting. John Piper, in *British Romantic Artists*, said that 'Romantic art deals with the particular'.[2] This is true of David Tress. His paintings at their most fluid and dynamic never dissolve the image; they record an encounter between inner and outer, the painter and some aspect of the external world. Piper also emphasised that the tradition of British landscape painting, established by Thomas Girtin and J M W Turner, shared its impulse to reveal the universal through the particular with the Romantic poets. 'They wanted to make landscape a means of reporting and recording, not places and things, but life.'[3] In the 1940s, the Neo-Romantic painters, such as Paul Nash and Graham Sutherland, with whom David Tress feels an affinity, had a similar sense of the 'poetic'. Far from meaning anything nebulous, this refers to embodied vision. It refers, for example, to Paul Nash's feeling for charged landscapes, for 'spirit of place' in ancient chalklands, and to Graham Sutherland's sense of 'presence' in the landscape. Later painters whom Tress admires include Peter Lanyon and, especially, Joan Eardley in her paintings of the north-east Scottish coast and sea at Catterline. Like Tress himself, all these are highly individual painters. What they have in common is a mastery of pictorial images of landscape and the natural world that embody elemental and spiritual power. They record the experience of life.

Tress's Pembrokeshire landscapes bear the imprint of thousands of years of human connection. They are sacred landscapes marked by Neolithic burial mounds and medieval pilgrim routes. In his depiction of the relationship between the aerial and the earthbound he is sensitive to what Wordsworth found at Grasmere: 'A blended holiness of earth and sky'. He responds keenly to what a later poet, R. S. Thomas, found in Wales: both a history of conflict ('the spilled blood/That went to

---

[2] *Aspects of British Art*, ed. W. J. Turner (London: Collins, 1947), p. 161.
[3] Ibid., p. 171.

the making of the wild sky'), and sacred mystery, 'the miracle of the lit bush'.[4]

David Tress's paintings evoke strong feelings. In a recent sequence of three paintings, *Green Winter Spring,* for example, the fluid interaction of green and yellow and black, in the foreground vegetation, against glimpses of blue hills and sky, produces a sense of awakening. This has the chill freshness of early spring, together with a new seeing of the near and far, the 'opening', which is accompanied by a vibration in all the senses, as one sees and feels the world anew. The excitement includes an element of raw discomfort, and is at once spiritual and sexual. Tress is equally capable of capturing the truth of an urban scene, as in his *Welsh Industrial,* where one can virtually taste the dust in the atmosphere and feel as physical sensation the relationship between indrawn valley terraces and distant view.

In his current travelling exhibition (2008-2010), *Chasing Sublime Light,* Tress pays homage to the beginnings of the British landscape painting tradition to which he belongs. In responding to landscapes painted more than two hundred years ago by painters such as Girtin and Turner, however, he is not copying their views. To do so would be false to the tradition itself, to its achievement of personal visions, well summed up by Thomas Hardy's description of Turner's late watercolours as 'a landscape *plus* a man's soul'. History too is implicated in perception of landscape, as we see in Turner's *Rain, Steam and Speed,* 1844, in which the artist has painted, not merely a train crossing a viaduct, but the experience of the new age. Similarly, Tress's *Kirkstall Abbey (Girtin's View)* is not a copy of what Girtin saw in the 1790s, but an experience of the scene now. In Girtin's serene view the abbey is at one with a natural order, sharing a sense of religious harmony with river, cattle and trees, and the human figures on the riverbank. In Tress's painting from the same viewpoint, all is jagged, disturbed, and vibrant with different energies stemming from road and railway, and the electricity pylon which now dominates the landscape, as the abbey formerly did. This is a depiction of the place experienced now, fraught with potent and dangerous forces. This too is a palimpsest, although in this landscape the different layers create a powerful dissonance. Here, as in his Pembrokeshire landscapes, David Tress paints the truth of experience.

---

[4] 'Welsh Landscape', *An Acre of Land*, (Newtown: Montgomeryshire Printing Co. Ltd., 1952), p. 26.'The Bright Field', *Laboratories of the Spirit* (London: Macmillan, 1975), p. 60.

Flooded with Light:
on the art of Elizabeth Haines

Colour is what strikes one first in looking at Elizabeth Haines's paintings. In *Flooded with Light* a warm yellow seems to flow into the canvas, in a way that does not drown the other colours, but makes them stand out, reds and browns and grey-white defining shapes of buildings, a tree, birds in flight, sky. Colour relates to shapes, from which an image emerges. In *Vortex for the Storm*, a war landscape, sombre reds stand out in relation to dark and light blues, and an image forms of trees on cratered and mounded earth. There is a feeling of menace, of a torn landscape stilled, held at a moment of explosive movement.

The title refers to a line from David Jones's *In Parenthesis*: 'The trembling woods are vortex for the storm'.[1] In view of the significance of David Jones's work and thought for Elizabeth Haines, however, it is important at the outset to emphasise that she is not illustrating his words. *Vortex for the Storm* may gain something for the viewer who recognises the reference to the 'storm' of battle in Mametz Wood, but the painting has the integrity of the artist's vision, and trembles with its own violent energy, at once beautiful and threatening.

Elizabeth Haines is both a sensuous and a sophisticated painter, who has developed her distinctive style over years of practice. She has absorbed influences from European modernism and from the British Romantic tradition. Her interest in the relations between the arts of painting, music and poetry has vitally affected her development. As well as resulting in her philosophical thesis, *The Web of Exchange*, for which she obtained a PhD from the University of Wales, Lampeter in 2002, her belief in the link between the arts informs a passionate way of imagining which helps to shape her painting.

Elizabeth Haines assents to David Jones's definition of the artist in *Epoch and Artist* as 'the person most aware of the nature of an art. The inception or renewal or deepening of some artistic vitality normally comes to the artist via some other artist or some existing art-form, not via nature'.[2] While this is true as far as the development of artistic form-

---

[1] *In Parenthesis*, p. 179.
[2] *Epoch and Artist*, p. 29.

making is concerned, however, it would be quite wrong to infer that nature did not play a significant part in the work of either David Jones or Elizabeth Haines. For both, nature in Wales was vitally important. David Jones's encounter with the hill-rhythms and streams of the Black Mountains in the 1920s helped to renew him as a painter. From this encounter sprang both his vision of landscape and his capacity to depict the past in the present, in painting and subsequently in poetry too. For Elizabeth Haines, experience of Pembrokeshire was equally important.

She was a young art student, with a degree in Graphic Art from Brighton College of Art, when she first came to Pembrokeshire in the 1960s. There, she met and married a shepherd, and there, since 1968, she has continued to live, in more recent years in a remote smallholding below the Preseli hills, where her studio is an eighteenth-century converted byre. From her base in Pembrokeshire she has made a considerable contribution to art in Wales, exhibiting widely for some 40 years. Her work is included in the collections of the National Library of Wales and the Contemporary Art Society for Wales. In 1987, she was Artist in Residence at the National Eisteddfod, Porthmadog. For all this visibility, however, too little has been said about what is distinctively Welsh, in terms of what she has absorbed and what she has given, of the work of this English artist living in Wales.

Coming to Pembrokeshire from Hertfordshire, it was, she has said, the 'wildness' of west Wales that impressed her.[3] Contrast between landscapes has continued to play an important role in her painting, and in the past ten years the landscapes of France have both provided her with a different spirit of place, and enhanced her sense of the 'otherness' of the country around her in Wales. Her Welsh landscapes are not confined to Pembrokeshire, however. *Llanthony, Barns in Snow* and *Under a Full Moon*, also inspired by the Marches, are among other, contrasting landscapes from Wales. But Elizabeth Haines is not a landscape painter in any literal sense. For her, the qualities of different landscapes – the colours and shapes and weathers, the different buildings and trees – are present as strong influences on her abstract compositions, and the images which emerge from them. Fleeting impressions and historical landscapes saturated with her own memories are equally inspiring; but the crucial factor in her mature work is what evolves during the process of painting.

---

[3] Except where otherwise noted, all quotations from Elizabeth Haines, and information about her life and work, come either from statements which the artist has provided for exhibitions, or conversations or correspondence with me.

As she has said: 'Almost all my paintings begin with an abstract play of shape and colour, and then have to undergo constant transformation, during which time I have to constantly pull them away from a too literal description which leaves nothing to the imagination'.

Pulling away from the literal subject without losing touch with it has characterised Elizabeth Haines's development. In the early years of marriage, the need to earn money led her to concentrate on illustrative work, including drawings for a children's encyclopaedia. The gift of close observation, required by this work, continues to be seen in her later drawings, in, for example, *Sketchbook from the Somme*, 2004, which includes detailed drawings of buildings, farmyards and war cemeteries, as well as landscapes. This is vital work. The painter, however, experienced a strong need to transcend the limitations of the descriptive and representational.

Her development of an abstract art, an art in which the motif or image emerges from compositions of colours and shapes, was in consequence a liberation from literalism. To call it abstract, however, is not to suggest that it loses touch with the particular, which John Piper defined as characteristic of Romantic art. Haines defines the style she has evolved as 'a style which is in a precarious hinterland between topography and abstraction'. Experience not of the observed world only, but of the world felt and lived in, known in the moment and bearing the experience of human life in time, informs the images that emerge in the process of composition.

The freedom from literalism which Elizabeth Haines has achieved as a painter, owes a great deal to her interest in the relations between the arts of poetry, music and painting. Poetry, and especially the 'music' of Welsh poetry, has had a special influence on her sense of pictorial composition. This may be understood with reference to Gwyn Williams's richly suggestive Foreword to *The Burning Tree*, his selection 'from the First Thousand Years of Welsh Verse', with his translations facing the originals. Williams writes of 'the absence of centred design' in old Welsh poetry, which he likens to 'the inter-woven inventions preserved in early Celtic manuscripts and on stone crosses, where what happens in a corner is as important as what happens at the centre'. The link between poetry, visual design, and a past-marked, sacred landscape suggests how Elizabeth Haines's experience in Pembrokeshire enabled her to draw on a connection between verbal and visual patterning. Initially, with a partial knowledge of Welsh, she heard 'the structure of cynghanedd as music. It was this underlying abstract quality to the poetry which provided the link with painting'. Her response to a particular Welsh poem illustrates how her sensitivity to poetry combined with her experience of Welsh landscape – the cultural landscape of Pembrokeshire, not wildness alone – to affect her mature imaginative development: 'Looking up to Carn Afr, especially when the mists swirl about, I think of Dafydd ap Gwilym's "Y Niwl", "a pale grey, weakly trailing fleece, like smoke, a hooded cowl upon the plain (Cnu tewlwyd gwynllwyd gwanllaes/cyfliw a mwg, cwfl y maes)". Then one experiences the essential characteristic of the Welsh aesthetic sensibility as an intricate, interlacing, meandering quality, rich in metaphor'. In the music and metaphor she found 'the alchemy which transforms ordinary material into something of imaginative significance'. This, she believes, 'underlies all the arts'.

What is involved here is something more than Walter Pater's idea of painting aspiring to the condition of music. Sound, and the echoing, pattern-making quality of sound, indicates principles of structure, similar to the way in which Gwyn Williams's links 'the idea of composition' in old Welsh poetry – which he perceives also in the writings of Dylan Thomas and David Jones – to 'the inter-woven inventions preserved in early Celtic manuscripts and on stone crosses'. Actual musical sounds also enter the paintings, as in *L'Arbre Abasourdi*, in which the colours of a vivid dawn combine with birdsong bursting from a tree, in the Charente, to produce a sense of the otherness of a dawn in France.

Elizabeth Haines's paintings have been described as 'dreamscapes'. The word is useful, providing it does not suggest anything fey, but refers to an art of imaginative transformation, analogous to the way in which dreamwork makes everyday reality soluble, and produces a new thing from elements of past and present experience. Again, the process has an analogy to the art of poetry, in which, if the poem works, meaning is discovered, not imposed, in the process of composition. Then, the poet will be the first person to be surprised by the new thing on the page. The keyword is 'transformation': the alchemical change of materials – words on paper, observations of the external world – through which the shape of meaning is revealed.

The importance of poetry for Elizabeth Haines appears also from the way in which she incorporates quotations from poems in some paintings. In *Mazy Charnel Way* the words are, again, from *In Parenthesis*, from a passage describing the battle in Mametz Wood, ('through which their bodies grope the mazy charnel-ways'.)[4] Here, in ink and acrylic on paper, the upright tangled forms suggest both men and trees, their black lines

---

[4] *In Parenthesis*, p. 179.

shot through with splashes of blood-red. *Deri yn Ymdaraw* incorporates words from 'Marwnad Llewelyn ap Gruffudd' by Gruffudd ab yr Ynad Coch, the poet's words invoking storm-tossed oaks beating together in wind and rain being made part of what is also their visual equivalent, the inks on paper producing an effect that is like a gust of fiery light.

The tree motif recurs in Elizabeth Haines's paintings. Again, close observation of different trees in the Welsh and French landscapes underlies paintings which express the deep symbolic resonance of trees, drawing on biblical, mythological, and literary references. As in *Mazy Charnel Way* and the passage from *In Parenthesis* that inspired it, trees are closely associated with humankind, a fact which, in the paintings, is shown also by their proximity to buildings. The connection between trees and human life is at once organic and imaginative, recalling the importance for Elizabeth Haines of Paul Klee's image of the tree for the artist's 'sense of direction in nature and life': 'From the root the sap flows to the artist, flows through him, flows to his eye'.[5] As Klee's metaphor shows, it is important to realise that the imagination is more than a mental faculty, that it draws on all the senses, and on memory and the unconscious mind, as well as consciousness, and is essentially transformative.

Gwyn Williams chose the title for his anthology of old Welsh poetry from a famous image in The Mabinogion: 'A tall tree on the river's bank, one half of it burning from root to top, the other half in green leaf'. In his Foreword he defined this as a metaphysical image which suggests 'the awareness at the same time of contrary seasons and passions, a mood in which the poet brings into one phrase the force of love and war, of summer and winter, of holy sacrament and adulterous love'. Describing poetry or painting as 'Metaphysical' or 'Romantic' can be a notoriously loose way of speaking, yet here, with this idea of the tension of contraries, is a potentially suggestive description. It applies not only to old Welsh poetry, but also to Romantic and Neo-Romantic landscape art. Ancient landscapes necessarily contain contraries; they are palimpsests, or layered sites mixing corpse-strewn battlefield and natural beauty. In poetry this vision discovered in Welsh landscape is exemplified by R.S. Thomas's consciousness of 'the spilled blood/That went to the making of the wild sky, /Dyeing the immaculate rivers/In all their courses'. In twentieth-century British painting it may be seen in the landscapes of David Jones and Graham Sutherland, and the death-haunted, sublime cosmic

---

[5] *Paul Klee on Modern Art*, with an introduction by Herbert Read (London: Faber and Faber, 1966), p. 13.

chalklands of Paul Nash. It may be seen, too, in Elizabeth Haines's paintings, and most insistently in those in which the tree motif occurs. Here, in these distinctive abstract compositions, are images of the fullness of life, which cannot be separated from the presence of death.

The symbolic tree embodies the entire life cycle. It is also an image of homeliness. This may be seen, in a number of Elizabeth Haines's paintings, in what might be described as a delightful neighbourliness. It is present in both Welsh and French landscapes, despite the differences marked by their contrasting tree-shapes and buildings. At times there is a feeling reminiscent of Samuel Palmer. In *Under a Full Moon*, for instance, sheep and cows feed in front of a village of red-roofed houses, with trees among them, and a church at the centre. The red of roofs echoes the colour of a blazing sunset, while that of the full moon echoes the colour of walls. The scene may be described as a pastoral, but what it reveals is the feeling that springs from the settled, peaceable scene, and holds all together. A sense of the sacred informs an image of temporal depth. One could say that light floods the scene. It would be truer to the work of the painting to say that the unified image emerges from the composition of colours and shapes. It is in the transformation of materials that Elizabeth Haines reveals a luminous borderland between topography and abstraction.

Ground

In order to know the ground we stand on we need to become aware of its strangeness. This paradox is central to the artistic treatment of 'place' or 'ground', as we see in the paintings of Ernest Zobole and the photographs of Ray Klimek.

Ernest Zobole, the son of Italian immigrants and a painter living in a community centred upon the coalmining industry before its demise in the 1980s, was to some degree an outsider in the place that he knew and loved. Ray Klimek, from a mining region of Pennsylvania, feels an affinity with the industrial wastelands of South Wales, which he sees, nevertheless, as a visitor. Both painter and photographer, therefore, are able to see the familiar with an outsider's eye. They know their subjects, but know them in a way that enables them both to recognise and to reveal the strange.

It is easy to look at a partly grassed over coal tip or some other feature of a post-industrial landscape without really seeing it, because one imports stereotypical ideas and images into the scene. Looking closely at Ray Klimek's photographs, however, one may see a subtle interplay of colours – greens and greys and black – together with different textures, shapes and rhythms. His photograph is a composition, an aesthetic object, but it also reveals truths about its subject, which is both material ground resulting from geographical processes, and historical ground, where man has reshaped the original terrain. The landscapes bear traces of the past, and their present moment is one of becoming.

The Rhondda, too, can be passed over without being seen, the very name conjuring up an *idea* of history that screens out the life of the place. The title of Ernest Zobole's *Black Valley* (1962-63) might seem to confirm the clichés – and indeed the Rhondda was black in the days of the mines; but the painting, with its colours and rhythmic arrangement of shapes, is much more than a study in black. With the figure passing the lighted window, it would be truer to say that it is a study in the interaction of light and dark, and thus an emotional statement about the place as seen and felt from within. Here, as in all his work, Zobole remakes his place in order to reveal it from the inside. Where there are human figures they are contained in place, as a fish is held in a stream, with the pressure of the element on its skin. Ernest Zobole paints the experience of total immersion, but also, in his finest work, combines it with different viewpoints, so that the inside is seen from the outside, too.

Ray Klimek's photographs carry the names of places – Cwm Bargoed, Blaenafon, Treorchy, Tylorstown – so that, in a sense, we know where we are. At first sight, though, there is nothing to show the human presence that makes history, and therefore gives a place its name. Yet what we are looking at is, in effect, charged with human presence. Everywhere in Klimek's landscapes nature has been subjected to human power, handled, moved by machines, and reshaped; and now, nature is in process of reclaiming the scarred and blackened ground, at the same time as humans are putting it to new uses, and making fresh marks. All is flux – a landscape bearing traces of the past; a ground of soil and dust, grass and water and concrete, in the process of becoming. In *6 Cwm Bargoed, South Wales* (2005), a red wheelbarrow is shown abandoned alongside a drainage channel. The image contains a witty allusion to William Carlos Williams's poem, which famously begins:

> So much depends
> upon
>
> a red wheel
> barrow…

Like the poem, the wit of the photograph carries a tribute. How small the wheelbarrow is, how monumental the landscape around it – the worked landscape, which the hands that wielded the barrow helped to make. The red of the barrow against the dark grey is aesthetically pleasing, but also, like the red in Zobole's *Black Valley*, it signifies a flame of defiant life.

'Everything springs from work.' Ernest Zobole was speaking of painting when he wrote these words.[1] He was right, of course; and his own art developed over his lifetime bears the marks of intense labour. Imagining is itself a crucial part of a painter's work. Zobole never forgot that what he was remaking, as a pictorial vision, was a world built on the work of other men and women, on humanly costly industry. Ground, as he painted it, was the life of the Rhondda, both the life of a community with a past, a present, and an increasingly uncertain future, and his own

---

[1] Quoted in Ceri Thomas, 'Ernest Zobole, Painter 1927-99: Out of and into the Blue', *imaging the imagination*, eds. Christine Kinsey and Ceridwen Lloyd-Morgan (Llandysul: Gomer, 2005), p. 125.

life-world, charged with personal memory and emotion. He was, in Ceri Thomas's words, a 'valley-dwelling painter'.[2] One crucial effect of this was that his mature vision became many-angled, for the person moving about in the valleys, climbing the hills and descending into the valley bottom, sees the same objects from different viewpoints, acquiring what might be described as a 'naturally' cubist way of seeing things. With this experience, the mountain or slagheap towering above becomes the humble mound seen below; and both images define the human vision. And this is only part of the complication of real seeing, which for an artist of genius, such as Zobole, is a continuum. Another important effect of his valley-dwelling was the sense of being contained and surrounded, whether indoors looking out or in the street.

A canvas such as *A Painting about myself in a Landscape* (1994-95) marvellously realizes the combination of opposing viewpoints, within the valley, inside the house looking out, and from an aerial perspective. Looking at this and other paintings, it is easy to understand why commentators should have referred to the 'daring fantasy' and 'amazing vision' of this Rhondda artist or seen a 'dream-like, lyrical, phantasmagorical quality' in his paintings. To Dai Smith, Ernest Zobole is 'the great Magic Realist of the most magical reality of Wales'.[3]

In coming to South Wales Ray Klimek brings with him both a stranger's eye and a sense of differences and affinities based on knowledge of the Pennsylvanian coalfields. He brings also a sense of the local seen from a profoundly democratic point of view, as in the literary tradition represented by William Carlos Williams, for example. It is a way of seeing things with strong echoes in the political, literary and artistic traditions of South Wales. Ernest Zobole said: 'To love a place strengthens me, it becomes the material for my painting'.[4] This was the spirit in which he knew the Rhondda. But his passion for the local was also a liberation, giving him a subject to which he applied techniques owing much to outside influences, from European painting, literature, and film. The very name Rhondda may suggest a stark realism corresponding to the life and death of a great industry, and a tragic and inspiring political history. But Ernest Zobole paints a fluid world, restoring subjective experience to his place. His imagined Rhondda makes us aware of its strangeness,

---

[2] Ibid., p. 132.
[3] Quotations from Ceri Thomas, *Ernest Zobole: a retrospective* (University of Glamorgan, 2004).
[4] Quoted in Ceri Thomas, *imaging the imagination*, p. 130.

as lived in, dreamed, and felt, and seen. Both Zobole the painter and Klimek the photographer awake us to realities that familiarity obscures – as dust once darkened windows in communities within the coalfields.

Putting the Poem in Place

'Men attach themselves to this world as certain kinds of seaweed cling to the rocks by the seashore.'[1] Clement of Alexandria, in the 2nd century AD, intended a reproach: men attach themselves to their earthly home, careless of their heavenly homeland. Detachment, however, is difficult. According to the idea of a fourth century Greek philosopher, transmitted by Aristotle, impossible: *To be is to be in place.*[2]

This has a bearing on Hamlet's famous question: To be or not to be. Contemplating suicide, he dreads what may follow death: 'The undiscovered country from whose bourn/No traveller returns'. Undiscovered, but still a country, a place. Nowhere is literally beyond the human imagination. All life occurs somewhere; as we say, 'takes place'.

My first landscape was the south coast in wartime: a shingle shore, salt water, eroded concrete seawalls, war debris among the flotsam, black-headed gulls. It was situated between Portsmouth and Southampton, both badly war-damaged. I was brought up at Warsash, and a few miles to the west, at Pennington, between the New Forest and the sea. In my book of poems published in 1978, I call my original home area 'Solent Shore'. 'Gull on a Post' expresses desires that may be incompatible, or perhaps complementary:

> Gull on a Post
> Firm in the tideway – how I desire
> The gifts of both!
>
> Desire against the diktat
> Of intellect: be single,
> You who are neither.
>
> As the useful one
> That marks a channel, marks
> Degrees of neap and spring;

---

[1] Quoted in Hugo Rahner, *Greek Myths and Christian Mystery* (London: Burns & Oates, 1963), p. 328.
[2] See Edward S. Casey, *Getting Back into Place* (Bloomington & Indianapolis, IN: Indiana University Press, 1993), p. 14.

Apt to bear jetties
Or serve as a mooring;
Common, staked with its like.

Standing ever
Still in one place,
It has a look of permanence.

Riddled with shipworm,
Bored by the gribble,
In a few years it rots.

Desire which tears at the body
Would fly unconstrained
Inland or seaward; settle
At will – but voicing
Always in her cry
Essence of wind and wave,
Bringing to city, moorish
Pool and ploughland,
Reminders of storm and sea.

Those who likened the soul
To a bird, did they ever
Catch the eye of a gull?

Driven to snatch,
Fight for slops in our wake.

Or voice a desolation
Not meant for us,
Not even desolate,
But which we christen.

Folk accustomed to sin,
Violent, significant death,
Who saw even in harbour
Signs terrible and just,
Heard in their cries
Lost souls of the drowned.

> Gull stands on a post
> In the tideway; I see
>
> No resolution; only
> The necessity of flight
> Beyond me, firm
> Standing only then. (*CL*, pp. 105–106)

The tension is surely a common human experience, between the desire to stay permanently in one place, and flight, freedom. My personal conclusion, paradoxically, is that being grounded ('firm/Standing') requires self-transcendence ('flight/Beyond me').

In a sense, I had already flown. The poems in *Solent Shore* were written in west Wales, in the hill country outside Aberystwyth, where I was teaching at the university. They both express *hiraeth* for my original home ground, and resist what in one poem I call 'the sludge of nostalgia'. What I had discovered for myself was the relationship between a sense of place and displacement. Poetry of place is generally a product of insecurity. This is true of great English poets of place, John Clare, his native territory changed by the Enclosure movement, Thomas Hardy, in his experience of social change. It is true of Welsh poets writing in English who straddle a border between Welsh and English cultural influences. At its simplest, there is the fact that seeing requires distance from an object. No one can see what they are part of.

During the period in the 1970s when I was writing the poems in *Solent Shore* some words of the great Welsh poet and painter David Jones became vitally important to me. In the Preface to his book-length poem *The Anathemata* he wrote: 'One is trying to make a shape out of the very things of which one is oneself made'.[3] A poem is 'a shape in words'. Its materials in many instances will be the very things that have made the poet – family, ancestry, history, culture, religion, language; all the things of place in the broadest sense; things that constitute the poet's being. But those aren't simply 'given'; they have to be identified, recognised, so that writing itself is a process of discovery. A sense of personal identity involving fundamental loyalties is involved in this process. A poet discovers who he or she is through making a shape out of the formative things.

My ambition is to make a body of work: poetry, criticism, and journal complementing each other, and informing my teaching. Coming

---

[3] *The Anathemata*, p. 10.

to live in Wales in 1965 turned out to be a determining influence. To me, first and last, Wales has been the other. Not quite an otherworld, as in the *Mabinogi*, but, compared to England, a foreign country.

I should qualify this. In Wales, I became part of something. As a literary critic, I involved myself with what we used to call Anglo-Welsh literature, and now usually refer to as Welsh writing in English. I formed friendships with writers. Anglo-Welsh literature was then a cause of struggle. Apart from a magic name or two – mainly Dylan Thomas – it was almost totally unknown outside Wales. Inside Wales it was usually ignored, or derided. I experienced first-hand the struggle to establish a course devoted to the subject in a Welsh university. I became a part of the small literary landscape. A simple view of things would be that as an English poet with a sense of place, I sympathised with Welsh poets drawn to write about their places. At a celebration of R. S. Thomas's 70th birthday, he said to me – I had been out of Wales for two years – 'This is where you belong'. I was grateful for the compliment. But belonging, as R. S. Thomas knew, is a tricky concept.

Hamlet, leaping into Ophelia's grave, exclaims: 'This is I, /Hamlet the Dane'. It is a wonderful affirmation of identity. The irresolute man, who had wondered whether to be or not to be, now proclaims himself his father's son, and the true king: 'Hamlet the Dane'. Shortly before, he has handled Yorick's skull: 'I knew him, Horatio … He hath borne me on his back a thousand times'. What makes this moment so poignant is that, for the first time, we see Hamlet the boy. The man is complete now; he is in possession of himself, his whole life. He is Hamlet the Dane; he belongs. But we are not Prince Hamlet. A modern poet is more likely to sympathise with Edward Thomas, who said of himself: 'Yet is this country [the south of England], though I am mainly Welsh, a kind of home, as I think it is more than any other to those modern people who belong nowhere'.[4] The complexity of the subject of belonging is compounded by the fact that, for many readers, the 'mainly Welsh' Edward Thomas is the quintessential modern English poet. But although displacement and modern self-consciousness complicate the sense of belonging, or being in place, they do not abolish it.

A friend once suggested to me that my poetry is primarily about continuity. Since he was heavily engaged with postmodernist theory, I suspected irony. But none was intended. The suggestion made me think. I could see grounds for it, in 'Curlew', for example:

---

[4] Edward Thomas, *The South Country*, 1909 (London: Dent, 1932), p. 7.

The curve of its cry –
A sculpture
Of the long beak:
A spiral carved from bone.

It is raised
    quickening
From the ground,
Is wound high, and again unwound,
    down
To the stalker nodding
In a marshy field.

It is the welling
Of a cold mineral spring,
Salt from the estuary
Dissolved, sharpening
The fresh vein bubbling on stone.

It is an echo
Repeating an echo
That calls you back.

It looses
Words from dust till the live tongue
Cry: This is mine
Not mine, this life
Welling from springs
Under ground, spiralling
Up the long flight of bone. (*CL*, pp. 116-117)

Curlews returned every year early in March to the marshy fields near where I lived, in a Welsh-speaking area of Ceredigion. After living in Wales for more than 10 years, I felt I had absorbed enough to write of where I lived. And it was of the continuity of life that the long-settled area under Mynydd Bach spoke to me. Whether in Welsh or the cry of a curlew, though, it spoke in a tongue that wasn't my own. The otherness or strangeness was part of the fascination. In another poem in the 'Under Mynydd Bach' sequence, I wrote:

> Where all is familiar, around us
> the country with its language
> gives all things other names. (*CL*, p. 118)

Where I lived had become familiar, but remained fundamentally strange. This no doubt influenced the non-possessiveness or self-transcendence characterising the sense of continuity in the poem: 'This is mine/Not mine, this life'. I have spoken in an interview of my sense of mystery at the heart of things. This owes a lot to my experience of living in Wales.

The finest passage about continuity I know occurs in a novel by the great modern American novelist Willa Cather. In *The Song of the Lark*, Thea, who is going to be a great artist, an opera singer, contemplates pottery fragments left behind by the 'Ancient People', the Pueblo Indians, in Arizona:

> The stream and the broken pottery: what was any art but an effort to make a sheath, a mould in which to imprison for a moment the shining, elusive element which is life itself – life hurrying past us and running away, too strong to stop, too sweet to lose? The Indian women had held it in their jars. In the sculpture she had seen in the Art Institute, it had been caught in a flash of arrested motion. In singing, one made a vessel of one's throat and nostrils and held it on one's breath, caught the stream in a scale of natural intervals.[5]

We can think of the stream of life in relation to what G. K. Chesterton called 'the eternal things, clay and fire and the sea, and motherhood and the dead',[6] or the American poet and ecologist Gary Snyder describes as the 'deep world', 'the thousand-million-year-old world of rock, soil, water, air, and all living beings, all acting through their roles'.[7] It is a function of poetry and the other arts to remind us of these things, to form 'a mould in which to imprison for a moment the shining, elusive element which is life itself'.

But the metaphor of the stream of life can be a problematic one, as we see in Willa Cather's use of it to link long-dead Native Americans to white

---

[5] Willa Cather. *The Song of the Lark* , 1915(London: Virago, 1982), p. 378.
[6] G. K. Chesterton, *G. F. Watts* (London: Duckworth, 1904), p. 59.
[7] Gary Snyder, *Back on the Fire* (Emeryville, CA: Shoemaker & Hoard, 2007), p. 34.

settlers and their descendants in a continuum of human creativity. In another Cather novel, *My Antonia*, her narrator studies Virgil's Georgics at university: "'*Primus ego in patriam mecum ... deducam Musas*': 'for I shall be the first, if I live, to bring the Muse into my country'" His teacher explains "that 'patria' here meant, not a nation or even a province, but the little rural neighbourhood on the Mincio where the poet was born". Virgil wasn't boasting. He was expressing "a hope ... that he might bring the Muse ... to his own little 'country': to his father's fields".[8]

The idea is attractive to a 'poet of place'. There is, however, always a larger history in which the 'little country' participates, whether as victim or aggressor. In the context of a colonizing or imperial power, such as the Roman or British Empire, one's 'father's fields' are likely to be an object of nostalgia, of longing for a simpler sense of belonging than the power affords. With the exception of a few Imperialists, English poetry of place has tended to take the form of local patriotism. In Wales in the twentieth century poetry is more likely to have a national focus, since in Wales poets are usually voices of resistance to external pressures. The Irish poet Patrick Kavanagh made a useful distinction between parochialism and provincialism. 'The provincial has no mind of his own; he does not trust what his eyes see until he has heard what the metropolis – towards which his eyes are turned – has to say on any subject.' 'The parochial mentality on the other hand is never in any doubt about the social and artistic validity of his parish.'[9] This applies equally to vital poetry of place in both England and Wales.

To the provincial the centre of life is always elsewhere, to be imitated. To the poet with a parochial mentality, it is where he or she is, in this place. But what is this place? People, certainly: family, friends, ancestors, neighbours, a human community. It is physical groundwork – rocks, soils – and all the shaping 'things': history, culture, religion, language. As we have recognised in recent years, it is the nonhuman world, too. I have emphasised the difficulty of seeing what one is part of, which makes poetry of place essentially exploratory. Add to this the necessity of always seeing anew.

According to Kavanagh, 'it requires a great deal of courage to be parochial'. Courage has been a necessary quality of the Welsh poet writing in English, especially in the period before it became established

---

[8] Willa Cather, *My Antonia*, 1918 (London: Virago, 1980), p. 212.
[9] Patrick Kavanagh, *A Poet's Country*, ed. Antoinette Quinn (Dublin: Lilliput, 2003), p. 237.

as a subject of academic study. The situation today is quite different from what it was in the 1960s and 70s, during my first period of living in Wales. With the exception of Dylan Thomas, it was commonly dismissed by English academics. More painfully, there was a tendency among Welsh-language writers and their readers to see it as not the real thing, even as a betrayal of Welshness. Not surprisingly, Welsh poets writing in English often felt painfully divided within themselves. Inevitably, the question of identity became especially important for poets in this period. At the same time, as voices of resistance, they were fulfilling a traditional function of the Welsh poet. Being an Anglo-Welsh poet might be experienced as a complicated, painful condition, but it meant something. It meant defending a territory against ignorance and prejudice, and the idea that it wasn't really Welsh. One's father's fields might be a coal tip or a street in Port Talbot, but they mattered; they were a centre of life, as important as any other, and more important to the poet.

There is nothing monolithic about poetry of place. It is a much larger subject than I can indicate here. In describing poets as voices of resistance, for example, it is important not to elide gender differences. The period I am talking about saw the rise in Wales of women poets, strong, independent voices such as Gillian Clarke, Jean Earle, and Ruth Bidgood. Individual poets, but with the common task of establishing the place of women's experience in a public arena dominated by the voices of men. Their achievement is one of three movements that have determined intellectual life in Wales over the past thirty years. The other movements have roots farther back in Wales: the work of socialist historians and thinkers, such as Raymond Williams and Gwyn A. Williams, and the nonconformist heritage, defined by Roland Mathias as 'that Puritan seriousness about the purpose of living, about the need for tradition and the understanding of it, about the future of the community as well as the individual'. [10] A word in passing about the latter. We are familiar in Wales with comic caricatures of Chapel culture, caricatures, in Caradoc Evans and others, driven by anger at what is seen as life-denying and hypocritical attitudes. But the time will come when it is more generally recognised that the Puritan heritage gave rise in Wales in the twentieth century, in the novels of Emyr Humphreys and the poetry of Roland Mathias, to a 'seriousness about the purpose of living' comparable to that of Hawthorne and the American Transcendentalists.

---

[10] Roland Mathias, *A Ride Through the Wood* (Bridgend: Poetry Wales Press, 1985), p. 206.

One thing these three movements – women's writing, socialist thinking, the Puritan heritage – have in common is concern for the individual as member of a community. Another is preoccupation with borders, understood in different ways. Raymond Williams, writing about Thomas Hardy, described 'the real Hardy country' as 'that border country so many of us have been living in: between custom and education, between work and ideas, between love of place and an experience of change'.[11] This spoke especially to people like myself, who had been the first in their families to go to university. It spoke to me all the more in that, from boyhood, I had read Hardy almost as if he were a neighbour. He described the Wessex I knew both geographically and socially, despite the changes. My carpenter brother working on houses in Oxfordshire read in *Jude the Obscure* his own story. Hardy helped me to recognise ideas about rootedness as the fantasies they are: life in place is change. Hardy was one of us because his subject was what in *The Return of the Native* he called 'the mind adrift on change, and harassed by the irrepressible New'.

Hardy's concern, like that of Raymond Williams and Welsh poets, was with the community as well as the individual. He was a realist, but here we need to exercise caution – human subjectivity is as real as the material world it transforms. Hardy described Turner's watercolours as 'a landscape *plus* a man's soul'. He described the Wessex of his novels as 'a partly real, partly dream country'. R. S. Thomas spoke of 'the true Wales of my imagination'.[12] In *Moby-Dick* Ishmael says of Queequeg's island: 'It is not down in any map, true places never are'. Thomas and Melville are playing wittily on the word 'true'. There is a truth of the imagination, which a gifted writer or painter persuades us of, so that we see with their eyes. Thus, we speak of Hardy's Wessex, of R. S. Thomas's Wales, of Ernest Zobole's Rhondda. We know that an individual vision is selective. But the place made over by a poet's or painter's vision is truer than a factual accounting, because the latter excludes the personal.

One of my beliefs as a teacher is that it is desirable to learn about the world by understanding where, in time and place, one is. In both Wessex and Wales, I have witnessed enthusiastic responses from students who discover their home ground through literary renderings of it. They recognise its peculiarities by seeing it with other eyes; by seeing it taken seriously, they realise that it matters, that this is where life is, as well as in

---

[11] Raymond Williams, *The Country and the City* (London: Chatto & Windus, 1973), p. 197.
[12] *Autobiographies*, p. 10.

widely advertised places.

    Roland Mathias, as poet, teacher, editor, historian, critic, was one who, living by this belief, did an immense amount to foster the study of Anglo-Welsh literature. His love of Wales was marked by humility. With his Puritan conscience, he honoured his inheritance, but felt himself unworthy of it. Without the Welsh language, he felt shut out of 'the house' of Wales. I saw him, rather, as a man who, through his devotion, truly belonged. Following his death in August 2007, I wrote a poem called 'Mathias Country', which unfortunately contains a factual mistake:

1

He will have imagined it like this:
cloud shadow on the Black Mountains
above the drowned valley,
that was once home ground.

He will have stood looking down,
or come like shadow on the water,
leaden and silvery, with a blade of light.

He will not have stopped at the soil
freshly turned among
older burials inside the chapel wall.

He will have looked death in the face,
knowing what he could not know.

2

Who knew this place as he did?

Family histories inscribed on stones,
marks weathered, marks erased
but held in his mind,
remembrancer,
poet of this country.

A book is closed here,
the pages closely written in his hand.

And who will read, who will care
to read with the care he showed,
this teacher, this scholar
of the dark and luminous word,
raiser of buried lives?

3

And he called himself a stranger,
a man standing with his face at the door
of a great house, looking in
at a life he would claim no part of,
thinking himself
unworthy to step inside.

At Aber, among his kin,
he waits for a judgement
no man can make.

But what we can say is this:
here, under sun-struck cloud
and shadow of the Black Mountains,
above the valley of the Usk,
the man who loved
and remembered has come home.[13]

The Brecon Beacons, not the Black Mountains, look down on the place where Roland is buried. That day, coming down from the Black Mountains to the Beacons, my mind was full of the former, which became, with the imagery of light and dark, integral to the poem. An additional reason for the error was my association of Roland with the seventeenth-century Metaphysical poet, Henry Vaughan, whose life and work he studied closely. Over the past decade or so, Henry Vaughan has become especially important to me through the Usk Valley Vaughan Association and its journal, *Scintilla*. In my case, this has contributed to a new direction in my writing – or the drawing out of one that was implicit from the start.

---

[13] The corrected version, which replaces 'Black Mountains with Beacons', appears in my book, *Scattered Light* (London: Enitharmon Press, 2015), pp. 33-4.

One of Henry Vaughan's most famous poems begins:

> They are all gone into the world of light!
> And I alone sit ling'ring here…

The poem is an elegy. But in expressing the poet's sense of loss for his beloved dead, it simultaneously makes a connection between 'here' and 'the world of light'. Henry Vaughan was a great religious poet, for whom place was sacred. His native country, the landscape of the river Usk, the Beacons and the Black Mountains, was a biblical landscape, imbued with the presence of God. The Marches were holy ground also for Vaughan's younger contemporary, Thomas Traherne, who recalled in *Centuries of Meditation* standing as a boy at the gates of Hereford, which 'were at first the End of the World'. 'The Dust and Stones of the Street were as Precious as GOLD.' It was the man who recaptured the boy's vision in his great prose poetry: 'all things abided Eternaly as they were in their Proper Places. Eternity was Manifest in the Light of the Day, and som thing infinit Behind evry thing appeared'. For other writers too, the Marches have been holy ground. In 1928, at Capel-y-ffin in the Black Mountains, David Jones began the writing that became *In Parenthesis*, the greatest work to emerge from the First World War. The time he spent in the Black Mountains profoundly influenced both his painting and his subsequent literary development. To David Jones, "man is a 'borderer', he is the sole inhabitant of a tract of country where matter marches with spirit".[14]

Raymond Williams's secular vision based on the same region was very different. One thing he shared with the religious poets, however, was the Welsh concern for community. Another was that he wrote in response to crisis. All these writers lived in critical times. Vaughan and Traherne lived through the Civil War. Raymond Williams lived through the Depression, through political and social conflict, and the Cold War. Like David Jones, he was a soldier. Their ideas of material and spiritual reality were quite different. What they shared was a sense of the communal life of place: place as ground of relationships, among the living, and between the living and the dead. Each also recognised the importance of the non-human world, and had what we would call a 'green' orientation.

Jane Aaron wrote recently of 'the liminal nature of border identities'; 'border communities', she says, 'make up a good third of the Welsh

---

[14] *Epoch and Artist*, p. 86.

population'.[15] So, in one way or another, many of us are 'borderers'; in David Jones's terms, we all are. In recent years, I have found myself thinking more and more about liminality – the condition of occupying a threshold. This 'border' state is a social and cultural phenomenon. But it is rich in metaphorical possibilities, too. It may be seen as a boundary between worlds, a frontier between the living and the dead, the seen and the unseen, surface and depth, language and silence.

My first landscapes were liminal, shores between land and sea, and forest and sea. This had a profound shaping effect upon my imagination. I can identify with what John Constable, my father's favourite painter, and a presence in my original home, said of his boyhood. He spoke of his love of 'the sound of water escaping from mill-dams, etc., willows, old rotten planks, slimy posts, and brickwork'. 'I should paint my own places best,' he said, "painting is with me but another word for feeling, and I associate 'my careless boyhood' with all that lies on the banks of the Stour; those scenes made me a painter, and I am grateful".

I identify readily with Constable's love of the sound of water, of old rotten planks, slimy posts, brickwork: these, or their equivalents, were among my first things. Poetry too is but another word for feeling. I associate my boyhood with all that lies on the shores of the Solent; scenes that helped to make me a poet, and I am grateful. My boyhood, too, was 'careless', in spite of the fact that my first memory was of being carried down into a shelter during an air-raid. But I grew up in the fifties, when, along with many others, I had an acute apprehension of the imminence of nuclear war. In consequence, from the beginning all my attachments were strengthened by a sense of their vulnerability. If, in the words of Clement of Alexandria, I clung like seaweed to the rocks by the seashore, and if I put a high value on place, it was due to the threat of placelessness – nuclear devastation, and the consumerist populism that would turn us all into provincials. I looked back through a family history closely associated with work on the land. The past draws me, as soil clings to one's feet walking across ploughland. Reading the Hammonds' *The Village Labourer*, I recognised an ancestor in a young man bearing my mother's maiden name. James Mould, transported for his part in the Captain Swing riots, inspired my poem, 'Elegy for the Labouring Poor'. I rejoiced, discovering in Richard Jefferies's *Hodge and His Masters* a reference to 'old Hooker, the hedge carpenter'. A Welsh definition of poetry is carpentry

---

[15] Jane Aaron, 'Teaching Welsh Writing in English', *English Subject Centre Newsletter*, Issue 13, October 2007, p. 20.

of song. And poetry, like carpentry, connects, and makes new. In writing the closing lines of one of my 'Under Mynydd Bach' poems I identified an ideal – as a poem will often tell a poet what he thinks and feels:

> around us
> the walls formed a deep channel,
> with marks of other lives, holding
> its way from worked moorland
> to this autumn with an open sky. (*CL*, p. 119)

Place connects us to the past; it is a 'deep channel' which bears the marks of other lives, the lives that made it, but where we stand it opens now, and to the future – the new, the place for our creative work.

I write often of water, real and metaphorical: channel, river, lake, sea; water from which we come, 'the shining, elusive element which is life itself'. Streams and rivers are part of places, often giving them their names; but they pass through, connecting the place with other places at a distance, and losing themselves in the sea. In one poem I adopt the persona of the nymph who tried to prevent Hades from abducting Persephone. She failed, and in her grief dissolved in tears, and melted into her pool.

CYANE

Finally a body that is water's own.

So at times words seem to come to me,
as though I could speak,
or as I remember speaking in another life.

I pool to a glassy stillness.
I move slowly, mirroring
shapes & colours of leaves;
housefronts, walls; a face;
the world entranced
gazing at the world.

Or quick, a stream
of silver – only

what I know is imageless,
except once, in another life...

My moods are stagnant,
turbulent, I circle circle circle,
or stand motionless, or pour out,
falling, scattering,
coming together with the smoothness
of a dolphin's back, an icy glide.

What was I before I was finally this?
Sometimes I dream that on my surface
I form a human face,
and look out at another,
red and glistening, a man's,
and arms, in which he grasps a woman,
binds her to him, drags her down.

And it shakes then: earth quakes,
and springs apart – they are gone.

And I shake, the being that I was –
                    skin blood bones
unbinding, flying into drops,
flowing with a constant tremor,
plunging down, shattering,
shaking out long and smooth,
always broken, always whole.

And over I go and over,
and under, and round and round.

But what is that but a dream
that I was human once,
who am pure spirit,
not bodied, not bodiless,
but water in water, quick
with a life beyond all words.

> Silence, then; or a voice
> that is the sound of water running,
> in which, if they listen,
> any one may hear a tale
> of terror at the roots of things:
>
> a tale that I tremble to tell,
> half remembering, or inventing,
> but as if, once, it were my own. (*CL*, pp. 319-320)

'Cyane' is perhaps my fullest expression to date of a liminal condition: between the human and the nonhuman, the material and the spiritual. It dramatizes an experience of becoming other, a version of the self-transcendence implied at the end of 'Gull on a Post'. In T. S. Eliot's words, 'Old men ought to be explorers'.[16] But why confine it to old men? Shouldn't it apply to all men and women, who begin, as children, exploring the world? As a teacher, it is what I seek to encourage my students to be – opening themselves to the experience of reading, and making discoveries, which are also self-discoveries. At the same time, writing is for me a parallel process – to change the metaphor, poetry is 'an art of seeing, an art by which, in my blindness, I learn to see'.[17]

> We shall not cease from exploration
> And the end of all our exploring
> Will be to arrive where we started
> And know the place for the first time.[18]

But knowing more is to see what we do not know. Poetry, if it is truly exploratory, continually comes to an edge. It may show something of the known shore, to which the poet clings. But the shore fronts the unknown.

---

[16] *Four Quartets*, 1944 (London: Faber, 1959), p. 32.
[17] From 'At the Edge', my afterword to Jeremy Hooker and Lee Grandjean, *Their Silence a Language* (London: Enitharmon, 1993), p. 75.
[18] *Four Quartets*, p. 59.

Index

Aaron, Jane, 257
Abbs, Peter, 233
Abstract Expressionism, 234
Adams, Robert, 202
   Beauty in Photography, 205
affectation, 43
American Civil War, 203
American Dream, 139
aphasia, 162
Aphrodite, 157
Applebee, Leonard
   Barns in a Field, 218
Aneirin, 10, 179
Arnold, Matthew, 16, 144
Aristotle, 246
Arthur, King, 232
Athena, 131
Auden, W. H., 10, 41, 127
   'The Wanderer', 217
Auerbach, Fred
   Primrose Hill, Summer Sunshine, 215
Auster, Paul, 132, 134
autobiography, 17

Baalzebub, 46
Bacon, Francis, 108
bardd gwlad, 72–73
Barlow, Robin
   Wales and World War One, 200–2
Barnes, William, 107
Barthes, Roland, 203
Baucis, 106
Beats, 10, 181
Becket, Thomas, 86
Benjamin, Walter, 159
Berry, Wendell, 108
Bidart, Frank, 125
Bidgood, Ruth, 11, 13, 42, 72–73, 83, 85–99, 180, 253
   Above the Forests, 95
   'All Souls', 89

'Butterflies at Wellfield', 93
'The Copy', 95
'Hawthorn at Digiff', 87–88
'Homecoming', 96
'Hoofprints', 91
Kindred, 75, 87
'Links', 86
'Little of Distinction', 95
'Llyn y Fan Fach', 76
Parishes of the Buzzard, 97
'Red', 76–77
'Riding the Flood', 86
'To the Fish Traps', 91–92
Bingham, Kate
   'Oxygen', 176–77
Bishop, Elizabeth, 77
Black Mountain poets, 12, 59
blaenau, 91
Blake, William, 100–1, 107, 135, 148, 181, 226
   'The Tyger', 149
Blau DuPlessis, Rachel, 137
   The Objectivist Nexus, 133
Blunden, Edmund, 53
Bohata, Kirsti
   Postcolonialism Revisited, 98
Bomberg, David, 214–15, 229
   Trendrine Cornwall, 213
Bonnard, Pierre, 229
'border', 257–58
Borges, Jorge Luis, 212
Boyle, Mark
   Bonfire Study, 220
Brady, Matthew, 203
Brân, 66–67
bro, 16, 99, 194
Brodsky, Joseph, 177
Brooke, Rupert
   'The Soldier', 43
Brwynllys, Bedo, 90
Buber, Martin, 137
   Between Man and Man, 42

I and Thou, 17, 79
Buddhism, 165
Bunting, Basil, 145
   Briggflats, 42

Casey, Gerard, 12
   South Wales Echo, 12
Casey, Mary, 12
Cather, Willa
   My Antonia, 252
   The Song of the Lark, 251
Catholicism, 227
Ceridwen, 71, 82
Cézanne, Paul, 227, 230
Chekhov, Anton, 157
Chesterton, G. K., 251
Chestov, Leon, 152
Christianity, 30, 77, 91
Civil War (English), 257
Clare, John, 95, 102, 107, 144, 248
Clark, Laurie, 105
Clarke, Gillian, 12, 70, 72–75, 82–83, 105, 179, 253
   'Blaen Cwrt', 172, 183
   'Cofiant', 73
   'Dyddgu replies to Dafydd', 73–74
   'Letter from a Far Country', 74–75, 180
   'The Water-Diviner', 171
Clement of Alexandria, 246, 258
Clemo, Jack, 42
Clifford, Susan, 105
   Trees Be Company, 105–6
Cluysenaar, Anne, 14, 179
Coleridge, Samuel Taylor, 59, 108, 217
   Biographia Literaria, 20, 32
   'Dejection', 29
   'Fears in Solitude', 44
   The Friend, 39
   Lyrical Ballads, 14–15, 20–23, 29, 33, 105, 214
   'The Nightingale', 25

   'The Rime of the Ancient Mariner', 30
Collins, William, 185
Colquhoun, Robert
   Church Lench, 216
Common Ground, 105, 108
Conran, Tony, 10, 14, 42, 179–81
Constable, John, 9, 34, 101, 105, 108, 111, 116, 214, 217, 221–22, 229, 233, 258
   Salisbury Cathedral from the Bishop's Grounds, 102
Cowper, William
   'Yardley Oak', 106
Crabbe, George, 23, 31
Crimean War, 203
Cross, 100, 104, 228
Crusoe, Robinson, 137, 139
cummings, e. e., 184
Cynddelw, 179

Dada, 152, 172–73
Dafydd ap Gwilym, 73
   'Y Niwl', 239
Dante, 189, 191, 225
Daphne, 106
Darwin, Charles, 108
David, 47
Davie, Donald, 190–91
   Essex Poems, 42
   To Scorch or Freeze, 191
Davies, Graham
   Oxygen, 174–75, 179
Davies, Idris, 72, 194–95, 198–99
Davis, Dick, 185–87, 191
   'Chagrin', 186
   'Getting Away', 186
   'I lay down in the darkness of my soul', 187
   Touchwood, 186
   A Trick of Sunlight, 186
   'Water', 187
   'William Macgonagall Welcomes the Initiative for a Greater

Role for Faith-based
   Education', 187
Wisdom and Wilderness, 186
Delius, Frederick, 112
Dewi Sant, 175
Dickens, Charles, 24
Dickinson, Emily, 45, 76–77, 185
Dilworth, Thomas
   David Jones and the Great War,
      200–1
De Quincey, Thomas, 21, 29
Dodman, 114
Donne, John, 178, 190
Duncan, Robert, 114, 116, 118, 120,
   127

Eardley, Joan, 214, 229, 234
   A Field of Oats, 216
Earle, Jean, 42, 72–73, 77–78, 82,
   105, 253
   'The Dancing Stone', 78
   'Escape to Felingano', 78
   'Every Day', 77
   'A Neighbour's House', 78–79
   'Peter, Dreaming', 79
   'The Picture of the Tiger Hunt', 78
   'Visiting Light', 77
'edge', 88–89, 166–67
Edwards, O. M., 98
Elijah, 46
Eliot, George, 24
Eliot, T. S., 12, 52, 59, 134, 261
   'East Coker', 41
   The Wasteland, 52, 139
Elisha, 46
Elphin, 71
Evans, Caradoc, 253
Evans, Christine, 70, 72, 83, 105,
   179
   'Cometary Phases', 81–82
   Cometary Phases, 79
   'Whale Dream', 79–82
Ezekiel, 132

Fainlight, Ruth, 107
Fell, Sheila
   Woman in the Snow, 218
feminism, 68
Fenton, Roger
   Valley of the Shadow of Death, 203
Ferlinghetti, Lawrence, 10
Finch, Peter
   'Hills', 172–74
   'A Welsh Wordscape', 172
First World War, 43–44, 103, 200–12,
   231, 257
Fisher, Catherine, 179
Fisher, Roy, 143–50
   'Abstracted Water', 150
   Birmingham River, 143–49
   'Calling', 145
   City, 42, 143, 150, 184
   The Cut Pages, 144
   'Every Man His Own Eyebright',
      148
   A Furnace, 145–46
   'Metamorphoses', 144
   'Our Own', 150
   'The Poet's Message', 150
   'Rudiments', 143, 149
   'Seven Figures From Anansi
      Company', 148
   'A Sign Illuminated', 146
   'Sikelianos', 145
   'Six Texts For A Film', 146, 149–50
   'Talking to Cameras', 147
   The Thing About Joe Sullivan, 150
   'Wonders of Obligation', 144, 150
Fisher King, 67
'Franciscan', 15
Fredman, Stephen
   A Menorah for Athena, 132, 135
French Revolution, 22, 25, 77
Friedrich, Caspar David, 102
Fulton, Hamish
   Seven days Alberta, 219
Fussell, Michael, 214
   Heavy Rain over a Marsh, 217

Gaia, 83
Gainsborough, Thomas
   Cornard Wood, 101
   Gainsborough's Forest, 101
Garlick, Raymond, 12, 171
Gauguin, Paul, 230
Gill, Eric, 228, 232
Gill, Petra, 63
Gill, Stephen, 21
Gillies, W. G.
   Eildon, 219
Ginner, Charles, 214
   The Window, 218
Giono, Jean
   The Man Who Planted Trees, 104
Ginsberg, Allen
   Howl, 10
Girtin, Thomas, 234–35
God, 135
Goethe, Johann Wolfgang von, 159
Gog, 116
Goldsworthy, Andy
   'Leaves' (exhibition), 108
Godwin, William, 28–29
Goldsmith, Oliver, 31
Grandjean, Lee, 9–10, 48–49, 108, 193–99
   Praise Awe Despair, 49
   Their Silence a Language, 48, 193
   Witness, 199
Graves, Robert, 71
   The White Goddess, 66–67
Green Man, 113
Grigson, Geoffrey, 110
Griffiths, Ann, 70
Gross, Philip, 161–67
   'Barry Island with Dante and Ducks', 163
   'Betweenland', 161–62
   'Brownian Motion', 165–66
   Deep Field, 161
   'The Duke of Nowhere', 166
   'Epithalamium, with Squirrels', 164
   'Fantasia on a Theme from IKEA', 164
   Later, 161, 166
   'Legacy', 166
   Love Songs of Carbon, 161–62, 164–65
   'Mould Music', 164
   'The Moveable Island', 161–62
   'Several Shades of Ellipsis', 162
   The Son of the Duke of Nowhere, 166
   'Something Like the Sea', 162–63
   'Storm Surge', 164
   'Thinks Bubble', 163
   'Vocable', 162, 165
   The Water Table, 161, 164
'ground', 19, 41, 242
Gruffud ab yr Ynad Coch
   'Marwnad Llywelyn ap Gruffudd', 208, 240
Gunn, Thom, 185, 191
   'The Cherry Tree', 106
Gurney, Ivor, 43
Gwalchmai, 179
Gwenallt, 10, 41, 198

Hades, 259
Hagreen, Philip, 63
haiku, 120, 123, 131
Haines, Elizabeth, 236–41
   L'Arbre Abasourdi, 239
   Deri yn Ymdaraw, 240
   Flooded with Light, 236
   Llanthony, Barns in Snow, 237
   Mazy Charnel Way, 239–40
   Sketchbook from the Somme, 238
   Under a Full Moon, 237
   Vortex for the Storm, 236
   The Web of Exchange, 236
Hamburger, Michael, 42
Hammond, J. L. and Barbara
   The Village Labourer, 258
Hardy, Thomas, 13, 15–16, 35, 40, 53, 95, 102, 119, 218, 225, 235, 248, 254

Jude the Obscure, 254
The Return of the Native, 254
Harmer, J. B.
   Victory in Limbo, 141
Harries, Howell, 91–92
Hass, Robert, 118–19, 126, 128–29
   Human Wishes, 123–24
   'Natural Theology', 124
   'On Squaw Peak', 124
   'Quartet', 124
   'Santa Barbara Road', 124
   'Spring Rain', 124
   Twentieth Century Pleasures, 123
Hatlen, Burton, 135–36
Hamilton, Ian, 156
Hawkes, Jacquetta
   A Land, 61
Hawkins, Coleman, 144
Hazlitt, William, 20–22
Heaney, Seamus, 43–44, 83, 219
   'Englands of the Mind', 43, 61
   'Exposure', 25
   North, 57
   'Now and in England', 43
   Preoccupations, 43
Heidegger, Martin, 18, 42, 44, 136, 138, 159
Heller, Michael, 41
Herbert, George, 189
Hermes, 119, 121
hiraeth, 13, 248
Hill, Geoffrey, 43, 145
   Mercian Hymns, 42, 57
   The Triumph of Love, 110
Hilton, Roger, 215
   January 1964, Red, 219
Hitchens, Ivon, 221–25
   Forest Edge no. 2, 224–25
   Garden Cove, 217
   Winter Stage, 224
   Woodland Landscape, 225
Hodgkins, Frances, 221–22
   Broken Tractor, 223
   Enchanted Garden, 224

Solva, 223
Wings over Water, 224
Hoggart, Richard, 144
Holden, Molly, 42
   'In this unremarkable island', 214
Hölderlin, Friedrich, 18, 42
'homelessness', 44
Homer, 16, 212
Hooker, Jeremy
   'Company', 57
   'Curlew', 249–50
   'Cyane', 259–61
   Ditch Vision, 15
   'Elegy for the Labouring Poor', 258
   'Englishman's Road', 55–56
   Englishman's Road, 37
   'Gull on a Post', 246–48, 261
   'Hill Country Rhythms', 37
   Landscape of the Daylight Moon, 36
   A Map of David Jones, 62, 64
   'Master of the Leaping Figures', 46–48
   'Mathias Country', 255–56
   'Matrix', 60–61
   'On a Photography of Southampton Docks', 53
   'Paintings', 34
   Poetry of Place, 35, 37
   The Presence of the Past, 37–38
   Solent Shore, 36–37, 53, 246, 248
   Soliloquies of a Chalk Giant, 36
   Their Silence a Language, 48, 193
   'Under Mynydd Bach', 259
   'The Witnesses', 196–98
Hopkins, Gerard Manley, 45, 56, 153, 158, 181, 184
   'Binsey Poplars', 106
Horovitz, Frances, 105, 215
   'Walking in Autumn', 216
Hughes, Aled Rhys, 200, 202–12
Hughes, Colin, 202, 211
Hughes, Ted, 10, 42–43, 83, 155
   'A Tree', 107
Hulme, T. E., 131

Humphreys, Emyr, 12, 42, 70, 198, 253
The Taliesin Tradtion, 36
Hyland, Paul, 42
Hywel ab Owain, 179

I-Ching, 67
imagism, 130–31, 137, 141
Impressionists, 34
Inanna, 93
'Influence and Originality' (exhibition), 221

James, Merlin, 226
Jarvis, Matthew, 85
Jefferies, Richard, 13, 15, 17, 35, 37, 45–46, 56
   Hodge and His Masters, 258
   'Meadow Thoughts', 217
Jenkins, Mike, 183
   Coulda Bin Summin, 181–82, 184
   'Gwyn Alf', 182–83
Jeremiah, 132
Jesus Christ, 20, 47, 58, 104, 189
John Barleycorn, 211
Johnson, Ronald, 42, 110–17
   The Book of the Green Man, 110–12, 116–17
Johnston, Dafydd, 11, 98–99
Jones, Bobi, 174
Jones, David, 11–12, 14–16, 39–42, 52–65, 71, 103, 106, 114–16, 118, 120, 127, 159, 178–79, 199, 209, 219, 226–32, 237, 239–40, 257–58
   The Anathemata, 16, 18, 39–41, 44, 61, 229, 248
   'Art and Democracy', 230
   'Black on gold', 49–50, 52
   Briar Cup, 229
   The Chester Play of the Deluge, 230
   Dai Greatcoat, 53
   Dancing Bear, 39

   Epoch and Artist, 236
   A Fusilier at the Front, 226
   Human Being, 228
   'The Hunt', 57
   Manawydan's Glass Door, 229
   'A Map of the Artist's Mind' (exhibition), 226, 228
   In Parenthesis, 40, 52–53, 57–58, 104, 201, 203–5, 207–12, 229–31, 236, 239–40, 257
   'Rite and Fore-Time', 58
   Roman Land, 228
   'The Sleeping Lord', 38, 52, 54, 218, 232
   Tir y Blaenau, 230
   'The Tribune's Visitation', 38
   'The Tutelar of the Place', 38, 54, 227
   Tree Trunks and Shed, 217
   Trystan ac Essyllt, 231
   Vexilla Regis, 104, 231
   'Wales and the Crown', 55
   'The Wall', 52, 59
   Y Cyfarchiad I Fair, 231–32
Jones, Glyn, 12, 17, 96, 99
   The Dragon Has Two Tongues, 98
Joyce, James, 57, 59, 184
Julian of Norwich, 104, 227
Jung, Carl, 120–21

Kandinsky, Wassily, 229
Kavanagh, Patrick, 15, 252
Keats, John, 18, 105, 153, 158
Kerouac, Jack, 184
Kierkegaard, Søren, 136
Kilhwch and Olwen, 90
Kilvert, Francis, 111, 113
King, Angela, 105
   Trees Be Company, 105–6
Kings, IV, 46, 49
Klee, Paul, 144, 162, 165, 240
Klimek, Ray, 242–45
   6 Cwn Bargoed, South Wales, 243
Kokoschka, Oskar, 144

landscape painting, 9, 34–35, 213–20, 233–41
Langland, William, 62
Lanyon, Peter, 234
  Soaring Flight, 220
Larkin, Philip, 43, 59, 110
  'Going, Going', 43
Latham, John
  Carberry Ring, 220
  'documentation', 220
Law, Robert
  The White Horse of Uffington, 219
Lawrence, D. H., 153, 158
Leavis, F. R., 144
Leslie, C. R.
  Memoirs of the Life of John Constable, 101
Lethbridge, C., 116
  Gogmagog, 114
Lewis, Gwyneth, 177–78
  'Zero Gravity', 177
  Zero Gravity, 177
Lewis, Saunders, 10, 72–73
Llywelyn ap Gruffudd, 63, 208
Llewellyn-Williams, Hilary, 69–70, 72, 76, 82–83, 179–80
  'Alder/Fearn', 66–67
  'Elder/Ruis', 67
  'Holly/Tinne', 68
  The Tree Calendar, 66–67, 71, 105
Lord, Peter, 10
Lowell, Robert, 59
Lowry, L. S.
  Seascape, 218
Luzatto, Moshe Chaim, 133

Mabinogion, 67, 240, 249
MacDiarmid, Hugh, 213–14
MacTaggart, Sir William
  Winter Sunset, the Red Soil, 218
Magog, 116
Mallarmé, Stéphane, 212
Mann, Sargy
  River Box, 217

Maritain, Jacques, 159, 228
Marx, Karl, 132–33, 135
Marxism, 18
Mary, Virgin, 58
Mathias, Roland, 11–13, 42, 88–89, 175, 179–80, 253, 255–56
Matisse, Henri, 222, 230
Matter of Britain, 61
Matthews, Caitlín, 71
Matthias, John, 11, 42, 110–17, 118, 129
  Beltane at Aphelion, 127
  'A Compostela Diptych', 128
  'Dedication to a Cycle of Poems on the Pilgrim Routes to Santiago de Compostela', 128
  'An East Anglian Diptych', 110, 114, 117, 127–28
  'Facts from an Apocryphal Midwest', 128
  A Gathering of Ways, 110
  'Poem for Cynouai', 128
  Reading Old Friends, 127
  'Rivers', 115
  Swimming at Midnight, 127–28
McCarthyism, 136
McCurdy, Michael, 104
McMichael, James, 118–19, 123, 129
  Each in a Place Apart, 125–26
McNeil, Helen, 76–77
Melville, Herman
  Moby Dick, 80, 254
memory, 67, 89
Merchant, Carolyn, 79
  The Death of Nature, 68
Meredith, Christopher, 11, 85–99
  Air Histories, 87
  The Book of Idiots, 92
  'Borderland', 88
  'The churches', 92
  'Colour', 94–95
  'Earth air', 87
  Griffri, 85, 90, 98–99

'My mother missed the beautiful
 and doomed', 93
'On Hay Bridge', 90, 94
'Prisoners', 88
Shifts, 85, 90, 98
'The slurry pond', 95
Merlin, 205
Metaphysical poets, 77, 190
Methodism, 91–92
Miles, Jonathan
 David Jones, 226, 229
Middleton, Christopher, 110, 151–60
 'At Porthcothan', 154, 159
 'Avocado Plant', 156
 'Bivouac', 158–59
 Bolshevism in Art, 151–52
 'Catacomb', 157
 'Discourse on Legend', 158
 'From the Alexandria Library
  Gazette', 157
 'Holy Cow', 160
 Intimate Chronicles, 151
 'Mandelstam to Gumilev 1920',
  152
 'A Memorial to the Room-
  Collectors', 156, 160
 'Moon Climbing', 157
 'On a Photograph of Chekhov',
  157
 'The Old Tour Guide', 156
 Pataxanadu, 157
 'Reflections on a Viking Prow',
  152, 155, 159
 Serpentine, 157
 'Small Carvings at Arycanda', 158
 'Wild Flowers', 157–58
 'Wild Horse', 154–55
Mondrian, Piet, 222, 232
Monet, Claude, 34
modernism, 9, 11, 14, 34, 41, 59,
 191, 221–22
Morgan, Edwin, 148
Mörike, Eduard, 152

Moses, 47
Mould, James, 258
'mystery', 103

Nash, David, 108, 217
 Ash framed with Ash, 220
 Larch framed with Larch, 220
Nash, Paul, 9, 38, 103, 206, 215–17,
 231, 234, 241
 Landscape from a Dream, 224
 Landscape of the Vernal Equinox, 103
 'Monster Field', 103
 Nest of Wild Stones, 216
 We are Making a New World, 103
Negative Capability, 153
Neo-Romantics, 9, 234, 240
Nesbitt, Paul, 108
Nicholson, Winifred, 214–16, 222,
 224, 229–30
 Cumberland Hills, 215
 The Red Flowerpots, 223
 View from Studio Window, 221
 Violas in a Window, 223
Nietzsche, Friedrich, 159
Nonconformism, 77
Norris, Leslie, 12

Oakshott, Walter
 The Artists of the Winchester Bible,
  46
Objectivists, 15, 41, 44–46, 130,
 132, 135, 137
Olson, Charles, 12, 41, 59, 127
Oppen, George, 17–19, 45, 120,
 130–42, 147, 159
 'Blood from the Stone', 44, 136
 'Of Being Numerous', 46, 130,
  136–42
 'World, World –', 135–36
Oppen, Mary, 131, 140
 Meaning A Life, 138
Ormond, John, 12, 16
Owen, Wilfred, 106, 183, 203, 205

Palmer, Samuel, 9, 111–12, 115, 215, 222
Pastoral with a Horsechestnut, 101
Under a Full Moon, 241
parochialism, 252
Pasmore, Victor, 215
The Snowstorm, 219
Pasternak, Boris, 93
Patchen, Kenneth, 10
Pater, Walter, 239
Peck, John, 118, 125–26, 128–29
  'Book of Life', 121
  'Early Summer Evening, Kanton Zurich', 120
  'On that high plateau', 121
  Selva Morale, 119–20
  'Spring-through-Fall Epistle to Hakuin', 120
Persephone, 259
Petersen, David, 206
Philemon, 106
photography, 200, 202–12, 242–43
Picasso, Pablo, 222
Piggott, Stuart, 56
Pinsky, Robert, 118, 125–26, 129
  'The Hearts', 121–22
  'Immortal Longings', 123
  Poetry and the World, 121
  The Want Bone, 121
  'What Why When How Who', 123
Piper, John, 238
  British Romantic Artists, 234
Pissarro, Camille, 34
place-names, 89
Plath, Sylvia, 59
Ponge, Francis, 159
Pope, Alexander, 111
populism, 199
Potter, Mary
  Sun on the Beach, 213, 216
Pound, Ezra, 12, 39, 59, 112, 120, 130–31, 153, 191
  Cantos, 80
  Cathay, 131
  'The Tree', 106
Powys, John Cowper, 11–12, 17, 45, 71, 146–47
  Wolf Solent, 225
praise poetry, 36–37, 70
Pre-Raphaelites, 234
Prince, F. T., 10
provincialism, 252
Psalm 23, 203
Pugh, Sheenagh, 70, 179
Puritanism, 77, 253–55

Quakers, 165
Quartermain, Peter
  The Objectivist Nexus, 133
Queen of Heaven, 228

Redgrove, Peter, 83
Reintjes, Liz, 221–23, 225
Reznikoff, Charles, 41–42, 44–46, 130–42, 147
  'Dream, Heavenly City', 132
  'Jerusalem the Golden', 130–34, 139, 141–42
  Testimony, 133
Rhys, Keidrych
  Modern Welsh Poetry, 168
Rich, Adrienne, 69, 75
Riley, Denise
  Poets on Writing, 146
Rilke, Rainer Maria, 159
Roberts, Lynette, 70, 179
robson, lloyd
  cardiff cut, 181, 183–84
Romanticism, 15, 105–7, 144, 147–48, 169, 234, 238, 240
'roots', 138
Rosenberg, Isaac, 106
Ruskin, 24, 45, 191

St Paul, 191
salmon of Llyn Llyw, 90, 98
Samaria, King of, 46

Sampson, Fiona
  Beyond the Lyric, 11–12
Sassoon, Siegfried, 202
Schachtner, Leonhard, 210
Schmidt, Michael, 118
Scott, William
  Slagheap Landscape, 220
sculpture, 193, 195–96, 199
Setch, Terry
  Penarth 111, 220
Shakespeare, William, 58, 105, 190
  As You Like it, 107
  Hamlet, 246, 249
  The Tempest, 164
shamanism, 67
Sheers, Owen, 182
  'Learning the Language', 175
Sheppard, Robert, 144
Sherman, Bill, 12
Shiel, Derek
  David Jones, 226, 229
Shulamite, 131
Shuttle, Penelope, 83
Sir Gawain and the Green Knight, 145, 149
Sisley, Alfred, 214
Sisson, C. H., 42
  'Burrington Combe', 218
Smith, Dai, 244
Smith, Captain John, 139
Smith, Stevie
  'Alone in the Woods', 106
socialism, 194
Song of Songs, 132
Sontag, Susan, 203
Spencer, Stanley, 227
  The May Tree, 101
Spinoza, Baruch, 135
subversion, 70
Snyder, Gary, 12, 45, 83, 251
  'Mother Earth', 80–81
Stevens, Wallace, 144
Sutherland, Graham, 234, 240

Taliesin, 10, 36, 66–67, 70–72, 79, 82, 84, 92, 184
Tanner, Tony, 185, 187, 191
Taplin, Kim, 42
  Tongues in Trees, 68, 105
Tauler, Johannes, 189
Tennyson, Alfred Lord, 144, 185
  'The Charge of the Light Brigade', 203
Theocritus, 187
Thomas, Ceri, 244
Thomas, Dylan, 14, 171–72, 176, 178, 239, 249, 253
  'Poem in October', 168–69, 183
Thomas, Edward, 12–13, 15, 17, 38, 43, 83, 95, 102, 116–17, 169, 249
  'The Chalk Pit', 103
  The Icknield Way, 116
  'Old Man', 93
  The South Country, 220
Thomas, Ned, 16, 99
  The Extremist, 10
Thomas, M. Wynn, 10, 85
Thomas, R. S., 10, 12, 52, 171–74, 234, 240, 249, 254
  'A Peasant', 104–5, 168–70, 173
  'A Priest to His People', 170
  'The View from the Window', 215
  'Welsh Landscape', 90, 173
Thompson, E. P., 24
Thoreau, Henry David, 15, 112
Tomlinson, Charles, 10, 42
  'The Marl Pits', 216
Torrance, Chris, 179
Traherne, Thomas, 101, 257
  Centuries of Meditation, 257
Transcendentalists, 253
Tree of Life, 100, 103–4, 106–7, 217
'The Tree of Life' (exhibition), 107
trees, 100–9, 240
Tress, David, 9, 233–35
  'Chasing Sublime Light' (exhibition), 235

Green Winter Spring, 235
A Hot Day, February, 233
Kirkstall Abbey, 235
Welsh Industrial, 235
Tripp, John, 12, 17
   'Soliloquy for compatriots', 170–71
Turner, J. M. W., 215, 222, 225, 229, 234–35, 254
   Rain, Steam and Speed, 235

Uncertainty Principle, 165
Upanishads, 123

Van Gogh, Vincent, 214, 230
Vaughan, Henry, 111–13, 116, 189, 256–57
   'Affliction', 51
   'The Night', 112
   'The Retreate', 112
   'The Waterfall', 191
Vellacott, Elizabeth
   Winter Trees, 217
Venus Genetrix, 58
Vietnam War, 119, 140
villanelle, 88
Virgil, 187, 252
Virtue, John
   Green Haworth, 220
'visual music', 221–22, 224

Wack, Amy
   Oxygen, 174, 179
Wallace, Diana, 11
Walser, Robert, 152
Walsh, James, 22
Wandil, 116
Watkins, Vernon, 71
Waugh, Evelyn, 93
Weight, Carol, 218
Weil, Simone, 45
Welch, John 42
Weldon, Fay
   Praxis, 68

Wells, H. G., 136
Wells, Robert, 185, 187–89, 191
   The Day and Other Poems, 188–89
   'The Forester', 188
   'The Winter's Task', 188
Welsh language, 75, 85, 98–99, 171, 175
White, Gilbert, 15, 108
Whitman, Walt, 12, 14, 18, 122–23, 203
   'Song of Myself', 113–14
Wilde, Oscar
   The Picture of Dorian Gray, 17
Williams, Charles, 71, 120
Williams, Gwyn, 14, 178–80, 239, 253
   The Burning Tree, 10, 208, 238, 240
Williams, Jonathan, 110
Williams, Raymond, 144, 170, 253–54, 257
Williams, Waldo, 10, 194, 198
Williams, William Carlos, 12, 15–16, 56, 112, 122, 144–45, 147, 159, 220, 223, 243–44
Williams, Rowan, 207
Williamson, Henry, 15
Wilmer, Clive, 185, 187, 189–91
   'The Falls', 191
   The Mystery of Things, 189
   'Stigmata', 189–90
Winchester Bible, 46
Winters, Yvor, 118–19, 121, 126, 185–87, 189, 191
woods, 57, 204–10
Woolf, Virginia, 82, 95
Wordsworth, Dorothy, 15, 21–22, 29, 31, 33
Wordsworth, William, 18, 37, 62, 78, 95, 102, 108, 111–12, 113, 116, 127, 143, 169, 215, 234
   'Expostulation and Reply', 20
   'Intimations of Immortality', 96

'Lines left upon a Seat in a Yew-Tree', 24–25
'Lines written a few miles above Tintern Abbey', 21, 27
'Lines written in early spring', 26
Lyrical Ballads, 14–15, 20–33, 44, 105, 180, 214
'Michael', 24, 30–32
'Nutting', 22
'Poems on the Naming of Places', 25
'A Poet's Epitaph', 27
The Prelude, 23
'There was a Boy', 28, 171
Wynne Rhydderch, Samantha, 182, 184
'The Lighthouse Keeper's Daughter', 181
Rockclimbing in Silk, 181
Wyn Griffith, Llewelyn, 203, 205–6
Up to Mametz, 201–2, 211–12
Wynter, Brian, 214
Landscape, Zennor, 219

Young, Edward
Night Thoughts, 28
Young, Louise B., 82, 84

Zobole, Ernest, 242–45, 254
A Painting about myself in a Landscape, 244
Black Valley, 242–43
Zola, Emile, 214
Zukofsky, Louis, 137

Lightning Source UK Ltd.
Milton Keynes UK
UKHW010646050720
365992UK00001B/74

9 781848 617087